TIGER CAGE:

An Untold Story

d.e. bordenkircher

as told to

s.a. bordenkircher

Abby Publishing

TIGER CAGE: *An Untold Story*

Copyright © 1998 by S. A. Bordenkircher

Published by: *abby publishing*

Library of Congress Catalog Number: 97-93396
ISBN No. 0-9661771-4-2

First Printing

Cover Design: *S. A. Bordenkircher*
Cover Photo: *Tiger Cage Cell Building,*
Con Son Prison, South China Sea
Photos: *Bordenkircher Family Collection*

Manufactured in the United States of America

All book correspondence should be addressed to:

abby
publishing

P. O. Box 114, Cameron, WV 26033

DEDICATION

To the men and women of the Office of Public Safety, who, under the direction of Byron Engle, gave form and substance to quality law enforcement throughout the free world. These men & their families stand as examples of the best in American values.

PUBLIC SAFETY OFFICERS KILLED ON DUTY
1960 - 1972

Norman Glowers	*Albert Farkas*
Michael Murphy	*Dan Metrione*
John McCarthy	*Dolf Owens*
Jack Wells	*George Miller*

PREFACE

To us, there's something innately decent about being an American. Call it a sense of honor, or a righteousness of spirit. Principled perhaps. Whatever it is, I felt its pride at an early age.

My father and grandfather, indeed all 21 of my blood relatives, were breathing examples of the pioneer spirit come of age in the Great Depression. By the time I was born, FDR was next to God himself and radio was everyone's thread to the world. When the devastation at Pearl Harbor occurred, I was five, already skilled in the tactics of survival and knew the financial and emotional hardships no family in America escaped.

In those days, you were either poverty stricken or a Vanderbilt. No in-betweens. The values of the working man were not those of the aristocracy or the financially able, even though most Americans, of all strata, recognized, rallied and decried the Nazi and Japanese threat.

As one of five children from an impoverished Ohio steel town, privation had been my life. But when the war was over, when the need to survive passed, when times got better, our family left behind wily survival techniques and concentrated once again on instilling the demanding ethics of our ethnic German heritage: self-discipline, hard work, honor.

It was then that FDR's reforms and the spirit of America gave rise to a fiscally able populace, and we, like so many other families, struggled to better our lot. The times had forced us to be contributors to the common good, not consumers--and contribute we did. We emerged as the great American middle class.

I knew even then I lived in the greatest nation in the world because of compassion for oppressed peoples as our forebears were once oppressed; because of freedoms fought for and won in our founding days; and because of a belief in a power greater than any man alive.

The Chinese say "Our greatest strength is our greatest weakness". After Vietnam, I re-evaluated my beliefs, deciding to continue on the same road. It may not always play well in Poughkeepsie, but I have to look at myself in the mirror every day.

I highly recommend the exercise.

CONTENTS

ACKNOWLEDGMENT

My wife of 37 years, Shirley, abused, shamed, wrote, edited, encouraged, and re-wrote every word written in this book. Without her, I wouldn't have started, much less finished the project.

I'm indebted to Randolph Carter Berkeley, III, those many years ago, for his shining example, his faith in me, and his unrelenting pursuit of excellence under the worst of conditions. He defines and personifies professionalism.

I'm energized by the late Frank C. Walton, who, until the day he died at age 85, never once wavered in his support of me, or this project. We remember him as a moral, remarkable man.

And I am profoundly proud to have served with them both.

No less significant are Byron Engle, Mike Mc-Cann, Jack Goin, John Lindquist, and John Manopoli. Each personify, in his own peculiar way, the very best of Public Safety.

While we bear a measure of guilt for pouring our lives into our work at the expense of family--our son, Chris, and daughter, Shannon, share our belief this story must be told.

And God himself has sent any number of kindly sorts to mentor us through each thought to written word. Our deep appreciation to these very special people.

My service in Vietnam was a scary, confusing, bumpy, thrilling, and bold journey for me. And it was also, a truly magnificent trip. I thank my wife and kids for the ticket.

Don and Shirley Bordenkircher

INTRODUCTION

God, country, mom and apple pie may be old saws, but we are ever more convinced those things are worth life itself, for a life worth living must have purpose; strive for balance; engender respect; seek justice; and be inspired by love.

It was those beliefs that caused me to accept a position with a small, elite government police advisory mission in 1967. I was hired from the administrative ranks of San Quentin Prison by the United States Agency for International Development - Office of Public Safety (USAID/OPS), as a correction's advisor.

I would spend nearly five years of my life in South Vietnam as the Senior Advisor to the South Vietnamese Director of Corrections and his forty-one correctional centers. One of these was the prison on Con Son Island.

I would never be sorry I served, nor apologetic for the job I did while there, nor would I ever be more ashamed of my countrymen, or my government. Which is not to say returning to the United States as a Vietnam survivor was easy. Returning from Vietnam was a little like having the newest communicable disease — some people were disgusted, some hostile, and others just avoided me. Or so it seemed.

Call me naive, but my Vietnam education in political reality was a blockbuster. I watched the world press, government officials, political expediency and incompetent bureaucracy join together, sometimes by design, but more often through negligence, ineptness, laziness and just plain fear, to foist upon our country more than one terrible injustice.

Hidden agendas, greed and power caused many a First Amendment privilege to be abused by the taking of First Amendment license. Honor, commitment, and righteous indignation got lost in the scramble for supremacy of turf. The good guys skirmished in the light, the bad guys in the dark, and who was who often didn't surface until the time was past to take action. Doing your job, doing it well, and doing it right, became a continual evasive action. That anything at all got done, is amazing; that anything of consequence was accomplished, is miraculous.

Even today, nearly thirty years later, the historical recollections of the Vietnam era placed to print and screen deal mostly with what America did wrong in South Vietnam. My story is about what some men did right. It is about a miracle of effort and commitment. And it is about how smoke and mirrors so easily destroyed the very substance of that effort.

In truth, there would be no story to tell were it not for my involvement in the so-called Tiger Cage Affair of 1970. I was just an advisor, like a lot of other advisors, doing their mundane job in a war torn country, meeting daily professional challenges, aspiring to make a difference, and trying to stay alive long enough to get home to my family. Nothing extraordinary.

But the tiger cage incident changed all that. By calling into question my very existence as an American, as a professional, and as a man, this most blatant example of exploitive manipulation changed the course of history, turning my competent service in Vietnam into a damnable segment of the era. In the following chapters, I'll attempt to bring you into the paradoxical prison system of South Vietnam. Why and how the United States became involved in a civilian prison system thousands of miles from its shores; what we did when we got there; and why we did what we did.

You will be introduced to civilian and military acronyms. Anticipate them to confuse you and perhaps try your patience. Be patient and do not allow confusion. Acronyms are designed to shield real people and their offices. They are a tool of the smoke and mirrors game.

I will clarify the convolutions of organizational structure surrounding the prison program. I will walk you through events which created a climate in which 60's zealots and a jaundiced press could aid the enemy, perhaps unknowingly, but nonetheless, effectively. I'll fuse the emotions of the times with the realities of those same times within the prison setting.

How the tiger cage drama of international attention played to the world is easily researched. Some of you may even recall snippets of the so-called atrocity. In the following pages, the atrocity will be reviewed in context. It will have a beginning, a middle, and an end, and it will be that part of the drama which never reached the eyes, or ears of the world.

Tiger cages are words of dramatic potential. The tiger cage episode was conceived and executed by men who knew how to work a crowd. They knew facts are never more tantalizing than when perceptions are stretched by the igno-

8

rance and emotions of the masses.

Although the tiger cage saga begins long before the Office of Public Safety was disbanded, it sped the process along. Public Safety became a casualty of the United States Congress under the 1974 Foreign Assistance Act, suffering a long and painful death.

Congressmen who backed the measure, led by Senator William Fulbright, D., Arkansas, contended the Public Safety program led to a multitude of sins in support of military dictatorships. Many members of the news media joined those who felt the program, advised by U. S. police advisors, was responsible for political repression, imprisonment, and torture of dissidents throughout the world.

While there was never evidence to support this conjecture, then, nor is there now, the tenor of the Congress in 1974 was more than modestly anti police and Vietnam. Congress wanted desperately to absolve itself of blame for the war. It was reactive, as political entities often are, and feeling the need to appease the media, the riotous youth of their constituents, the anti war groups, and a public tired of a war it was increasingly certain we could not—or would not—win. So much was going on in the anti arena, resolve was fading, and multiple scapegoats were needed to extricate themselves, and they believed, the country.

As the best advertising executive knows, the masses aren't difficult to sway when emotions run high. And so, Public Safety became one of the many sacrificial lambs left to flame on the pyre of the times. According to some, it was inevitable. Actually it was a coup of brilliance. And it was easily done.

The general public's first exposure came on July 17, 1970, when a LIFE magazine exposé paraded the tiger cages of Con Son Island Prison. A Congressional Committee Aide, solicited and was paid, $10,000 for the photographs. The deal was made before the photos were in hand; before having seen anything; before leaving the U.S.

TIME magazine, and other print media followed with spins of their own; a U. S. government subcommittee held hearings, the world shuddered at the atrocity depicted, and the negotiators at the Paris peace talks—North Vietnamese, Viet Cong, and Americans—accused and defended respectively. The tiger cage incident, and the media's accounting of it, was excellent theater.

A California congressman said to a gathering of colleagues in early 1970, that he was out to "find a factual basis for an emotional response to end the war in Vietnam." He and others *found* the tiger cages—contriving and orchestrating an emotional frenzy. Their justification was regal—if it helped end the war—if it helped end the Office of Public Safety, then so be it. But little they depicted was supported by fact.

The aide's premise was not questioned. That his facts and pictures were skewed to achieve his end was not, apparently, worthy of active consideration. The few efforts made to correct the misinformation fell on deaf ears and lazy minds. Independent investigation of a firsthand nature was not encouraged, in matter of fact, the option was actively denied to those few who raised the question.

Granted, everyone has a story to tell. Myth, legend and fable spring naturally and take on a life of their own. The Tiger Cage Story is a brilliant example of that phenomena. But there is another side to the story, and for it to be believed historical documentation is required.

My wife began active research for this manuscript in 1988. I continued to buck her efforts feeling no one cared, and besides that, I couldn't prove to the last detail everything I knew and had lived through. After interviews, numerous correspondence and telephone calls, our search for missing pieces ended in late 1994.

We received another in a series of communications from Frank Walton, retired Director of the Public Safety mission in south Vietnam. He was in Hawaii, well into his eighties, and still swimming each morning in the surf off Waikiki.

"I'm sending some boxes; everything's yours, if you want it. It's too late for me to write about . . ." One week later, Frank Walton died.

Soon after, we received three hundred pounds of original documents, copies of originals, memoranda, data inclusive of program planning and budgeting, photographs, congressional responses, fact sheets, personal notes and letters. And every monthly report of the Corrections & Detention Branch from 1967 to its termination, declassified about the time Walton retired, though we didn't know that until recently. We could now speak out.

While none of us may ever know, in minute detail, what transpired outside the eyes of Corrections and Detention, or the Office of Public Safety, concerning the tiger cage incident, we now have support documentation which demonstrates intent and motive.

We're reminded a conclusion is a judgment formed after much thought; and a fact is a deed, an act -- something stated

to be true. We choose to hybridize the two into Faclusion -
an opinion, or personal judgment, formed after much
thought, based on deeds, acts, research and data provided
one as truth. Such is the beginning of our story.

Thirty years after leaving Vietnam, we are led to several
sobering and painful conclusions:

§ Ambassador William Colby (CIA) was being
strangled by the United States Senate's Foreign Relations
Committee's penetrating investigation of his pacification
program, with focus on the clandestine Phoenix component.

§ The Office of Public Safety did serve as a cover
and front for the CIA. Public Safety's Correction & Detention Branch was administratively within Phoenix, under the
umbrella of ICEX. CIA funds were the backbone of the
Corrections/ Detention advisory effort in South Vietnam, to
include the infamous Con Son Island prison complex.

§ Colby's pacification committee's damage control
objective was to save the CIA before the Senate Foreign
Relations Committee. The Office of Public Safety was
Colby's tool, assuring a protective cover for CIA covert
operations.

§ The tiger cage story, put out in 1970, stands as
one of the most successful operations ever undertaken by
Hanoi's Department of Psychological Warfare.

The public outrage began when a self-styled, freelance
journalist accompanied visiting Congressmen and their Administrative Aide, a 1992 presidential candidate, to Con Son
Island in search of the so-called Tiger Cages. The cells were
depicted as cement lined pits roofed with bars and too
shallow for a man to stand. Statements were cited from
prisoners, and select students, who said they were tortured,
unable to exercise, and lost the use of [their] legs through
atrophy.

Our collection of facts encourages us to the Faclusion
these men brought discomfort, shame, and embarrassment to
the United States government and its mission to South
Vietnam by facade and deceit. The tangled liaison woven by
the record suggests a damning conspiracy, but -- facts thus
far support only needs and motives of greed, power, ego and
self-service.

Research supports the view the two men shared a need
for notoriety, and money -- basic necessities for any aspirant
to higher levels of purpose.

One would sell books and articles - thus spreading his
subjective word of injustice, perversity and shame. At the
same time, while claiming expert status, be elevated with

credibility to the pinnacle of the radical left -- ombudsman for the oppressed.

The other, a young man impatient for a future, and the affluence and supremacy he had heretofore been denied, needed money to continue his education - a universal ambition. But his cravings were more complicated. It was necessary to fuse political competence to personal aspiration in such a way as to camouflage the depth of his hunger, and the willful prostitution of principle.

The two men quickly recognized a mechanism and a vehicle capable of fulfilling their personalized obsessions. The mechanism was a medley of media, Congress, and the times. The vehicle was a contraption of South Vietnamese prisoners, American POW's in North Vietnam, organizations and individuals sympathetic to the enemy's cause, the Office of Public Safety, and its Correction and Detention Branch. They were the right men, in the right place. Was their association a fortuitous fluke? Maybe. But I don't believe it.

What is clear to me, is the story they told the world used doctored photographs, misrepresentations, embellishments, and distortions of fact, and all was fictionalized for impact. They stretched advocacy style journalism to its limits. Perhaps beyond. In so doing, they helped the enemy, and hamstrung American negotiators. The stories printed by the media about the so-called tiger cages, based solely on purported findings of two obscure men, strengthened the hand of communist negotiators at the Paris peace talks by amplifying passions on capital hill.

It would be fair to say these same participants would not agree with this assessment. And I don't expect them to. I expect them to say -- however improbable it may appear to me -- their single goal was to end the war. A lofty goal, indeed.

My question is if the total abandonment of moral and ethical principle is justified by their goal. But that isn't the point to be made here. At issue is not which story is *the true* story; or even if there is one true story. At issue is my right to tell mine. Theirs has been told--in infinite detail--and now it's time for, as Paul Harvey says, "the rest of the story."

And one can only wonder how their actions affected the treatment of America's POWs held by North Vietnam. This haunts me still.

Colby knew their statements were distortions, fallacious, and in many instances, out-right lies. Everything done in our program required approval and signature of Colby.

Frank Walton said it best, "He [Colby] couldn't afford to let me tell what happened." Frank believed Colby's agenda was best served by letting the distortions stand. And I agree.

Colby had the power, authority and political clout to save Public Safety. Someone or something had to take blame for the Phoenix program and its purported excesses. He gave them Public Safety.

We freely admit this reconstruction is infused with our opinions and judgments. However, we've labored to be as objective as possible about the people and the events put to these pages.

We are compelled to tell this story. We tell it for what lessons it can teach. We tell it because we believe in justice, and because we care. We tell it because it, too, is a piece of the puzzle that was Vietnam.

This story is what I lived, and it is historically relevant. Whether or not it is ideologically relevant, is ultimately a judgment individual readers must make for themselves.

War is an ugly thing, but not the ugliest of things; the decayed and degraded state of moral and patriotic feeling which thinks that nothing is worth war, is much worse.

A man who has nothing for which he is willing to fight; nothing he cares about more than his own personal safety; is a miserable creature who has no chance of being free, unless made and kept so by the exertions of better men than himself."

– author unknown

ONE

Feet first — OPS, ICEX, PHOENIX & me

Dawn in Saigon is extraordinary. There is no wild and crazy traffic. No motorbikes and trucks choking the roadways. The streets have been cleaned. Street vendors aren't yet clogging the roadside. The corrugated doors of shops and restaurants are closed and quiet. The pungent aroma of cooking food is not yet consumed by the odorous vapors of gasoline and truck exhaust. And the tree-lined boulevards are pictures of southern serenity.

Indeed, morning was the time to savor the elegance of this historic and ancient city — very beautiful, despite the ravages of war. Morning in Saigon was before reality.

I was assigned the job of Senior Advisor to the Directorate of Corrections (DOC), and counterpart to the South Vietnamese Director, Le Quang Mai. One morning, when I arrived at work, Mai was waiting for me with sweaty palms and a solemn face.

His extended family of eleven lived in the countryside near Hue he said, and asked for my help to rescue them. He missed his parents, and his six daughters needed their grandparents. He wanted them safely in Saigon. He had no idea how we would accomplish this feat, but assured me he would not return without them. They meant a lot to him and with or without my help, it was something he must do.

Smuggling nationals from one province to another wasn't my specialty, but I said I'd do what I could. An apocalypse of roadblocks, check points, sniper fire and contested travel documents swirled through my brain. We left within the hour.

In the first weeks of May, 1968, in the company of Director Mai and Mr. Gi, my Administrative Assistant/Interpreter, I had surveyed five of the six provincial civilian prisons in I Corp. Our last stop was to be a prison in Thua Thien Province, where the city of Hue had been under siege since the Tet Offensive.

The raging battle for control of Hue was past but sporadic fire fights were still in evidence. The ancient city

15

was a shambles -- bridges out, buildings listing and vacant like cardboard boxes pitched in a dumpster. Sculptures of twisted metal lined the main roadways. Glass crunched under the weight of boots and jeeps, and the stench of raw sewage, gunpowder and death hugged the city like vaporous mist hugs a bayou.

When we arrived in the city, I raked the province communications advisor out of bed and sent a message to Saigon--need flight space/13people/ThuaThien/Saigon/day after tomorrow. I'd pick up the response at Lou Spalla's province headquarters.

Lou was an Office of Public Safety (OPS) province advisor and a good friend. He was from Arizona, had been with OPS just a while longer than I had, and we were bunking the next night at his place. I knew I could count on his help and I was right.

We reached Lou's, and Mai left to gather his family at the prison by dawn. The next morning, Mai wasn't there, but nine new prisoners were. Half-way through the inspection, Mai dropped off two more prisoners, and we completed the survey of the prison together. Meanwhile, Lou was doing his part, picking up my flight message, confirming our Air America space.

A prison truck was loaded with the eleven prisoners and Director Mai. I sat opposite the truck's driver, and Lou and the province Police Chief rode ahead of us in his jeep. We hit a couple of roadblocks and one sticky checkpoint, but we bluffed through without anyone checking the "prisoners" papers. An airport gun battle, two days, and many prayers later landed twelve happy people in Saigon.

I cabled Berkeley, my boss, requesting Ambassador Komer intervene with the Minister of Interior (MOI) to allow Mai and me to proceed with a survey of II Corps civilian prisons. Concluding the cable with an overview of my survey and inspection of I Corps' prisons, I typed, "It's so bad — if this is an indication of what we'll find in the remainder of these prisons -- then we've got something more than a big problem." The situation was critical and overwhelming. Really bad.

We were directly responsible for making a difference, and there was nowhere to go but up. Still, I felt like running back to the states. Instead, I swallowed hard and vowed to do the best I could -- as fast as I could. Mai caught up with me in Da Nang.

The Ministry had told the chief jailer of each province prison about the upcoming surveys. We were very aware of the problems we would confront and knew how to surmount them, but we feared the GVN-Ministry of Interior wouldn't support us, nor give us the time we needed to upgrade. Still, there was excitement in the air. At least, now I would have my chance to see the real world of Vietnam.

I sent Gi back to Saigon. Mai spoke English fluently and I spoke some Vietnamese. He would better serve us at the Directorate, turning my daily field scribblings into translated reports.

We completed II Corps June 6, 1968. From dawn to dark, seven days a week, Mai and I visited at least two centers a day. Daily, in depth, analysis on each center (civilian prison) visited, inspected, and surveyed, was sent to Berkeley by courier. Each morning, Gi picked up my pouch enroute to the office.

By the end of June, our inspection and survey of all thirty-seven provincial prisons was finished. The four national centers could be completed later. We returned to Saigon.

Every nook and cranny at every civilian prison was inspected. I arranged with each Chief Jailer to line up every prisoner so I could personally count them, nose by nose. I compiled a definitive list of the strengths and weakness of each prison and its staff, and developed budget requirements for the upcoming fiscal year.

Thorough documentation was an absolute during my years with OPS in Vietnam and Washington. It became a habit and an ability which continues to serve me well, but then it was an extremely time-consuming task which slowed, what I perceived as, my real work. Gi rose to my paper demands early in our association and became adept at meeting them. He had translated my handwritten field notes into typewritten reports in two languages before my return flight touched the tarmac.

The other Correction & Detention (C&D) advisors had also been busy. Randolph Carter Berkeley III, my immediate supervisor, maintained two offices. His primary space was at the Military Assistance Command Vietnam (MACV) headquarters at Tan Sha Nhut Airbase, adjacent to William Colby's office. A secondary location was at USAID II, just down the corridor from John Manopoli's OPS headquarters.

Berk developed a handbook on the legal processing of

national security offenders. He was a taskmaster who did his share and more. It wasn't unusual for him to work until midnight keeping our paperwork moving. His military career had given him an edge in dealing with the corkscrew path of bureaucratic process and he used it to the advantage of C&D.

Phillip "Swede" Severson, a former Director of Prisons in Alaska, was assigned the post of Senior Advisor to the Detention program in liaison with the National Police. He was feverishly working with the Director General of the National Police on the establishment, staffing, and operation of a national jail system. Simultaneously, he was developing construction plans and protocol. Our plans were to build eight thousand nine hundred additional jail spaces in strategic locations, quickly. Swede had office quarters at USAID II. (27)

Bill Secor, a retired military Colonel and former Sergeant at San Quentin Prison, and I had a full time working office at the South Vietnamese Directorate, and space to hang our hats when at the USAID office. And we preferred it that way.

Bill had worked under me at San Quentin as death row Sergeant, and we had roomed together while training in Washington. He was a tall, large man with a flat, pug-nosed face, and a squinty grin. After having his say, he followed orders, was dependable in a crisis, and understood chain of command.

We had a good working relationship, but socially we weren't much of a match. Bill was gregarious, and liked the camaraderie of the boys, while I'm a homebody who doesn't mind being alone. I favor small gatherings, avoid crowds, and am very shy. Small talk isn't easy for me, even now, though I've learned to be more at ease about it.

In Vietnam, the two of us continued to lead our separate after work lives. Without family around, I mostly worked, but occasionally ran into Secor at some cocktail party or another when my attendance was expected. It was a satisfactory arrangement. Other than prisons, Bill and I had little in common.

Bill was my second, and held down the office at the Directorate, backstopping my crisis-ridden, nonstop, inspection and evaluation tour. He continued the implementation of the extraction program -- a name implying something other than moving excess prisoners/detainees from province prisons vulnerable to Viet Cong attacks. Primarily national

18

prisons were the destination, more specifically, Con Son Island.

I spent little time in any office. We were a new project, and it was critical to know everything first hand. I regularly canvassed prisons countywide with Gi. Director Mai accompanied us when he could.

During the first four months of settling in, and while I jumped from one side of the country to the other, major changes were taking place. General Creighton Abrahms replaced William Westmoreland as the MAC/V Commander. In April, President Johnson announced he would not seek reelection.

About this time, Ambassador Komer assigned William Colby, his assistant, as a direct U.S. counterpart to the Minister of Interior, Tran Thien Khiem [General]. LTC. Loi Nguyen Tan, was General Khiem's man in charge of the Vietnamese Phoung Hoang/ICEX Directorate. Tan's marching orders came directly from Khiem and those orders never skipped a heartbeat from the will and pleasure of Colby.

May 5, General Nguyen Ngoc Loan, the plucky head of the National Police, was seriously wounded. Loan was a commander of the highest order and OPS would mourn his absence. Col. Tran Van Phan, General Khiem's personal choice took his place.

Doug Valentine reports in his book, THE PHOENIX PROGRAM, what Evan Parker says about his patron, William Colby. "The interesting thing was his relationship with Khiem . . . they would travel around the countryside in the same plane, each sitting there with his briefcase and a stack of working papers, working like mad, answering memorandums, writing memoranda, passing memorandum back and forth. . . there's your coordination."

ICEX was a newly conceived entity and it was Komer's baby, but the CIA had long been in Vietnam. To fully understand the usefulness of ICEX to the CIA, and to Colby, it's helpful to know how ICEX came to be. How my own agency, the Office of Public Safety, came under the wing of William Colby, the CIA, Phoenix, and ICEX is part of the same, intricately woven cloth.

I knew nothing of ICEX when I arrived in Saigon. My arrival was three months behind that of my fellow recruits. Much to my dismay, my aptitude for foreign language, shown while training at the Foreign Service Institute, put me into Vietnamese language submersion classes. No way. I was tired of Washington. And I was more than anxious to move on to my assignment.

In the Navy, I had trained in Russian as requisite to being a cryptographer based in Kamasaya, Japan. I'd enjoyed it. But now, after three months in foreign service classes, I was eager to start working. I petitioned my superiors at OPS to move me along to post. No luck. The rational was basic. I was one of only two recruits to ever make it into the language school and that feather would stay in OPS's cap.

Byron Engle, the Director of Public Safety, listened to me for a bare second, leaned over the table and nailed my eyes. "You'll do as directed." he said, dropping eye contact with a wave of his hand. "In the meantime, enjoy it."

I stood and saluted. Nobody argued with Engle.

Although at that moment I resented being held in D. C., knowing Vietnamese - however poorly - would become one of the better tools at my disposal during my tenure in Vietnam.

By February 21, 1968, when I landed at Tan Sha Nhut Airbase, I was like a racehorse high on protein supplements - lean, mean, and ready to run. The day fit my mood. It was 7:15 a.m., and Saigon was bright yellow. It was also just three days into the battle that has become known as the Tet Offensive.

Smoke curled across the city in every direction. Buildings burned uncontrollably. Gunfire was constant. The roof of the airport customs building was blown away and the resultant debris dappled the tarmac as far as I could see.

Vietnamese police and army units were scattered around the airport area and throughout the terminal. I was one of many in a very long line waiting to pass through customs. Two hours later, I had my luggage and stood, as instructed, outside the terminal waiting to be picked up.

My orders were to report to USAID II, CORDS Compound, Saigon. At noon I gave it up and grabbed a taxi.

The CORDS building was located eleven miles across town from the air base. In route, detours were necessary to avoid army and police units, as well as, gunfights blocking many of the through streets. An hour later the taxi chugged to a stop near the USAID II building.

Inside the building, the halls were deserted. There were no people. Anywhere. I had pictured OPS Saigon as a bustling enterprise. This wasn't the case. I zigged and zagged until I found a cluttered cubby hole with an American sitting in it.

He introduced himself as Charlie O'Brien. All OPS advisors in Saigon had been detailed as armed guards for busses transporting U.S. employees to various work sites in the city. Because of the Tet situation, he apologized-- someone should have met me at the airport. At his instruction, I went to the top floor to find Carberry, the man in charge of OPS personnel in country. He confirmed my room at the Kings Hotel on Hong Tap Tu Street, one block off the infamous Tu Do Street in downtown Saigon.

The C&D branch had just moved into the building, and their offices were on the first floor - left at the bottom of the stairs, second room on the right. Carberry wasn't certain if anyone would be there - routines had been radically disrupted by Tet. I would find out quickly there were no routines in Vietnam, even in the calmest of times. Except, maybe, the noon rest hour when the entire country shut down.

The National Police Compound, where all weapons were checked out, was still in a state of shock over Tet, and weapons were at a premium. We weren't required to carry weapons, but at my request Carberry offered to loan me two of his own.

I loaded the .45, stuck it securely in my belt; loaded the carbine, placed it on safety, and thanked him. Much, much better. It was already apparent to me, Vietnam for an OPS advisor was a do-it-yourself operation. I intended to be prepared.

Entering the Corrections & Detention office on the first floor, a giant of a man stepped forward. He was at least six foot seven inches tall, blond, weighed about two sixty and towered over me by nearly a foot. I stuck out my hand and introduced myself.

"Phil Severson," he said.

"I was told to report to the boss. You him?"

Severson laughed aloud and said, "Man, let me tell you everything's all f___d up around here."

He told me he was slotted to manage the C&D operation, but a new outfit by the name of ICEX had taken over and displaced him in favor of a man named Berkeley. Severson didn't sound happy about the change, or Berkeley as a boss.

"What's ICEX," I asked, ignoring his arrogance.

"It's CIA. You'll find out soon enough."

I didn't debate his statement though it was news to me, and asked about Secor's whereabouts. He was in the 7th Field Hospital located in the Cholon district of Saigon. A week earlier, Bill had suffered a kidney stone attack and had undergone major surgery. The phone rang.

Severson waved me away with, "Berkeley wants to see you."

"Good. Where do I find him?"

He just laughed.

A Deputy Director's instruction when I left Washington was to "go with the flow." The words rattled in my ears as I located Berkeley's office, an hour and a half later, in the MACV Compound -- at the air base where I had arrived nearly six hours earlier.

BERKELEY C&D marked the door next to Ambassador Komer's. In the outer office sat Berkeley's right hand, a LTC. on loan from the U.S. Army. He introduced Randolph Carter Berkeley, my new boss.

Berkeley was extremely apologetic. No one had informed him of the day I would arrive. He assured me, had he known, he would have driven his vehicle a quarter of a mile, met me, and brought me to his office. He was genuinely embarrassed.

Business was never mentioned. Berkeley was interested in hearing about my background and credentials, but he quickly suggested I check in, get some sleep and a good meal. He would pick me up in the morning - at seven sharp - and we would "hit the ground running."

At my hotel, I rode something resembling an elevator up to the third floor, put my bags by the door, and laid the carbine on top of them, fumbling in my pocket for the door key. When it hit the keyhole, four deafening shots rang out, and the door in front of me splintered.

Next thing I know, the .45 is in my hand and I've spun around to stare at a woman in the doorway of the room directly across from mine. An automatic handgun, held by two quivering hands, was pointed directly at my chest. The American holding it was hysterical--visibly shaking all over and screeching, "Unload this damn thing!"

I shouted some choice words as I grabbed her arm. "I know, I almost killed you," she sobbed. "I couldn't figure it out!"

Relieved of the weapon, she sunk back against the door

frame whispering an apology as she shoved the gun into my flesh. I jammed it under my belt and went directly down-stairs.

When I returned, I had the manager with me, or some-one who thought he was the manager, or someone I thought was the manager. The corridor was by now filled with people, which struck me as odd, for the entire place appeared abandoned when I arrived. It's still unclear where they all came from. I would learn to view this as an Oriental phenomenon from which one does not escape. One is never alone in Asia.

My new location on the second floor looked okay as I put the key in the lock, turning to check the nooks and crannies behind me. Satisfied things were relatively secure, I opened the door and kicked my bags inside. To this day, all I can remember after that is sitting down on the bed for just a moment.

I awoke, fully dressed, at five the next morning. Within minutes I was showered, unpacked, and downstairs facing an American style breakfast. By six a.m., dressed in a tropical suit and coordinating tie, .45 in my belt, carbine in my right hand, I stood in the street waiting for Berkeley. The suit and tie lasted only a day or two, but these weapons and then some would be my able and constant companions until I left Vietnam.

Punctuality was part of Berkeley's bible. He drove up at seven sharp in his 1962 Mercury Comet, a symbol, I would find out later, of CIA affiliation. He wore his uniform--dark dress slacks and a white cotton shirt, unbuttoned at the neck.

"Good night's sleep?" A nod was my response. I was too embarrassed to tell him about the hysterical American and her misplaced bullets.

Berkeley deposited me in his office, and spent the entire day shuttling in and out to previously scheduled meetings. My day was spent digesting the orderly contents of his file cabinets. It was a unique chance for me to get a handle on this thing called ICEX. Severson had piqued my curiosity.

The files revealed policy statements by the pound, each one open to interpretation. What follows is my appraisal of those documents.

The CIA had strongly influenced the selection of Ngo Dinh Diem, a Catholic Mandarin from Hue, as the President of South Vietnam. Nguyen Ngoc Le was appointed Diem's first Director General of the National Police. Le was a long time CIA asset. Diem's "denunciation of the communist campaign" was managed by security committees chaired by CIA advised security officers.

Shortly after the U.S. National Security Council (NSC) endorsed Diem, Michigan State University (MSU) provided South Vietnam technical assistance in public information, public administration, police administration, security services, finance and economics. MSU added overt police advisors, most former Michigan state troopers and professional police officers, to the Civil Police Assistance unit, diluting the number of CIA officers working undercover as professors.(261)

In actuality, the police technical assistance program was initiated by Michigan State University's School of Police Administration under contract with the International Cooperation Administration (ICA). The ICA was an agency created within the U.S. State Department to administer the foreign aid program. A small staff of CIA personnel in Washington, D.C. managed the affairs of an ICA sub program entitled Civil Police Assistance. The ICA was renamed the United States Agency for International Development (USAID) in 1962.

This civil assistance program was the vehicle through which the CIA became involved in the management of the South Vietnamese Special Police. Covert CIA officers advised the Vietnamese Bureau of Investigations (VBI), known as the Cong An. One of the program's original CIA managers was Byron Engle. The CIA's Saigon Deputy Chief of Station, in the spring of 1959, was William Colby, who would later become Director of the CIA. (26,261)

Colby managed the station's paramilitary operations. Simultaneously, he increased CIA advice and assistance to security forces. At that juncture, MSU ceased being a CIA cover.

The newly elected President, John Kennedy, was distrustful of the National Security Council. One of his first actions in office was to organize and establish the Special Group-CI (counter insurgency) to study guerrilla warfare and unconventional military tactics. The membership of the group was illustrious, quiet, and personally chosen by the President. Indeed, all were trusted Kennedy friends.

The distinguished Averill Harriman was appointed chairman. The members, Allen Dulles, CIA; David Bell, ICA; Robert Kennedy; and Edward R. Murrow of the United

States Information Agency (USIA) were empowered to circumvent the NSC, and reported only to the President.

At first, the group focused on military training, but ultimately the program included police training to foreign nationals. Third world countries clamored to learn the latest methods of traffic control, identification systems, and arrest procedures, as well as, how to get and use the newest communications equipment.

Byron Engle, a long time Harriman associate and friend, was assigned by Dulles to direct a sub committee authorized under the Special Group-CI. Engle astutely engineered, through that group, Kennedy's reorganization of counter-insurgency entities. In this way, an interagency study group to address civil police assistance within foreign aid programs became an element of counter insurgency programs.

Confronted with Khrushchev's threat of wars of liberation, Kennedy chose to face the menace at its level of origin--civil disorder. He wanted a democratic civil response because he, and I believe rightly so, did not believe a military response appropriate at this level. (291, 292, 261)

Acknowledging the necessity and contribution of the Civil Police Assistance program, Kennedy ordered the State Department's AID agency to absorb the CIA officers associated with it. The Civil Police Assistance entity was renamed the Office of Public Safety (OPS).

The name Public Safety was selected as camouflage. It was less meaningful within the budget framework than police assistance, and provided sufficient bureaucratic layer to cover its CIA birthplace, nurturing and nursing. Byron Engle became the Director of the new office, known in Washington as USAID/OPS.

In late 1967, while I was training in Washington, RAMPARTS magazine seized the moment. Their exposé on Michigan State as a cover for CIA agents and activities was timely. The anti war sentiments building in the United States flamed on this new information. In an editorial, and a blazing article titled simply PACIFICATION IN VIETNAM, the magazine laid out a grizzly scenario that hung MSU, OPS, and anyone and anything else even remotely, or ever, touching the CIA, at the end of a rope twisting in the wind. The windier it got, the more twisted the facts became.

The legitimate press and anti war liberators swallowed the rope whole, expanding and expounding, layering and clouding, until sorting out the details became impossible.

That no one really cared to delve deeply enough to sort it out was a sign of the times -- and inevitable, given the shroud of secrecy surrounding the CIA. Secrecy, like so many other images in life, has multiple faces.

RAMPARTS did have the players straight—as far as they went. But it didn't have the game plan right. How could they? As we noted in the introduction, smoke and mirrors is a mystical game and acronyms are part of the design and meant to confuse. By the time I arrived in Vietnam, we were very aware our program was fertile ground for issue exploitation--by our own and by the enemy. It was just a matter of time.

Robert Komer, who was a member of Kennedy's National Security Council, and William Colby, CIA, Washington, D.C., were good friends of Engle's. The three men had served together in the CIA's front runner agency, the Office of Strategic Services (OSS).

That Komer, Colby and Engle had been OSS colleagues was of little consequence to OPS operations. Occasionally, their social paths crossed, but their work paths were more like wheel spokes than railroad tracks. Purportedly, the CIA became Engle's past and OPS his future. But until retirement, he continued his CIA affiliation and status, although the details, indeed, the awareness of the alliance, was obliterated by years of silence to the subject. (261)

Engle, a country boy from the Midwest, was a bespectacled and engaging man who enjoyed hunting safaris and tromps in the woods. He was a stickler for detail, and seemed to never forget a face, or a name. And you never, ever, wanted to be on his list. He could, would, and did make your life a living hell. He was also a masterful and wily bureaucrat within the Washington political structure, and an astute, interesting and lively conversationalist who acknowledged and nurtured junior members with ease. His leadership style was quiet, steady, and if need be, authoritarian. He built a loyal, proud and committed organization by encouraging each man's singular talents.

The ultimate consequence to OPS would not be known for years, but most would agree, under Engle's tutelage, OPS succeeded where others had failed in the area of civil disorder.

The objectives of the Public Safety division in South Vietnam were to strengthen the capability of the civil police and paramilitary police forces through specialized training. They would learn to enforce the law and maintain public order with minimum use of force; be encouraged to develop responsible and humane police administration policies; and discover ways to become more closely integrated into the community.

Peculiar to this mission, was Public Safety's concurrent advisory assistance to the South Vietnam Directorate of Rehabilitation. The effort began, with one advisor, in 1961, at the insistence of provincial OPS advisors -- men who pleaded with their boss, John Monopoli, to provide help and assistance to the provincial civilian prisons, which they described as wretched.

The province advisors, most of whom were former policemen, knew little about corrections systems. The initial advisor to the program was William Benson, a police advisor. He had difficulty getting into the prison system, but eventually, through sheer perseverance, freedom of access was granted.

In 1966, our country's most prominent spokespersons, doves and hawks alike, openly threatened Ho Chi Minh with dire reprisals if he hurt, or executed, captured American pilots. Ho referred to American pilots as war criminals, and continued violating international guidelines for handling POW's. (5)

Ho's response was, essentially, that our escalation of the war would cause him to kill his American prisoners. This statement pushed the Washington hierarchy to the wire. The President, not Ho Chi Minh, would get the blame. Not an acceptable circumstance. The escalation debate raged on.

Simultaneous with these verbal gymnastics, was a report Byron Engle received from his friend, Harriman. The communication was from Ho Chi Minh and Madam Binh, the Viet Cong's representative, to the Geneva Peace discussions. It concerned prisoners-of-war, theirs and ours, and it was chilling. (6,11, 261)

"Ambassador Averill Harriman . . . advises . . . Madam Binh, . . . stated, 'those prisoners that you have confined in the prisons of South Vietnam are our patriots. Whenever we receive word of mistreatment and maltreatment of our comrades in your prisons, you have diminished the life span of your war criminals held in camps in North Vietnam.'" (11, 261)

Binh's message couldn't have been more clear -- captured United States personnel were in crisis if we didn't take care of men and women confined in civilian prisons. Even though the prisons were civil prisons, not prisoner-of-war camps, we had no choice but to believe, and pray, that if we diligently worked toward improving the quality of life for civilian prisoners held in South Vietnam's prisons and jails, then the improvement would directly affect the quality of life of Americans held captive in the North. Quid quo pro.

So serious was this statement that, on May 18, 1966, Deputy Assistant Secretary for Public Affairs, Robert J. McCloskey, conducted a press briefing with international news correspondents. At the gathering, McCloskey announced Governor Harriman (Ambassador- at-Large, W. Averill Harriman) would assume the general supervision of the State Department's actions concerning prisoners held on both sides in the conflict. (6)

The State Department and Special Group CI's interpretation of Madam Binh's statement was to require impetus be given the U.S. advisory effort to South Vietnam's corrections system. The health, welfare, and safety of Americans being held in the prison camps of North Vietnam had become a priority.

The directive to increase advisory and technical support to the prison system was issued to OPS. Byron Engle wasn't the only state department chief who didn't want the task assigned to his section. Aside from the peculiarities of the particular situation, correction's personnel and police officers labored under a history of miscommunication. Subtle disdain for each other's roles and contributions to the criminal justice organization, where neither side conceded the other's job as far more complicated, difficult and extensive than the stereotypical allows, was ever present.

It was this subtle disdain and oblique understanding which caused agency chief after agency chief to call in his due bills to avoid having to hire corrections advisors. Finally, more as a favor to his old friend, Harriman, Engle agreed and proceeded with good grace. (261)

President Johnson built on Kennedy's concept. He identified and was concerned about two wars in South Vietnam. Bureaucratic foot-dragging in the insidious people's war exasperated him. He believed we could not prevail if we continued to insist on fighting a soldier's war, while our enemy focused on a peoples war.

The enemy's shadow government -- a precise replica of the South Vietnamese structure -- sought to infiltrate every level of society and every administrative element of the legitimate government through meticulous and covert organization, persuasion, nationalism, care and kindness. When that methodology failed, they turned to coercion, threats,

28

terror and death. The President perceived the enemy as winning the people's war, and activated a response.

Johnson appointed Robert Komer as his Special Assistant, and directed him to supervise the U.S. response to this people's war. Komer's orders were to "beat the program into shape" He was uniquely suited to the task. His management style was authoritarian--balanced perilously close to totalitarianism. He was master of group psychological dynamics and came by his in-country nickname, Blowtorch, honestly.

Komer requested William Colby, then on assignment at CIA headquarters in Langley, Virginia, be assigned as his Deputy. The President agreed, and Colby joined Komer. (8)

In May 1967, Robert Komer arrived in Saigon as the White House Assistant for Pacification. He wasn't in country very long before he conceived a way to coalesce and fuse the divergent civilian elements of the pacification program. (290)

According to Colby, quoted in FACING THE PHOENIX, by Zalin Grant, "Komer knew that if you put pacification under the military it would be lost, because the military would go out and shoot everybody. Komer also understood. . .the military would never accept anything but a unity of command. Therefore, the only way to make it work was to structure pacification under the military, in civilian hands. He had the genius to see that." (291)

Using the heavy hand of the presidency, Komer convinced General Westmoreland of the merits of reorganization. And reorganize they did. Westmoreland became the commander of the military war and the people's war. Komer was his Deputy for Pacification (people's war).

Komer named his pacification organization Civil Operations and Revolutionary Development (CORDS). His personal short title was DEPCORDS. He quickly moved to organize civilian advisory units into one bureaucracy under his command, embroiling him in the bureaucratic politics and institutional prerogatives of all the agencies concerned with Vietnam. The Department of State (DOS), the Agency for International Development (AID), the United States Information Agency (USIA), the Central Intelligence Agency (CIA), the Department of Defense (DOD), and their many elements, were instantly redefined. (291)

Komer expedited establishment of a general staff presence composed of the highest ranking inter agency members of the Military Assistance Command-Vietnam (MACV), DOS, CIA, USAID, USIA, the Embassy, and DOD. Voilá, a

Pacification Council.

Within the Pacification Council, a specialized branch was developed for coordination of all intelligence gathering. This sub group drew personnel from the CIA, MACV, the Embassy, and CORDS, affording each agency equal representation.

Komer and Colby knew the communist hierarchy had developed, and had in place, a shadow government comprised of party committees in every province, major city, district, village and hamlet in the south of Vietnam. These recruits were support elements for North Vietnam's army and the Viet Cong fighting units. Thousands of them were covert/clandestine communist party members. Weapons were at their disposal, but for the most part they didn't carry them. Each of them had fighting unit bodyguards, and they used weapons only if capture appeared evident.

These party members organized their geographical areas with men, women and children who would support their communistic, nationalistic, anti-American, anti-Thieu causes. Their mission was to handle propaganda, medical, rest/relaxation, communications, food, water, and labor, in support of the fighting units of their shadow government.

These people could be communists, but many were not. Many were nationalists who felt, or were manipulated to believe, the U.S. would occupy the south forever. That the U.S. would spend billions of dollars and spill gallons of blood in their homeland -- and then leave -- was inconceivable. There were others who got offers they could not refuse from communist organizers, and some were merely caught up in the sheer thrill and power of the game of anarchy and terror.

At any rate, none of these people were arms carrying. Therefore, if captured, they could not be classified as prisoners of war according to Geneva Convention guidelines. So, they were called Communist Criminals and treated as any other civil criminal.

Komer and Colby called these non arms bearing people Viet Cong Infrastructure (VCI), knowing they must be neutralized and put out of business if pacification was to succeed. Their newly organized intelligence coordination group, within the pacification program, was code named ICEX. The long title for ICEX was Intelligence Coordination and Exploitation of the Enemy.

ICEX general staff was divided into three separate units.

The Intelligence Unit, composed of two officers--one from MACV and one from the CIA--would evaluate the effectiveness of the attack on the VCI.

The Plans and Programs Unit was composed of three program managers. They were responsible for intelligence collection; coordination and reaction operations; screening, detention, and judicial processing of VCI civilian defendants.

The third unit managed the capture and interrogation of VCI captives and defectors. It was the activities of this unit which would eventually destroy the entire Phoenix program as one rabid dog taints the pack. And it was this unit which caused us, in C&D, a lot of grief. (261)

Having a reputation for terror and accusations of operating death squads, the ICEX managed Interrogation and Exploitation Unit fell to manipulations of definition, perception, and assumption. Indeed, ICEX, shrouded in secrecy, was self-defeating. Rumor prevailed.

As an example, ICEX published the names of VCI members, and provided these lists to U.S. and ARVN military units. Military sweeps of areas would result in fire fights. When published VCI members were killed, ICEX would be credited with the kill, and for the record the word eliminated would be noted next to the member's name. The media and political detractors, seeing these statistics, assumed the VCI member, killed in battle, had been assassinated, discarding traditional definitions in favor of sound bite eloquence, and the lazy comfort of assumption.

The jargon of the intelligence community is far more exciting and colorful than the actualities of action -- as any insider knows. But the perverse manipulation of the vernacular colored the newsprint stateside where advocacy journalism was in full bloom. And they knew exactly what they were doing.

I personally witnessed many of these sweeps during my travels across the south. There was never a time when I saw a sweep unit without a media type traipsing along for a first hand glimpse.

Komer's ICEX plan was endorsed by Ambassador Bunker and General Westmoreland, and delivered to the White House where it was subsequently approved. He quickly set up shop, choosing Evan Parker, a senior CIA officer, to manage the ICEX program. To quote Komer, "ICEX is born." (278)

It was Parker who brought OPS onto the ICEX staff. John Manopoli was the senior in country OPS advisor. He was counterpart to Director General of the National Police.

Manopoli, a retired New York State Police Lieutenant, had served with Michigan State University as a civil police assistance advisor in Vietnam from 1956 to 1959, returning in 1966 as the Chief of OPS. He had no advisory authority over the Special Branch of the National Police, a fact which bothered neither Parker, nor the CIA, a whit. (278)

As Senior Advisor to the National Police Chief, Manopoli was responsible for their administrative needs, as well as, the needs of ICEX as directed to him. ICEX was not organizationally responsible and accountable for the police, or for the military. or anything else for that matter. ICEX simply gave those particular organizational units a directive in the name of MACV, or DEPCORDS, and expected the directives to be carried out.

ICEX was an organizational nightmare. OPS was speechless -- almost -- and helpless to extricate itself from ICEX demands. That OPS wasn't the only agency opposed to the convoluted processes and excesses of ICEX did little in the end to keep it from harm--nor its C&D branch from censure by association.

ICEX's location was on the second floor of the USAID #2 building in downtown Saigon. Its first task was to clearly delineate goals and objectives. The major objective of ICEX, as laid out by Komer, was intelligence, intelligence coordination, and exploitation for attack on VC infrastructure. This objective was clearly outlined in what is commonly known as MACV directive 381-41. This directive marked ICEX, as a formal entity, on July 9, 1967.

Robert C. Lowe, was the Assistant Director for OPS in Saigon. On July 13, a report, prepared by OPS advisor, Bill Benson, and Lowe, was given to Manopoli for presentation to the ICEX general staff. This report outlined the manner in which communist prisoners were processed in the field, and was based on Benson's first hand findings.

OPS defined the major issues plaguing the Directorate of Corrections. They developed screening mechanisms to learn who to interrogate, jail, imprison, or release within the civil prison system. They clearly identified a judicial system lacking due process, habeas corpus, arrest warrants, and lawyers. People were languishing in interrogation camps, jails and prisons without trial for as long as two years.

Public Safety acknowledged this condition, and overall found the situation reprehensible, moving quickly to have ICEX correct it, under signature of Komer. (4)

It was this information provided by OPS, and the dogged prodding and prompting of OPS to the ICEX staff, which caused Robert Harper, a lawyer on contract to the CIA, to come on board as an ICEX team member. All the while, Byron Engle, Bob Lowe, John Manopoli, and Frank Walton, Manopoli's Vietnam replacement, are feverishly recruiting and hiring prison professionals for the now prioritized OPS/ICEX C&D Branch.

The Human Sciences Research Corporation, a Washington based think tank, hired Randolph Carter Berkeley, III, a retired Marine Corps Colonel, to do a study on civil affairs in military operations. Specifically, Berkeley's study focused on the prisoner-detainee problem in Vietnam. At that time, neither Komer nor Manopoli, nor any person on their staff, knew of Randolph Carter Berkeley.

The think tank provided the White House with a copy of Berkeley's study. Shortly after the new year of 1967, Komer was at the White House when Berkeley was summoned to brief him on his report. (261)

Komer immediately liked Berkeley, and he liked what Berkeley told him. Komer hired Berk, on the spot, as Senior Advisor for Prisoners-Detainees. Berkeley had no formal experience or training in corrections or jail administration, in fact, his entire experience was military. However, he was shipped to Saigon as the Senior Advisor on such matters, a full member of the ICEX staff, and manager of the OPS C&D Branch.

Recently retired, with a young child at home, and no job, Berkeley was ecstatic -- and not just about having a job. He found he was fascinated and challenged by the subject of corrections and detention, and looked forward to his involvement. His outward demeanor belied his intense commitment and enthusiasm.

He was methodical, gracious to a fault, yet demanding, small in physical appearance yet larger than life in the composure department. His humor was dry and casual, and business was serious stuff. Elegance in all its embodiments probably describes him best, overall.

Still, no one in OPS knew of Randolph Carter Berkeley, or the fact he had been personally hired by Komer to handle C&D matters. OPS, given the task of hiring corrections professionals for this program, was proceeding post haste.

Berkeley had no counterpart. The counterpart method of organization was used extensively in Vietnam wherein our organizational structure was mirrored by the host government. It was not uncommon to hear an American advisor introduce himself as counterpart to . . . This advisory procedure brought the Vietnamese and American ICEX Directorates into closer coordination and standardized operating procedures. And it worked quite well.

The Vietnamese had no literal translation for the term ICEX so they developed the term Phoung Hoang. The logo of Phoung Hoang mimicked a mythical bird representing grace, peace, virtue, and concord. Americans manned the ICEX directorate and our Vietnamese counterpart agency manned the Phoung Hoang Directorate. One more twist in the pipeline. Berkeley was breaking new ground.

At 11:30 p.m., when Berk dropped me at the hotel, starved, tired, and full of questions, I fell across the bed to immediate, excruciating pain. The gun I'd acquired from the incident the night before was on the bed. The right side of my nose and right eye began to swell and blacken, and scrapes on the right cheek drew blood. I went for ice.

Next morning at seven sharp, Berk's eyes riveted on my face. My explanation was short. "Fell on a gun," I muttered. Perhaps he found my story hard to believe. He just stared.

And this was just the first day!

TWO

Who we were & why we were

From the very beginning, Berk found great humor in my intense and serious demeanor and relished leading me astray. He quickly learned to anticipate my mask, and baited me unmercifully. It became a game he played to get me to "lighten up." He was then, and to my mind remains, a mentor I was lucky, indeed, to know, but it took me a while to read beneath his unruffled exterior. And he did have a way with words.

"I must have forgotten to tell you," Berk said smoothly. "You're accompanying the GVN correction's people transporting a thousand prisoners to Con Son Island. The LST leaves at 5:45 a.m. tomorrow."

I thought because I was the youngest, and the least senior member of the branch, I was tapped to make the trip. My first reaction was that transporting prisoners was -- well, been there, done that -- and I felt my talents were best used to attack the myriad prison problems we faced -- immediately. But it was an opportunity to survey the island prison, so I said I'd go under the condition I would survey the prison.

Berkeley's response was vintage. "That's the great thing about being an American; you have the freedom to voice your opinion." I readied for the trip.

Bill Benson arranged an audience with the Director of Corrections, Le Quang Mai, my counterpart, who would also be on the LST. This was my first opportunity to put my Vietnamese language training to use.

Benson, Berkeley and I entered the Director's office. I was about to say something extremely profound in Vietnamese when Mai stuck out his right hand, and said, "This must be the new guy, Don Bordenkircher." He even pronounced the last name correctly.

During our short meeting, Mai told me he was a graduate of the University of Southern Illinois, and had earned a degree in criminology there. While he was impressing me with his credentials and background, I heard very little. All the hours I was trapped in Washington, a town I detested, listening to those damn language tapes!

After our tour of the Directorate, Berkeley assured me he would make more amenable arrangements for me - a stock of food, a permanent abode and, perhaps, a vehicle. After all, there was plenty of time - the round trip to Con Son would take four days or more. All in all, it had been another bummer of a day. And I was hungry.

As it turned out, I was wrong about going on that trip. Mai and I had four days to get to know one another, and it gave me access to the Vietnamese perspective on the corrections program. It was an invaluable initiation.

Berkeley arrived at 4:25 a.m. and we drove to the Saigon Naval Yard to catch the LST. Mai, and Mr. Quang, his Administrative Assistant, waited for me while discussing last minute arrangements with the jailers.

There were seven armed jailers from Chi Hoa Prison and with them, sitting in a squat position in straight even rows, were eleven hundred male prisoners who were to be transported. I was amazed. Not one prisoner wore hand cuffs or leg irons. They simply squatted in perfect rows, taking orders from one old, and formidable, Chief Jailer.

At 5:15 a.m., Mai and his staff began to load the prisoners, who were called by row. In an extremely orderly fashion, they marched single file onto the boat, sat on the floor, put out their right leg, and were hobbled.

The leg iron assembly consisted of a one inch diameter steel bar, approximately 25 feet long and a U shaped one inch diameter leg cuff. At the end of the U was an eyelet large enough for the long pole to slip into and through. Each prisoner was given one leg iron. He placed the U portion of the iron on top of his ankle so the two eyelets were positioned at his heel.

When all prisoners in a row had their iron in place, the jailers passed the long pole, and man for man they slipped the pole through the eyelets of each U bolt. At the far end, on each side of the pole, the jailers snapped a huge lock into place.

During the entire time, there was not a single sound nor order given. Hand signals were the only communication used between jailers and prisoners. Everyone seemed to know what they were doing, how to do it, and it was done.

Mai and I were assigned a cubicle on the LST. The trip was smooth and uneventful. I truly enjoyed the ride through

36

the waters of the Mekong Delta and the South China Sea. Almost every waking moment was spent with Mai; the two of us sitting on the fantail of the ship. He obligingly, and in detail, told me about the DOC. He was articulate and knowledgeable, and he cared deeply about his country. He, like many others I worked with, was a Catholic and a Northerner. He would become my valued friend.

Two days later, at ten a.m. on a morning straight out of heaven, the LST landed on the beaches of Con Son Island. The huge gate, or front door, of the boat lowered into the water. Prisoners, row by row, disembarked to the beach through about two feet of water. When the prisoners reached the beach area, Con Son jailers merely pointed to a spot on the ground where the first man should stand; the others followed, rank and file, in perfect lines, without a sound. Once everyone in a particular row was in line, the entire row of prisoners would squat on their haunches in the sand. Never a word was spoken. Eleven hundred prisoners were off-loaded without incident.

After all my years of working in U.S. prisons, the silent, orderly loading and unloading of these prisoners boggled my mind. Prisons in the U.S. are manufacturers of noise and battlegrounds of aberrant behavior. Unbelievable, had I not seen it myself.

Berkeley and Benson, having arrived by aircraft earlier that morning, waited on the beach. Military trucks appeared, between two breathtaking mountaintops, driving toward us. The prisoners would be transported by truck to the prison camps clustered around the island.

LTC. Ve, Commandant of the Con Son National Prison, arrived and Benson introduced us. Ve was very aloof towards me, but spoke in glowing terms to and about Benson.

My first sense of Ve was cursory. He made a spit and polish appearance — his uniform was impeccably pressed and creased and his demeanor confident, alert, and pleasant. He definitely had presence. My Vietnamese was as good as his English -- which left a lot to be desired on both counts. He preferred the French language and was fluent and eloquent when he spoke it. Somehow it suited him. He was definitely the chief rooster. I was impressed but decided to reserve judgment until I knew more about him and his prison.

Soon after our arrival, Ve became visibly upset and

turned on Berkeley, blaming Berk for causing his most recent misery -- eleven hundred additional prisoners from mainland provinces to integrate into his camps. Berkeley was sympathetic, but reminded Ve, Con Son was the only answer to the problems of maintaining secure custody of these prisoners. The Tet offensive had caused serious damage to various prisons. These prisoners had to be moved from the mainland for their own safety and as a way of keeping them securely confined.

When the last truck was loaded, Ve jumped into his jeep and led the convoy up the mountain and out of sight. I again suggested I stay on the island. It was lush and very beautiful, but I itched to get moving on my surveys. I could do nothing really constructive until I know who, what, where and how much.

But Berkeley wouldn't budge. That particular set of orders didn't please me, and I let Berkeley know it. He smiled, a rarity I was to discover, and said, in his best imperturbable manner, "The great thing about being an American is that you have the right to complain." Various versions of this phrase became his mantra, and part of the repartee between us.

I never quit telling him what I thought, and though he valued my daring, he never gave up trying to channel me to a smoother course. We also had a healthy respect for each other's competence, and that helped make our alliance creative as well as productive. Our opposite styles strengthened our ability to find solutions that worked, and our program was the beneficiary. But this understanding would come later. At that moment, I boiled.

On the return trip, I continued to pick Mai's brain concerning Vietnam and the prison system. And I learned a few things about Mai, too. He was a Northerner from the Imperial City of Hue, a tall, handsome fellow with six tiny daughters he adored. He was embarrassed by the snail's pace of his government and the Directorate, and equally embarrassed at his embarrassment.

Mai had been toiling in the ranks as a dedicated Inspector for the Directorate of Rehabilitation when he was noticed by Bill Benson. Benson recognized his potential and arranged for him to attend the International Police Academy (IPA) in Washington, D. C., and for his further schooling in criminology at Southern Illinois University--all with the blessing and funding of OPS.

IPA participants were handpicked for their professional ability and potential as career officers in their own country. They were usually exceptional in some way, stood out among their peers, demonstrated leadership qualities, and generally were top track people who it was felt would benefit from additional training in their field.

As time went on, I marveled at Mai's fluency in four languages and his dedication to family; and delighted in his ability and willingness to get things done. He was too Americanized for a political hierarchy choking on change, and he had no highly placed patron to back him should he ruffle too many feathers. He was impatient and creative, and we were to make an excellent team.

On July 1, 1968, Berkeley grouped all personnel to hear a first hand reporting of my survey. Distribution copies of the report -- one thousand ten pages exclusive of Polaroid film photographs, prisoner count sheets, and budget drafts -- were passed around. Evan Parker was there and listened intently. We met at 8 a.m., and tossed questions and answers around until 3 p.m., working on the details until midnight. Exhausted and exhilarated, finally, we had something to build on.

Some of it was dry reading, even for us, but it was all important from the standpoint of planning. It told us where we were. And it was mandatory reading for those unfamiliar with the nuts and bolts of a prison environment. Even in those days, the public perception of a prison was skewed by catchy journalistic portrayals of prisoners as in the Bird Man of Alcatraz, and Cool Hand Luke. Not that abuses don't and didn't occur. But that's another subject. Here I'm talking about the purpose of a prison and how that purpose is best fulfilled. Misconceptions abound.

First, prisons aren't intended as bastions of torture. Basic punishment is the loss of freedom to live your life as and where you choose. This is a matter of degree as measured by time. Period. The ultimate punishment is loss of life, in other words, permanent loss of freedom to live your life as and where you choose.

Sub-categories of punishment can be defined as:

Retribution: Implies restitution, i.e., "You're going to get what's coming to you." A part of retribution is restitution. Ideally, it is decided by a court, using law and legal precedent as a guide, and may take the form of time, money, life - any, all, or none. Hopeflly, it will be just, i.e. fitting to the crime.

Special Deterrence: Teaches a lesson as in—"We're going to punish you so you won't do it again."

General Deterrence: Sets an example as in—"We're going to punish you so that others won't do the same thing."

Incapacitation: Confine and separate from opportunity to repeat. "As long as you're being punished, you won't be out doing something to others."

Rehabilitation (We will reform you through the prison experience) and reintigration (Contact and interact with the positive rather than the negative elements of society in halfway houses and social agencies) are modern day concepts, and are really misnomers as applied to prisoners.

Rehabilitation returns to, or restores to, former capacity or condition. I don't think that's what society intended in this instance. Habilitation is what we really mean. Habilitation, or reintegration, cannot occur and should not even be attempted, until first, basic necessities are in place; and second, the prisoner has accepted responsibility for his own behavior.

In any event, a person who is hungry, cold, burning up, worried about his safety, dirty, unkempt, and sick is in no mood to work toward changing himself. Survival is man's first priority.

The society and law which creates prisoners has every right to expect the prisoner will be clothed, fed, kept safe, clean, and generally in good health, not be housed in conditions unfit for humans, nor be subjected to cruel and unusual punishment. All expectations, except the last one, are easy to define, grasp and to put into practice. I'll leave discussion on the last aspect for a later book.

The job of the prison administrator is to provide an environment which meets the basic needs of a human being, and after that, to expand the environment to include recreation, education, and emotional support. And while it's true a man can eat cockroaches and stay alive, I think we can agree a higher level of sustenance is necessary to maintain life as we know and expect it.

The survey produced a specific accounting of what we needed, and where we needed it; what and where our priorities should be. Wrapped into the next chapters is a shortened account of what I found on my first country wide survey. It's a singularly important document in that it set the basis for our program.

40

THREE

Facing the provinces - civilian prisons & prisoners

When the LST returned to Saigon, Berkeley had a couple of surprises for me. Phil Severson would be the Senior Advisor of the Detention Section, and I would be the Senior Advisor of the Corrections Section. "We felt," he said, "it would be great if you moved in with Benson."

Fine with me. Benson's home was a vintage, pock-marked villa built by the French. The backyard was bordered by concrete and barbed wire fences. Over the fence was the National Police Compound.

The villa was immaculate and sprawling. Bill had a Vietnamese cook and housekeeper, both of whom had been with him since 1961, and they prepared a sumptuous Chinese meal that evening.

I hadn't seen Secor since he left Washington a few months before. Bill had been released from the hospital, and moved in with Benson and me that evening.

The stroke of midnight had a sobering effect on the three of us. Without warning, we were in the shooting war. The VC near and about the National Police Compound were tossing mortars. Many missed their mark, falling short into our front and back yards. Nonetheless, we monitored all night, weapons in hand, manning doors and windows, and putting out fires.

We didn't want to draw fire, but decided firmly anyone entering would be immediately shot. That first night in my new quarters was very long. I didn't know it then, but it would be one of fifteen consecutive nights we would sleep in shifts monitoring VC skirmishes next door.

For the next few weeks I was a shadow to Benson, immersing myself into learning as much as possible about the Corrections system - as seen through the eyes of an American. There was no reason to mention the four days I had spent with Mai on the same subject.

In the interim, Berkeley and Severson worked with the Officer In Charge of Construction (OICC) for the new detention facilities (jail). I assigned Secor to advise the

41

wardens of Chi Hoa, Tan Hiep, and Thu Duc. His priority was in depth surveys of those three national facilities. I would study the DOC, its myriad offices, Vietnamese policy and procedure, and also handle Con Son.

With Benson leaving, there wasn't much time to get the basics out of the way. I had witnessed the reverence the Vietnamese had for Bill Benson. He was more than their advisor, he was their grandfather. They didn't cherish the thought of losing him, and they had no great faith in my ability to assume his role.

I overheard one ranking Vietnamese officer say, "The boy's only in his thirties - Benson's in his sixties; what can this young man do for us?"

Secor and I spent hours listening to Benson preach about how to advise foreign governments - his philosophy was fist and glove with the training I'd received at the Foreign Service Institute. Bill insisted we recognize our status as mere visitors. Vietnam was host and we were guests. We should not enforce or impose our personal values, principals, or ideals upon these people. We could share our views, but they had the right to accept or reject as they saw fit.

Theoretically, I could buy it. In practice, I had my doubts. And I had a whole lot of reservations. I now knew what corrections was going to require. I bit my tongue, and decided to play it close for awhile.

The day of Benson's departure came and correctional cadre from all over the country piled into Saigon to shake his hand. It was a sad day. Benson was going. The youngster would be warming his chair.

After Benson's tearful farewell, I was a bit more than surprised at the large contingent of Vietnamese on hand to welcome me at the Directorate--7 Dinh Tinh Houng, Saigon--the next morning. I was now the direct U.S. Counterpart to the Director of Corrections. Petrified, elated and challenged, I was eager to set up a functional working relationship within the Directorate. I worried for nothing as the attitude was: Benson is gone. You're the advisor. That's life. Let's get started.

The Vietnamese are nothing, if not adaptable.

The DOC compound presented its own set of problems. The facility was previously a French sûreté (police) head-quarters. The Director of Corrections, his Assistant Director, Inspectorate, and twelve bureau chiefs and their staffs had offices here. All records, on every facet of correctional operations, were kept in the same building. The Director's job was to keep a paper trail of all national and province prison operations; support the four national civil prisons under the immediate purview of the Director and; provide backup support to province prisons.

The Deputy Director and members of the Inspectorate were military officers. Bureau chiefs were older Vietnamese who had formerly worked for the French under the Director General of Rehabilitation. All workers supervised by bureau chiefs were civil servants.

The building itself was antiquated, poorly lit, lacked sufficient work space, and in general, was literally falling apart. The entire place needed extensive renovation. Records and files on corrections operations and prisoners went back one hundred years, and I believed it--there were files and papers stacked floor to ceiling everywhere. There were no filing cabinets. It could take a month or more to retrieve a specific document, even with 154 personnel!

The legal arretés (decrees) governing the system were catalogued here, however, it didn't take much to determine the decrees were just so much ink and paper. The employees perceived their Director as a clerk for the MOI, and perceived their own very low wage and dirty working conditions as the result of the Ministry's penchant for utilizing DOC laborers as cleaning ladies, while staffing management levels with MOI personnel.

Most employees were openly verbal about the situation. This made it difficult for USAID staff, like Gi, to act in liaison with Directorate employees. Gi's salary was higher than Director Mai's.

Because the DOC functioned only at the will and pleasure of the MOI, it was, in my opinion, a driver without a map. The DOC had many difficulties, but it had only one problem: The correctional system did not have a single administrator.

Their organization was sophisticated and confusing. There had always been, in one organizational form or another, a DOC. Direct and meager U. S. involvement began in 1961, with a single advisor, when it was known as the Office of the Directorate General of Rehabilitation. The South Vietnamese Directorate General received his appointment from the President, and reported directly to the Minister of the Interior.

The Director General of Rehabilitation was downgraded in 1967 to a lessor Directorate administered by an ARVN Colonial, or a civilian. A Directorate had insufficient clout to keep and maintain the enlightened support and concern of the province chiefs throughout the county. It was the province chief who was fully in charge of the correctional facility in his province and the DOC, in Saigon, was simply a support arm for materials, supplies and equipment.

The province chief was an ex-officio warden, too. He usually had a chief jailer who was on site and in charge of the actual day to day management of the prison. The chief jailer was appointed by the Director but the appointment required the approval of the province chief. This system did not generally serve the best interests of prisons or the DOC.

The DOC provided all funds to operate national and provincial centers through his annual budget, but he didn't have operational control over those centers. In order to retain some control over funds given to the provinces, the Director was empowered by the MOI to have his Inspectors make monthly checks.

Correctional personnel at the centers were called cadre. Their duties ranged from general supervision of the work-shops, grounds, and work details to record keeping and paper shuffling. The average ratio of correctional staff to prisoner in most provincial prisons was one jailer for each 172 prisoners.

In thirty of the thirty-seven centers, police officers were covertly on staff. Frequently, they worked as intelligence agents to ferret out trouble-makers, plotters, hard core communists and what were often called hardheaded criminals. Since much of their work was done covertly, it was usually conducted under the guise of being a convicted communist criminal. There were also police officers who supplemented the security forces on an overt basis.

Each center had a civil service clerk, responsible to the chief jailer, and he or she had assigned to them several prisoner helpers. It was not unusual to find inmate clerks who were better informed on the administration of a given center than either the chief jailer, the civil service clerk, the province chief, or the Director. All correctional paperwork, for any purpose, was written in longhand and the filing system was totally inadequate by any reasonable standard.

Finding filed papers was haphazard and depended mostly on the memory of the clerks. It may sound like a small matter, but we couldn't find anything quickly. Finally, at my wits end, I asked my wife, on one of her visits, to come up with some way to relate a single file to three languages and specific subject matter. She devised a color coded system with a comprehensive key which did the job.

The chief jailers of the province centers averaged seven years work experience within the system. They were sometimes appointed from other branches of government. The chief jailer was usually a lackey of the province chief who had provided the job in return for favors owed to friends and relatives.

The pay of a jailer was two hundred piasters per month. This equated to about US$3. Although the jailers considered this very low pay, they were happy not to be foot soldiers. Qualifications for a jailer were minimal -- be able to read and write and enjoy reasonably good health. He and his family were provided a small room, on the compound, as their living quarters at government expense. Neither was it unusual to find living quarters of the chief jailer and his subordinates substandard to that of prisoner quarters in the same compound. A jailer could be transferred from one province center to another, or from one part of the country to another, without recourse.

Discipline for correctional staff was swift and rigid. They were severely reprimanded verbally, or beaten up, or transferred quickly to another province. The employee was responsible for his own moving and travel expenses. In some centers, a staff member would be punished by adding duty assignments to his regular schedule. This, however, was ineffective as most employees regularly worked a twelve to sixteen hour shift, and considered a six-day week a luxury.

Because Vietnam was in a state of war, it was necessary for all prisons to utilize a number of external security forces to guard the perimeter walls. These forces were usually Vietnamese Civil Guard. In some cases, however, the provincial police would assist with external security. The average number of armed guards for the exterior of a center was thirty-six--split on three shifts.

Monthly inspections of all provincial prisons were conducted by the local staff of the province chief and inspectors from the Directorate. But, there were no official government prison standards in the country. These inspection groups lacked any knowledge of what a standard should be and lacked the authority and the means to correct any deficiencies they detected. The standard, therefore, became no bitching, serious illness, or catastrophic event, either by act of God, or war, and the prison received a passing mark for being in good shape.

The Vietnamese method of counting prisoners every four hours was adequate. A chief jailer and the correctional cadre subordinate to him were without any sort of weaponry inside the centers. Firearms were never allowed inside. Chief jailers did not have tear gas at their disposal and there were specific reasons for this. It was next to impossible to keep tear gas on hand in Vietnam because of climate and weather conditions without expensive, controlled warehousing. Vietnamese military units did, however, use tear gas in their operations and, on rare occasions, did provide tear gas to the centers.

Even if there had been an inexpensive way to provide warehousing for the gas, the employees did not have gas masks or other equipment to prevent their own gassing. Further, use of weapons and tear gas inside the centers would be of no real use to jailers and correctional cadre. Staff was simply outmanned by prisoners. Had prisoners wanted to take control of any center, they could have done it, anytime they wanted.

A substitute for tear gas was used in most centers. The lime concoction, produced by burning ocean coral in kilns, made a satisfactory surrogate. Mixing the resultant powder with water made a suitable, non-toxic paint facsimile which was used extensively throughout the country to whitewash buildings at very low cost. We used it to paint prison walls. Further, at all prisons the coral lime was used by prisoners to freshen their individual honey buckets.

It's interesting to note the similarity between the lime concoction the Vietnamese depended on for so many uses, and the compound called tabby used by the early settlers in the U. S. Examples remain in states along the eastern seaboard. Tabby was a powdered seashell mixture, often with shell particles apparent and non-toxic, used for caulking, building, and whitewashing.

In most centers, trustys and other of the chief jailer's favorites handled the keys. In several centers, the key to the key control chest was in the hands of a trustee. This was not unlike most prisons in the U.S. at that time, and a condition which exists in many to this day. There was no control to speak of. All tools were deposited at the end of the day in a wooden chest which was kept unlocked. Any prisoner had ready access.

Locking devices in almost every prison were old, obsolete, and most did not work. Often cell doors were locked with padlocks easily picked by an amateur. At other centers, inmates had keys to the padlocks on their cells. Most cell doors were made of wood. Such things as emergency doors and exits were nonexistent, even in relatively new centers.

Understanding the prisoner classification framework and the legal mandates of this war torn country, as concerned prisoners, is mandatory to understanding the limitations, expectations and problems of the civil correctional system of South Vietnam. Indeed, the unwillingness or inability of politicians, activists, muckrakers, et al., to acknowledge the propriety and effectiveness of the OPS mission stems from, besides their advocacy agenda, three basic errors of understanding.

First, a jail is not a prison. The terms are not interchangeable in usage or meaning. However, nonprofessionals, including most of the media, even today, skew the meaning by misusing both words. While Rome, Jonathan and Winesap are all apples, subcategorized red apples, every good cook knows a specific composition dictates a specific use if one expects specific and optimum results. And so it is with jails, prisons and prisoners.

A jail is a confinement space specifically designed to house unsentenced citizens until sentencing, and sentenced citizens who commit minor (misdemeanor) offenses, for terms up to one year.

A prison is a confinement space specifically designed to house sentenced citizens who commit major (felony) offenses, for confinement exceeding one year and a day.

Secondly, a prisoner of war, although a person detained against his will, is not the same as a prisoner detained against his will for a crime against civil law. The POW is a situational prisoner, while the common criminal/prisoner is a person breaking the civil law of any given society.

A political prisoner is not a recognized category or sub category of prisoner in any arena. A political prisoner has a political ideology or revolutionary distinction, and a free world prohibition. The term political prisoner was taken from the rhetoric of the revolutionary, and disseminated by the media as a way to characterize confinement by political ideology alone. It is a purely subjective, arbitrary designation, devised by revolutionaries, to emotionalize and polarize the masses.

This evaluation depends solely on which side of the fence you are on. If your views are bent toward the political power in place you are a patriot and visionary. If your views are against the entity in power you are the enemy, and hence, may be a pure political prisoner.

The functional category for a person imprisoned for his ideology and armed support to it would be a prisoner of war, but people characterized as political prisoners are not members of the armed enemy, its military, or its support elements; rather they are overt supporters of an out-of-power ideology, and damning of the government in power. Therefore, the elements of the POW category are not met.

A further reduction in the ability to identify a true political prisoner comes from the fact that most countries have defined acts such as sedition, espionage, and treason as crimes. A person whose activities constitute such crimes, despite his ideological motivation--cannot be held to be a political prisoner. That person is a common criminal--a civil prisoner, although the crime is a more uncommon one.

Five types of prisoners were found in civil prisons in South Vietnam:

The COMMON CRIMINAL was one charged and convicted by the civil court system for various degrees of murder, rape and pillage -- in other words, civil crimes against society. These societal, or more correctly, civilian criminals were held in various prisons and jails throughout the country.

The MILITARY OFFENDER was a member of the military who was charged, and convicted of committing a civil crime and/or absconding from the military service while on active duty with the Army of the Republic of South Vietnam. There were a large number of this type of prisoner held in DOC prisons.

The COMMUNIST CRIMINAL prisoner fell into one of three subcategories but all categories had two characteristics in common -- they were unarmed and were either communists or communist sympathizers supporting the ideology of North Vietnam.

Their most important distinction was the *unarmed* designation. They were the enemy, but the Geneva Convention referenced POW's as arms carrying.

Therefore, the COMMUNIST CRIMINAL, who by definition did not carry arms, could not be held in South Vietnam's POW camps. Instead, the GVN was forced to stuff them in civil prisons -- where they didn't belong either -- *by declaring these persons criminals*. In the same way, the North Vietnamese declared our pilots to be criminals, but not for the same reasons. The GVN simply had no viable, alternate, lockup facility fit for human habitation. It was a Catch 22.

A COMMUNIST CRIMINAL Category A was identified as one holding a political leadership position in the Viet Cong infrastructure, and membership in the communist party. These people were not armed. They were a North Vietnamese shadow government -- a replica mimicking the hierarchy of the South Vietnamese government structure, poised to step into place to take over the governmental chores of South Vietnam at the very moment of a northern communist victory.

Viet Cong Infrastructure (VCI) was the term William Colby and Ambassador Komer introduced to define this enemy/criminal group. The word's literal origin -- the Latin infra, meaning below, paired with structure, equaling below structure -- its original definition was permanent military installations . . . of NATO. However, in the evolution of general usage and exposure, infrastructure conjured images of government financed sewer pipes and interstate highways, instead of the structure of a government itself. The public embraced the media interpretation of the Viet Cong -- political prisoner--and the concept inherent in that term, rather than use the more cumbersome, and less dramatic word, infrastructure.

So, while infrastructure was specific and meaningful to Colby and Komer, indeed, it had exactly the type of obscure connotation favored by CIA nomenclature types, most people were confused by it when used in the context of people. Did not these two very smart men anticipate the problems that would plague their programs because of this misconnotated word? Probably not. The choice suited their history to a tee.

To simply name the opposing entity a Shadow Government, or even SG, would have saved much grief for everyone. SG coupled with other acronymic indicators would have been a definite plus--even in the convoluted world of Vietnam. In any event, after this, we will substitute shadow government for infrastructure in the interests of clarity.

COMMUNIST CRIMINALS Category B's, also unarmed, were listed as cadre or members of the Viet Cong shadow government involved in direct support roles to fighting units. These people earned their midmanagement positions in the communist party. Their duties, whether identified as overt, or covert, were as propaganda teams. They collected taxes, provided comfort, food, and medical supplies to the VC and North Vietnamese fighting units.

COMMUNIST CRIMINALS Category C's, again unarmed, referred to low level followers and sympathizers who were noncommunist, were not yet accepted as full members of the communist party, and were relegated to doing the most menial tasks -- carrying rice, cleaning honey buckets, hiding guns and ammo, carrying messages, and feeding the armed units.

Interestingly, not all Category C's wanted to be communist party members. Many were staunch nationalists, and many were just nonpolitical peasants who were forced to pick a side. Both groups chose to align themselves with anyone other than foreigners or turncoats, which were, in their minds, the U. S. and the GVN. Most were not sufficiently informed, or savvy enough, to realize the Soviets and Chinese had armed and bankrolled these homegrown communist nationals.

All these Viet Cong shadow government detainees (Communist Criminals) were held under warrant of the Police Special Branch, a division of the National Police. *The Police Special Branch was advised only by covert CIA personnel*, not by Office of Public Safety Advisors.

Sentenced prisoners of Categories A, B, and C were to be housed in prisons. If, when arrested, they were carrying weapons, they met Geneva Convention criteria of a POW, and were subsequently, and properly, sent to POW camps under the jurisdiction of ARVN and U. S. military.

The *armed* Viet Cong, soldiers arrested during sweeps of the districts and provinces, were confined in local jails until they could be transported to regional, civil prisons pending transfer to military POW camps as a bonafide prisoner of war. DOC records referred to this group as ARMED REBELS while in transit at the province prisons. There were generally 30-40 such prisoners in various province prisons during any given month.

Another 28-30 ARMED REBELS were *formerly* POW's

which we knew were housed at Con Son. These previous prisoners of war were convicted of murdering fellow convicts at a POW camp. They were charged, adjudicated, and committed by civil courts to a civil prison, for that crime.

The fifth and final type was prisoners such as members of the Cao Dai, Hoa Hao (considered religious zealots), members of the Binh Xuyen (Vietnamese Mafia), or just plain anti-Thieu folk. From these groups came the *authentic* POLITICAL PRISONER.

Three such prisoners were housed at Saigon's Chi Hoa prison and were openly categorized by the Directorate of Corrections as POLITICAL PRISONERS. They were the strong, vocal, charismatic, and sometimes zealous, political adversaries of President Thieu. They were charged with no civil crime and were not criminals. They were simply against President Thieu and his policies. Never, during my tenure, did this type of prisoner total more than five throughout the country. At any given time, the count was three to five. [29]

All prisons, excepting Con Son, had both male, female and juvenile prisoners. There were attempts to segregate them but because of serious overcrowding they were generally all housed in the same building. Juveniles found in the province centers were children of prisoners, had been sentenced as petty thieves, or had been identified as sympathizers to the Viet Cong. These juveniles were mixed in with the adult population.

In company of these prisoners, the chief jailer, or warden of the facility, had to also accommodate the prisoner's infant children, pigs, goats, sheep, chickens, and other personal properties. They brought such items from home when they were sentenced by the courts, or accumulated them during their incarceration, through gambling. The prisoners were simply afraid of losing their personal properties while in prison, so they brought everything with them. There was nothing in the law to prevent them from bringing their belongings. Thus, we had males, females, juveniles, and livestock sharing the inner compounds at most of the prisons.

In late 1967, the entire population of the Vietnamese civil penal system was thirty-two thousand. I know because I counted every damn one of them. Over 70% (22,400) were communist criminals. Twenty-one percent (6,720) were common criminals and the remaining 9% (2,880) were military personnel who had committed civilian criminal acts while in uniform. Women represented less than 8% (2,560) and there were only a few more than 600 juveniles, of both sexes, throughout the system.

Now and again, at province centers one would find a local politician held in protective custody by the Police Special Branch. This was at the insistence of the province chief, and lasted until the election was over. Although rare, one might also find a businessman who was *too* successful (taking business away from a relative, or friend, of the province chief) lodged in the provincial centers.

These individuals would be charged with suspicion of some kind of act against the government, such as black marketing, price manipulation, or corruption. He would be picked up, placed in a correctional center, and held for trial. More often than not, after six months or so, the charges would be dropped as an unfortunate mistake and the individual would be released to find his business absorbed by competitors.

Of the twenty thousand plus communist criminals, less than three of every ten had their day in court. This figure included female prisoners. Juveniles were tried by the juvenile court and, after sentencing, sent to a juvenile training center for boys near Thu Duc, or a special training center for girls--both under the Department of Social Welfare, an arm of the Ministry of Justice. There was simply no place, other than the province prisons, to hold juveniles awaiting transfer. (30-39)

The physical plants of the prisons were divided into three separate types. The first type was the facility constructed before W.W.II, generally of French design. The second was comprised of makeshift, inadequately constructed, or converted buildings. The third category was mostly new construction of Vietnamese design.

In almost every case, the facilities were of modest size and failed to provide an atmosphere necessary for what non-Asians would consider adequate correctional treatment. In all centers, there was severe overcrowding. All were dirty, lacked reasonable sanitation and were in dire need of health delivery systems.

As South Vietnam needed additional prison spaces at province level, they resorted to conversion of old, unused buildings of various kinds. Warehouses were the most popular, or available, structure to convert into prisons. It was easy to convert a warehouse into a prison as most had very few windows and all had heavy doors. Bars were added to the few windows and, sometimes, windows were walled over. Steel sometimes reinforced the heavy, wooden, outside doors, but that was not the norm.

At every province prison, the bathing and toilet facilities were outside the housing areas, were inadequate, unsanitary and best described as nightmares. Every center had portable honey buckets for each cell and/or dorms. These buckets were usually freshened with lime and cleaned daily.

An old Archives of the Minh Mang Dynasty, in Hue, was converted into a temporary prison and was still being used. This building was constructed more than one hundred and fifty-five years ago. In other places in the country, former residences, shops, offices and barracks were also converted into holding centers.

The Vietnamese government had built a few prisons using mostly grass, or thatched roof huts encircled with barbed wire fences of all types. Any prisoner determined to escape could easily walk away, but fences did provide some deterrent effect, by slowing him down.

There were a few of the newer provincial prisons which were reasonably well designed and constructed, but all were too small to do the job intended. They were planned or constructed when the prison population in the province was at a low, and were severely overcrowded. Even the best of these left little room for expansion, training, or industry.

Housing units in prisons constructed by the French were still in use, although most of them were under continual repair. All correctional camps were badly overcrowded by American standards, and some were overcrowded even by Vietnamese standards.

The provincial center of Dinh Tuong, at My Tho, was probably the worst. This center had a usable area inside its walls of 3,100 square feet. It contained 1,400 prisoners, each with barely enough room to squat Oriental style. The prisoners slept in shifts. All of these prisoners spent most of their time in the cell house, leaving only for meals, political lectures, and an occasional bath.

There were numerous features of the physical plants which were in dire need of improvement. But the kitchens were, without a doubt, in the greatest need. While two or three of the kitchens were clean, well-lighted, and ventilated, the remainder were dirty, dark, and usually in a bad state of repair. Each could boast of a horrendous fly population. It was commonplace, nearly mandatory, to put a handkerchief over your nose and mouth to assure you wouldn't inhale flies.

Regrettably, these kitchens mimicked many village kitchens I had observed throughout the countryside. Some of them had the advantage of open air ventilation, or tent covers, to protect kitchen activities and food from the sun, but that was rare.

The stoves were built of brick and concrete and set in continuous rows, or banks, with cooking kettles embedded in the top. The firebox opening was in the front of the bank or the row, and dirt from tending the fire filtered up over the cooking pots covering everything in sight with ash particles and dust -- including the cooks. As few of the kitchens were vented, grease, smoke, and steam soon blackened the interiors.

The kitchens were fire hazards, too. All created a health problem. Floors in most, originally made of concrete, were pitted, cracked, and dangerous through fair wear and tear and lack of preventive maintenance. Some concrete had been dug out, or was repaired with a caulking of dried mud resulting, at least, in a sweepable surface, if not a scrubbable one.

The area outside the average prison kitchen was poorly drained, with many low spots, and excess water accumulation. No effort was made to police dropped food, and this, mixed with the filth already present, created a breeding place for disease, flies, bugs, and vermin. Many of these critters were first time finds for me. I hadn't given much thought to the possibility of so many variations of bug life, and marveled at finding new sizes, shapes and colors until the day I left.

Chicken, dogs, pigs, and cats had the run of the prison compounds. They ate, slept, and defecated wherever they wished. It wasn't unique to find a chicken or pig pen in the same building as the kitchen or adjacent to it. Nor was it unusual to find a latrine located adjacent to the kitchen--it had been the case for years.

I recall one announced inspection where it was rewarding to see the enormous amount of work completed since my previous visit -- trimmed walkways, roofs repaired, dormitories and housing areas scrubbed and sparkling inside and out with fresh coats of paint and whitewash. Clearly, staff had taken to heart my laborious explanation about the necessity of keeping latrines, honey buckets, and waste dump piles away from kitchens, wells, and housing units. My exact instructions had been profanely clear.

Smugly optimistic, I rounded to the next area where I noticed an unusual outcropping. Against the long exterior wall of the kitchen structure, glistening in the summer sun, a freshly painted configuration of lumps bulged like a pile of cottage cheese into the yard area. Upon closer inspection, my pride vanished--the staff had taken great care to shovel and mold a mountain of sewage waste into a form smooth enough to paint.

After a very short investigation, I was able to determine how my instructions on separation of water supply, sewage dump, and kitchens had been misunderstood. It wasn't my faulty Vietnamese, or the jailers' English skills. Priority instructions had to be dramatically emphasized in order to be taken seriously. Thereafter, I remembered to combine broad gestures, solemn facial expressions, and a menacing tone when ordering the exact site for waste disposal, or storage.

They tried, I'll give them that, but reiterating the health reasons for making such an effort in the first place became one of my litanies. Somehow the connection between death, disease, sewage and water source was a difficult concept to grasp. They had been doing it this way for years and they were still alive, right? Eventually, however, when the death rate inside the prisons dropped, the jailers and prisoners alike became advocates, and worked hard to keep their inferior surrounding clean.

The cost of 600 grams of rice was the basis of the prisoners' ration. The cost of rice varied province to province, but the average cost of 600 grams of rice was about 10 piasters, or US$ .15 cents a day. Six hundred grams of rice was considered sufficient to keep a man alive and working. The rice ration was supplemented with 150 grams of fish, meat -- pork and beef, 150 grams of vegetables, and nuoc mam (Vietnamese fish sauce). The amount of nuoc mam was not specified, but apparently was sufficient. In some locations, bean sauces and other special condiments were added.

The average daily menu of the prisons generally fol-lowed this bill of fare: Rice soup -- congee -- for breakfast; rice, vegetables and fish for the noon meal; and the same for the evening meal. Tea and nuoc mam were available at mealtime. Fish replaced meat once a week, depending upon the generosity and budget of the chief jailer and/or province chief.

A considerable amount of rice was lost by poor preparation. Allowed to burn in the kettles, or cooked until tasteless, prisoners refused to eat it. This also applied to the preparation of many of the vegetables. When fish was available, it was placed in a large sieve and submerged in water. The fish was boiled until the heads and bones separated from the flesh. The bones were usually served with the flesh, and occasionally, eaten. The liquid remaining was served as a sauce.

The meat, either pork or beef, was prepared in the same manner, and often in the same kettle. It, too, tasted like fish. Almost every part of the animal was used. After a pig was prepared for cooking, only the ears and hoofs remained. With beef, everything except the hide went into the pot. But even that wasn't wasted, it went to the tanner, or craft master.

Vegetables were of poor quality. Carrots, beans, corn, and taro were seldom seen in the mess halls. Cabbage was never served. A gourd like vegetable, common and cheap, was served most often. Greens, such as watercress, were quite common, especially when they could be grown and harvested by the prisoners. Vegetable gardens at most centers failed to produce sufficient food. The only exception to this was on Con Son Island during the rainy season. A few prisons raised pigs and chickens, but these were usually sold in the marketplace and the money added to the prisoners' social fund.

It was a rare facility that had a member of its staff assigned to the kitchen to supervise the preparation of food. It wasn't unusual for prisoners to be in total control of mess operations. Cleanliness was unheard of, or else it was considered unnecessary. A group of prisoners, representing prisoners' interests, supervised the weighing of all food for prisoner consumption. It was hard to determine how carefully this process was followed. It was equally difficult to tell if prisoners' representatives, could or were, calculating correct quantities, costs, and number of servings.

The food was weighed in with all waste material attached. There may have been sufficient food to keep the prisoners from hunger, but the quality was questionable.

Friends and relatives were allowed, under Vietnamese law, to bring food to the prison for their loved ones. On each and every day, at every correctional center, there was a continuous procession of family food bearers.

When one speaks of medical services in the provincial prisons, you must address the totality of the DOC medical delivery system. DOC didn't have a prison hospital, however, there was a prison wing at Cho Quon Hospital, managed by the Public Health Ministry, which was located in the Saigon's Cholon District. The ward had a capacity of two hundred patients. Saigon Municipal Police provided security for this special wing.

Chi Hoa Prison had a clinic staffed with a full time doctor. The doctor handled sick call and also visited the patients in the Cho Quon clinic. He was on twenty-four hour call for emergencies. A dentist was there part time and the gist of his practice was extractions and rough fillings. Dental equipment was obsolete.

There were ten nurses on the clinic staff. They provided little more than first aid to the prisoners. About seventy-five prisoners who had some medical training were recruited to help the regular nursing staff of the clinic. The center had a large pharmacy and dispensary, and there were eight cells reserved exclusively for psychiatric patients pending transfer to the mental health ward at Cho Quon Hospital.

Seriously ill prisoners were sent from provincial prisons (including Con Son) to the Chi Hoa Prison clinic. If the doctor felt they could not be properly treated there, the prisoner was referred to Cho Quon. This procedure also applied to those found to have a mental health problem.

Every prison had at least one staff nurse, and most had more than one. The majority were assigned to the provincial Public Health Department and were available only during certain hours of the day for prisoner sick call. All centers recruited prisoners with any sort of medical training to supplement the Public Health nursing staff.

At Thu Duc, the women's prison, two mid wives were employed, as well as, several female nurses. The dispensary was old and in the process of being enlarged for the purpose of providing a delivery room. Nurses treated small injuries, skin diseases, gave shots and dispensed certain medications such as aspirin and anti-malaria pills. Each were trained in western medical methods, but it was not unusual to see them treating patients with herbs, acupuncture and other Oriental remedies.

Chinese herbal remedies were used regularly. They were administered by placing the herb on the skin and forcing, or driving, it into the skin with heat. Seriously ill females were transferred from province facilities to Thu Duc Prison. After treatment, they were returned.

Water supply directly effects health. A few provincial facilities received water from nearby city systems. Sometimes, the water was piped in, but there was often only one common spigot to use. Many had to truck their water from outside sources as they had no wells, or the water in the wells they had was unfit for human use. Salt and alum were the chief problems of provincial water systems.

Overcrowded conditions and lack of proper bathing facilities resulted in skin diseases throughout the system. While the medical personnel could treat, and in many cases cure, the malady, the source and cause, was still there and the disorder continued. Prisoners bathed regularly when given the opportunity, but washing their hands before handling food, was not, as an example, considered important. In general, prisoners were reasonably healthy in spite of the conditions under which they lived.

Another common malady, which affected health delivery, was the lack of electrical power. Because of the war effort, centers fortunate enough to be hooked into the electrical systems of the province were subject to rationing.

Some province prisons had small generators which provided the minimum amount of lighting for three hours each night. Centers relied heavily on Coleman gas lanterns for security lighting. Most centers, however, had their electric power rationed to the point their security was completely inadequate, both internally and externally. Less than one half of the centers had electric power during the day, and all provincial generators were turned off at night. Most of the offices and shops were dimly lit buildings and the lack of light resulted in little or poor work.

Cleanliness was monitored by an in-house hygiene group. These groups spent the bulk of their time sweeping and policing troublesome areas, but little was done to ensure latrines, bathing, dish washing and kitchen areas were cleaned and well drained. In most places, the only effort made to eliminate flies was a few prisoners swinging fly swatters.

From time to time, malaria teams entered the prison

compounds. Cockroaches, ants, beetles and rats were commonplace--as they were across most of Vietnam. They were so numerous one might be of the impression prisoners were raising pets rather than living with pestilence. The staff would arrange to spray kitchens, eating and sleeping areas with insecticides, but latrines, drains and other breeding places for insects and pests were not touched.

Each of the thirty-seven prisons had one or more members of the Directorate's Rehabilitation service cadre assigned to handle and supervise academic training. The cadre also conducted civic action instruction for both civil and communist criminals. The number of service cadre from the Directorate were assigned solely on the basis of the size and population of the province prison.

Prisoners categorized as communist prisoners were subjected to several hours of lectures each day. Usually, cadre lectured two to three hours in the morning, and held discussions in the afternoon. Where there were prisoners the chief jailer felt to be stubborn, the lectures were not permitted unless the center was blessed with having a public address system. In those cases, the lectures were piped into the cell houses.

Academic subjects were taught in every province prison. Every center had a school for illiterates. Several provided courses that would qualify students for high school examinations equivalent to our GED. Prisoners usually taught these courses under the supervision of the Department's Bureau of Rehabilitation. It was common practice to have at least half of the prisoner population engaged in some kind of academic instruction, if only to keep them occupied.

Vocational training was limited, but in force. There was a small apprenticeship class in virtually every prison. The classes handled repairs and alterations to the fair wear and tear of the individual correctional facility. It's difficult to say where vocational training began and industries took over. Many prisoners were involved in vocational trades, but most were engaged in their own private and independent industry.

Prisoners were employed within the institutions but most of them received little or nothing for their work. However, it kept them busy and in most instances the individual prisoner learned a new skill or craft. Usual work assignments for prisoners were as cooks and cooks helpers, hygienic crews, clerks, nurses, woodcutters, water crews, electricians, and maintenance men -- very similar to U. S. prison work assignments.

Other prisoners were employed outside of the centers and assigned as janitors, street sweepers, beachcombers, refuse disposal, house servants, caretakers, gardeners, and clerks. Many of the military criminals were recruited as special trustys to help jailers, and as service cadre to maintain order.

All, but five, prisons in the country had places for prisoners to worship. The majority had both a Catholic chapel and a Buddhist pagoda. Most of these houses of prayer were built by the prisoners with funds donated by local communities, although none of the centers enjoyed resident clergy. The MOI and DOC permitted religious programs at every center, but did not do much to support or encourage them.

Recreation was along the same line as found in prisons of the U. S., except it was on a much smaller scale. There simply was not enough room in most facilities. The national centers had sufficient room for soccer fields and had them. Volley ball and basketball courts were available in a number of locations and were used extensively, and table tennis was popular. Where tennis courts were available, only staff were allowed to play tennis, but badminton could be played on the same courts by the prisoners. Actually there was a reason for this, and it wasn't punitive.

As I remember the logic -- there were few tennis balls available and no money to purchase more, but the prisoners were able to make very adequate birds out of corncob chunks and feathers -- therefore -- it only made sense to restrict tennis ball usage to members of the staff. I couldn't argue when I'd seen decisions of more gravity made with less thought.

Every prison had musicians who put on concerts for prisoners. Several centers had theatrical groups to present plays and other productions on a regular basis. One special group of entertainers visited Con Son monthly. The troupe handled all lighting and even constructed portable stages they transported from center to center. These musicians and theatrical groups later became unified into the Bang Song troupe--DOC's political retraining arm.

Occasionally, motion pictures were shown to the prisoners. Unfortunately, most centers didn't have the electric power to operate a projector even when they had one.

There were three programs virtually unknown in the penal system of South Vietnam. They were classification, parole, and probation.

While a prison system can exist without probation and parole, classification is essential to a competent system of correctional custody, security and control. Classification of prisoners was absolutely lacking. In fact, was non-existent throughout the entire system.

Discipline in the prisons was usually handled by the chief jailer in the most expeditious manner possible. There were chief jailers who, before they could punish any offender, were required to receive the province chief's permission. Others only had to report that they did, in fact, punish, or intended to punish, some violator. In a few locations, a committee of jailers and correctional cadre handled disciplinary cases. The cases were reviewed and approved by the province chief before any disciplinary action could be initiated.

As a rule, minor violations or first violations were handled by the jailer or cadre who witnessed the act, but they could be brought to the attention of the chief jailer, for possible reprimand. In the case of serious or numerous violations, the chief jailer usually called in the violator along with the cadre witnessing the violation. The chief jailer ordinarily followed the advice of his cadre and severely reprimanded the individual, withdrew his privileges, and/or confined the inmate to a disciplinary cell, with or without restraints. Those who acted out with violence were shackled.

The universal disciplinary action taken by chief jailers was to make the offender, once found guilty, eat subsequent meals in the indoor dining room. The Vietnamese, an agrarian culture, very much enjoyed eating their meals outdoors where squatting in groups, talking to their friends about their families, and sharing the news of the day was a social highlight of their existence. Prisoners disliked being forced to sit indoors at mealtime, the logic of which escaped many U.S. visitors.

One such visitor was Congressman John Conyers from California. Conyers and others insisted we construct stateside style dining rooms. Indeed, he even convinced a guilt ridden Congress to allocate monies over our strenuous objection. So, we built dining rooms when we needed kitchens.

As we anticipated, the dining halls we were forced to build were never used for meals; they were relegated to use as disciplinary quarters. I'm sure Congressman Conyers slept better knowing he had prevailed on the side of humanity, but I didn't -- my nights were spent trying to figure out how to make dirt floored, open air kitchens into sanitary preparation areas, with no money.

The prisoners considered the loss of privileges a severe penalty. Loss of privilege could result in restricting, over a set period of time, a prisoner's family from bringing in gifts of food. It might mean loss, or reduction, of other privileges such as recreation time, mail, working on hobbies, or the prisoner's personal money making projects. Or perhaps, being required to eat in the dining hall.

Confinement in a disciplinary cell could last from a few hours to several months, depending upon the center, the violation, and the violator. A typical disciplinary cell looked very much like a portable outhouse, but was big enough for a prisoner to move around and lie down.

In summary, the thirty-seven provincial prisons of South Vietnam were sub-standard to any reasonable man. With very few exceptions, the centers were intolerably overcrowded and inadequate in every component. Each province center would require a transfusion of money, manpower, renovation, rejuvenation, training -- and time.

Simply stated, we had real problems. Big ones. If Hanoi's propagandists were to judge the manner in which civilian prisoners and unarmed communists were housed and maintained in the provinces of South Vietnam, our POW's in Hanoi were in serious trouble. We all agreed on that point.

FOUR

National prisons, the Directorate, & Con Son Island

Bill Secor surveyed the four national centers. He portrayed them, Chi Hoa, Thu Duc, Tan Hiep, and Con Son, as having physical plants equal to, and in some cases superior to, prisons he had seen in the United States. I'd seen them all as well, and echoed his sentiments.

One of the last prisons constructed by the French was Chi Hoa, formerly called Central Prison, which was built in 1939 and used by the Japanese during their occupation. Chi Hoa sat on thirty acres on the outskirts of Saigon. It was a four story octagonal design with sufficient space, based on ten square meters per prisoner, to house 6,000 prisoners.

Bill Benson, and Mai, who was then a training supervisor, developed the National Correctional Academy in the early 1960's at Chi Hoa. Correctional cadre were brought into Saigon at least once a year for training, or better, to re-establish themselves as staunch supporters of the Thieu administration.

The training consisted of numerous hours of political instruction, some history of Vietnam, psychology, sociology, and techniques of instruction. After a month of lectures and theory, the cadets were taken to prisons around Saigon where they lectured prisoners. Prisoners were tested to determine the degree of retention and persuasion.

The idea was to convince the cadre to grasp the philosophy and mission of the academy to train new hires, and conduct in-service training on correctional operations. The academy was a priority in view of the massive program of construction, renovation, extraction program, health, sanitation, and inmate training programs we intended to establish. It was imperative training programs be inclusive and focus on gaining the enlightened support and concern of those who really ran the system--correctional personnel.

The national prison at Tan Hiep was a 1,500 prisoner facility for young trainable, male adults. It was the nation's model correctional center for male prisoners, and required continued advisory support. Sophisticated correctional industry and vocational training programs were in full process at Tan Hiep. It kept a lot of prisoners busy. The major industry was a contract with Vietnam's Army, making uniforms.

All inmates were kept busy at Tan Hiep and all inmates were paid for their work. Money received from the sale of handicraft items was meted out on a percentage basis. Ten went into the social benefit fund, enabling the startup of a substantive handicraft program. Another 10 went to the prison general fund, and 20 percent went to the individual inmate to spend locally. The remainder reimbursed for materials and supplies.

Female prisoners were exclusively housed at the national prison at Thu Duc. It was a, beautifully landscaped facility, of French design, very well kept and manicured. The exterior stucco walls were the color of blended pink and yellow tea roses. At the main entrance there was a guard tower with a tiny chapel tucked in the bottom level for passerby to use. Inside the perimeter walls various varieties of trees swayed with the breeze and the dormitories were as clean and neat as grandmother's house.

This was the one correctional facility everyone wanted to visit. It was, in every respect, an enlightened program for the inmate and the staff very much enjoyed working there. It needed a better kitchen and some paint, but overall it was in good shape. A sophisticated industry and vocational program, where all inmates were employed and worked daily, was in place. We decided Thu Duc deserved our continued advisory and dollar support.

The oldest correctional center in the system was built at Con Son Island in 1862, by the French. The penitentiary complex was six separate, but adjacent, prisons referred to as camps. All were clustered around the tiny hamlet, or town, of Con Son.

The history of the penal colony on Con Son dates before the twelfth century when the island was known as Rotating Island. Later, the Chinese renamed the island Con Lon Dao. The Vietnamese imitated the Chinese and referred to the island as Con Non. The Europeans referred to the island as Poulo Condore. Through the centuries, Con Son was owned by Spanish, British, Chinese, French, Cambodians, and Vietnamese.

There was always a prison or jailhouse of some sort at Con Son, and the island became infamous across the region.

But it was also an island paradise with beaches, mountains and lush greenery everywhere. Many famous and wealthy people spent holidays there over the years.

At the beginning of the first quarter of 1968, the number of prisoners housed on Con Son was nearly 8,000. I spawned the idea of tent camps as a quick fix for overcrowding and health concerns, giving us time to construct a permanent compound. Two tent camps were set up, housing 2,000 prisoners each. Together these tent camps made up what was known as the 7th Facility.

Every camp on the island was in serious need of renovation. Over the years adequate funds were never provided to keep pace with fair wear and tear. Perhaps the most infamous part of the penal complex was the disciplinary cells located in Camp Four. A prisoner would be housed in these cells a few hours to several months, depending upon the nature of disciplinary action. Camp Four cell blocks were more secure than other housing, which wasn't saying much, but the structures were built by the French for the tropical climate. They were well ventilated, well lit, with thick walls, and except for the doors, were sound.

Con Son housed the most hard core of the nation's communist criminals. Each camp was highly organized by the prisoners according to ideological party lines. LTC. Nguyen Van Ve, the island's administrative leader, was concurrently the warden of the penal complex. He, his staff, and the Director viewed the most serious inmate infraction to be refusing to stand at attention during the morning flag-raising ceremonies while the national anthem played.

All prisoners were expected to stand at attention and salute. Those who failed to do so were remanded to disciplinary cells. Reverence and respect for the symbol of country was mandatory, and upheld as the Commandant's prerogative. While in our country, at this point in time, this might appear a spurious order, to the Vietnamese it was the ultimate symbol of allegiance. And Ve went by the book.

Prisoners referred to these disciplinary cells as tiger cages--in the same way prisoners in the United States refer to isolation as the hole. Con Son's prisoners, much as prisoners the world over, looked upon disciplinary cell confinement as a badge of honor and courage.

Disciplinary confinement might include being placed on rations of rice, without salt, and water. This was equivalent to the bread and water diet at U. S. prisons in years past. At night, prisoners housed in this section of Camp Four were immobilized by shackles. There was one jailer on duty after dark, and since the doors to the disciplinary cells were wooden slats, it was necessary to shackle to prevent escape attempts.

Berkeley blended my report into courses of high impact action, sending completed drafts through the ICEX committee. He addressed crash screening, corrections, and detention systems programs. The title of the major document was SCREENING, INTERROGATION, AND DETENTION OF THE ENEMY. ICEX code named the document SIDE.

SIDE outlined goals and objectives of the United States corrections advisory effort to the DOC, their national prisons, and the provincial prisons. Essential elements were policies for the jail program, funding arrangements, and maintenance.

This massive document was approved by Evan Parker, signed by Komer, and sent to the regional ICEX/Phuong Huoang committees for implementation. General Westmoreland and Ambassador Bunker endorsed the program, as did the Secretary of State and the White House.

One week later, Berkeley delivered ten million Vietnamese piasters, CIA money, to the officer in charge of construction. ICEX was operational. (11-16)

We were poised to get things done. I knew I could count on Mai to handle the GVN part satisfactorily. In my opinion, our greatest asset was Mai. He knew everything I knew about DOC plans and programs, and we worked well together. But I predicted logistical problems for us in the advisory group. I would prove right on both counts, but as it turned out, the logistical problems became a battle of timing and creativity, and the blessing of Le Quang Mai was not to be mine for long.

FIVE

Building dams & bucking tides

My stress level was high and I needed a pit stop. Home and family was then, and still is, my refueling station. Within hours, my wife and kids would be arriving at State's safe haven post in Taipei, Taiwan. Having a safe haven assignment for my family was something both Shirley and I were excited about. From Taipei, she could take advantage of the several times a year wives were allowed to visit in Vietnam, and I would be able to visit for a week, every 6 weeks or so. That's how it was supposed to be anyway. At this point, I hadn't seen them in almost a year, but couldn't squeeze out more than a few days.

It was a great visit. My son, Chris, and daughter, Shannon, six and five, were old enough to appreciate the adventure, yet young enough not to be fearful of new and unknown things and places. My wife worked hard to foster that attitude in them and the transition to their new home was full of excitement and wonder.

On August 6, 1968, I arrived back in Saigon a happy man. Within the hour, news of Mai's removal as Director of Corrections had reached me. He was suspected of corruption. My gut told me he would be cleared, and the real story, when it surfaced, would have something to do with political maneuvering at the Ministry of Interior. Mai wasn't politically connected; he just did his job. He was transferred to the Ministry of Interior pending the outcome of an investigation, and LTC. Tran Cong Hau, the Deputy Director of Corrections, replaced him.

Mai's removal was devastating, personally and professionally. It was lousy news to come back to, but that's the way it was in Vietnam - stress hovered like a hummingbird over a spring blossom. Thanks to my prison experience I was more prepared than most to handle the constant, and high, levels of pressure we worked under. Still, Mai's fall from grace was a burden to us all.

Before leaving, I submitted a budget for all the prisons. We had to organize well. Once the money for materials and supplies was in our hands, the regional C&D advisors could ramrod their respective prison projects to completion. Equipment and commodities had to be transported for issuance to the chief jailers. Early on I took on personal management of that task. Materials and supplies were being stolen, hijacked, or blown up. Or so I thought.

Losses were nearly non-existent as long as I rode with the delivery, and followed up daily on projects. Hijacking was a threat, but not all that common, no more than the other hazards of war. The real problem was the province chiefs and jailers. And I can't say I was unsympathetic. Given some of their circumstances, I might have done the same thing. What they did wasn't stealing in the strictest sense of the word, but from an American perspective it amounted to the same thing. Only we'd probably call it extortion.

For example, I'd compute we needed so much rebar, concrete, bricks, mortar, and tin to build a sanitary kitchen. The materials would be ordered and delivered. A week later I'd arrive to inspect the new kitchen and find, instead, a half finished kitchen building and a new concrete parking area for employee's bicycles. The jailers would tell me they didn't have enough material to finish the kitchen project -- I must not have ordered enough. Their justification was simply a matter of priority. Theirs.

They would tell me the new kitchen was a really nice idea, but they could make do with what they had. However, they had never had a vehicle, or a bicycle parking lot, or whatever, and that's what they really needed. So they bought it, or built it before completing the project C&D had funded.

After this happened a time or two, I devised a way to keep everyone happy - me included. On every project I factored in a particular jailer's priority. Often I'd arrive in a used military jeep to deliver their project materials. I'd turn over the keys, stay the night, and by the time I came back the next week, the assigned project was completed to my satisfaction.

It's true that it was simply a prestige thing in many cases. Some jailers and their employees couldn't even drive, but I'd see prisoners shining and polishing the vehicle. It was status. It was transport. It meant they were special. They'd never had a vehicle before and now they did. Comparatively, the national prisons and their employees had everything -- sophistication, education, supplies, weapons -- and in the provinces they had next to nothing, and often just plain nothing, with which to work. They had lived under these abysmal conditions for so long, their longing for acceptance as equals was even understandable. In many respects, it was kind of amusing, they were like little kids waiting for Christmas. And it was sad, too.

From the perspective of some Americans, this was graft and corruption of the highest order. Spending U.S. dollars for status symbols rather than necessities. Perhaps I played into their hands by adding on these requests as if they were priority items. However, not one Vietnamese jailer ever hid, sold, or profited from the diverted materials that I could find. I could account for every stick of rebar. None was sold on the black market; it was all used to improve the prison in some way. So we funded a pet project here and there, projects were still finished, and the lot of prisoners improved—our goal, after all. A proud jailer was a happy jailer, and that made everyone's job easier.

I often wondered what the difference was between this and the U. S. and international inspection and oversight groups, AID inspectors, amnesty and church groups who come in, each with their own agenda. They would walk through and make recommendations such as: Father Drinan's view that the way the prisoners ate, sitting on their haunches, was barbaric and wasteful. Build dining rooms he and Congressman Conyers said. And we did. The dining rooms didn't change the prisoners' eating habits, though it did help with disciplinary problems. Expensive disciplinary response, but it did the job.

And then there was the VIP who said: "Don't these poor people get to see movies or have any fun?" Soon after, crates of the board game Scrabble arrived. The visitor didn't want to hear there was no electric generator to run a movie projector, no doubt thinking his Scrabble gift a more suitable leisure activity for French and Vietnamese speaking players.

The Scrabble kits were never used. It wasn't the type of game Vietnamese relished. The games were kept packaged, clean, and stacked for all to see. Kind of like keeping Auntie Myrtle's ugly gift displayed so as not to offend her.

I don't know of one VIP type who ever had any experience with prisons or prisoners. By that, I mean living life day to day as a prisoner or employee. While it is true a prison can be likened to a small municipality in many respects, it is still made up of citizens with needs peculiar to their situation. What an outsider thinks they need to make a better life is often a nicety, but more often a waste—especially when the most rudimentary goods aren't available. Seems to me it's a little hard to enjoy a game when fighting a case of amoebic dysentery.

Many well meaning people don't exercise their brain along with their heart when it comes to prisons. This kind of thing isn't exclusive to Vietnam. It's something I've seem in every U. S. prison I've ever been in. True bleeding hearts seem to think they have a corner on compassion, and those of us tasked to keep criminals locked up, have none. Guess it's natural to distrust the gatekeeper, but to me it demonstrates a lack of common sense as applied to individual circumstance.

From another perspective it can only be viewed as shameful.

Meanwhile, our budget was approved and we received everything asked for, except a fishing trawler for Con Son. Things were definitely looking up.

By August 15, the President and the Prime Minister had approved boosting correctional personnel by one thousand. And Mai's replacement, Colonel Nguyen Phu Sanh, assumed the position of Director. Sanh was a personal friend and confidant of General Khiem, the MOI.

As Colonel Sanh's Chief Advisor, I found him to be a nice enough guy, a good family man, and extremely passive. He reminded my wife of a bantam rooster, and eventually I agreed. When his tail feathers were ruffled, his cheeks ballooned and reddened, and he looked as if he would explode. His wife towered over him, and his seven daughters jumped to satisfy his every whim. He doted on them. He spoke little English, but was fluent in French. His passions, likes, dislikes, education, affiliations, religion, past—he never talked about, and I never asked.

After his appointment, I spent hours with Sanh discussing the ICEX/SIDE program. He had copies of my prison survey, including the assessment. His reply was cautious. He would study them. By this time, I was close to caustic. There was no need to study them -- I had already studied them. What we needed was to get busy -- now.

He repeated, "I will take everything under advisement."

I kept my anger under wraps long enough to get to my car and drive off. By the time I parked at our Saigon office, I had a solution.

Berkeley's office, next door to Colby, had closed and his

files and working papers moved to the USAID II office. John Manopoli became our sole reporting channel. Colby still managed everything, but now he was much more insulated, and we were, as well.

Back at CORDS USAIDII, I grabbed Berk on my way to Manopoli's office. As I saw it, in order to meet the requirements of OPS and ICEX, and to assure fair, humane treatment of our POW's held by the North, we had to knock off the subtleties of friendly persuasion. The mental gymnastics required to save Vietnamese face were exhausting. Cross cultural understanding at the expense of our POW's was unacceptable. My idea was to start kicking ass and taking names.

What had to be done couldn't be done by the book of State Department Diplomacy or the Protocols of the Foreign Service Institute. We had a U.S. military police LTC. in each of the four corps to handle Corrections & Detection matters for us, and they in turn communicated with and received assistance from local provincial Public Safety advisors. It was time we raised hell and made things happen on a high priority basis -- from Saigon, to the Corp, to the province. I was wild.

It seemed utterly ridiculous to spend any time at all pleading with the Vietnamese to get this horrendous job done while our own POW's were languishing in North Vietnamese camps. And I got wilder.

I intended to make things happen rather than wait for a Vietnamese permission slip. We could earn our respect easy or hard, fast or slow -- or never. It didn't matter to me. The best that could happen was the problems would be handled, and the worst was the Director of Corrections and MOI could ask Manopoli to send me stateside. To describe my manner as angry would be, well, I was nearly savage by the time I finished my tirade.

Manopoli looked at me for a few seconds, tipped his 250 pound bulk back in the chair, and laughed until tears spilled down the front of his shirt. He put on his best cop face to say, "Get it done."

True to form, Berk's response was monochromatic, "Splendid."

Colonel Sanh listened intently as I told him clearly and succinctly exactly what our priorities would be with the DOC, and what I expected him to do. A bare moment later, tail feathers high, he smugly sputtered, "But -- you can't do that."

My response was not diplomatic. Essentially, he was told I could, and would. We were going to start that very minute, and if he didn't, I'd see him guarding some obscure tree in Da Nang. Then I brought out the big guns -- Ninety-eight percent of every dollar spent on *his* prison system was U.S. money -- and I controlled it.

Sanh flashed a smile, deciding instantaneously. "We need each other", he said, pumping my hand. I left to meet with my Vietnamese staff. The remainder of the year was a flurry of activity -- an amazing number of work projects were designed, implemented and completed.

By end of August, 1968, Phoung Hoang/ICEX committees were established in all provinces. The term ICEX, however, lasted only for another thirty days. Through osmosis, ICEX was transformed into Phoenix. The official rumor was a Staff Sergeant of Komer's took the Phoung Hoang logo, made minor changes, and developed a picture of the mythical Phoenix -- a bird perpetually rising from its own ashes. As the American drew it -- a bird, omnipotent, predatory, holding a black list in its claws, selectively snatching prey, symbolized the new entity. (28,38,278)

In November, Richard Nixon was elected President. He developed the honorable withdrawal doctrine called Vietnamization. Nixon appointed his friend and fellow Republican, William Colby, as DEPCORDS, replacing Komer. Colby reported to General Abrams, Ambassador Bunker, and Henry Kissinger, the then Presidential National Security Advisor.

With full support from Kissinger, Colby spawned his vision of the pacification program in support of Vietnamization. Philosophically, South Vietnam belonged to the South Vietnamese and we would let them run the programs. Rural Development (RD) was set up to spearhead Vietnamization. RD was incorporated into CORDS, and USAID advised the program.

Within RD, Colby created the Accelerated Pacification Commission (APC). Part three of the APC concerned internal security--the old ICEX program renamed Phoenix. CIA policy was to withdraw from programs, as fast as they could, to enhance Vietnamization. The base line--if the CIA could not control a program they would abandon it. Within days, Colby held a press conference to announce the new program managed and operated by Vietnamese--Phoenix/Phoung

Hoang.

By creating the Central Pacification and Development Council (CPDC) as his personal staff, Colby maintained a private channel to the new Prime Minister, General Khiem, allowing him both freedom and control. A member of Colby's personal staff was Harry "Buzz" Johnson. Colby gave Johnson responsibility for territorial security under CPDC, and assigned him an office outside Minister Khiem's at the Ministry.

By December, the CIA station chief informed Colby the CIA had fulfilled its overt function. Phoenix was now functional under MACV and CORDS. The CIA withdrew all management, abdicated responsibility for the pacification program, and reverted to covert roles in various segments of the government, including advisors to the National Police Special Branch, under which the Province Interrogation Centers (PICS), and District Interrogation Confinement Centers (DIOCCS) operated.

The change this made in our lives was minimal, at least on the surface. We remained affiliated with Phoenix funding sources, but Walton became a member of Colby's general staff which changed our reporting channels--and our autonomy.

The efforts of the C&D branch of OPS were as extensive as were their accomplishments. GVN apathy toward the prisoner detainee problem was converted to genuine concern and positive remedial steps were taken. The MOI and the Director of Corrections were energized by aggressive new leadership. Four thousand three hundred prisoners/detainees were shifted from provincial prisons to more secure locations, and 3,600 of those transferred to Con Son.

All of the captive VCI in I Corps, categorized most dangerous by the GVN, had been moved to Con Son. In spite of 18 attacks on prisons after Tet 1968, no prisoners had been released by Viet Cong attack nor did any escape. Our bunker design, security systems, and training of units charged with defending the centers were major factors in repelling VC attacks.

This was the result of an earlier action Mai and I had conjured up. Unlike any normal free world penal system, the Vietnamese Directorate of Corrections had to function in spite of attacks and harassment by the enemy. The Viet Cong first singled out the penal system in 1967. That year they launched a number of successful attacks, freeing over 2603

Viet Cong prisoners. Six months into the next year, 2223 more prisoners were released by these attacks. Seventy-three prisoners were known killed by the Vietcong, and 261 were wounded in the attacks.

Of the 4,826 freed prisoners, 1,022 returned to their respective prisons, asking to be placed back inside. They didn't want to die the way their fellow freed prisoners had been forced to die. The Communists had sent freed prisoners into battle as a first wave--never to be seen again.

The purpose of the murders was simple—terrorize jailers and others wanting to be jailers, thereby denying us staff to run the prisons, thereby filling vacant ranks of the VC.

In addition to prisoner casualties, 19 jailers, their wives and children (19 mothers/wives and 57 of their children) were executed by the VC. This is well documented in C&D, Embassy, and DOC reports.

And the executions of jailers and their families were especially grizzly. If a correctional center had metal main gates, the enemy would first shoot the jailers, their wives, and children, and then use barbed wire to hang them from prongs fastened on top of the gates facing the outside of the prison. If the correctional center had wooden gates, then the dead babies, women, and jailers would be nailed to the gates by driving spikes through their throats, shoulders and abdomens. An unspeakable death; an unspeakable sight.

Some local jailers were petrified, and quit their jobs at the centers. Who could blame them? For a time, we were forced to recruit jailers from Saigon, and we trained them specifically to meet this threat in the provinces.

Our reaction was to build new outside fortifications and watch towers at every correctional center. RF/PF forces were stationed in the defensive perimeter positions, and the GVN, with full U.S backing, announced the new policy to every prisoner, correctional worker and private citizen: If the Viet Cong breached the walls of the prison, the prison, and the prisoners, would be blown up.

I provided the explosives and helped wire and set them at those centers known to be favorite targets of the VC. Overall security of the system was dramatically improved. After 1968, in spite of continued VC attacks, prisoner escapes stopped. Checkmate.

And there were other measurable results, too. Some dramatic. Directly attributable to improvement to sanitation, food, medical care and living conditions, the mortality rate of prisoners in 1968 fell to 22 per month, in contrast to 43 per month a year earlier.

Berk was ecstatic. He made sure everyone upstairs knew these improvements had taken place during the war's most active period, and during a steep rise in prisoner population. His reports raved on about how regular monthly inspections were instituted, and improvements in cleanliness, security and correctional techniques were on-going in every prison. Political retraining, education and medical treatment programs were expanded. Dispensaries, beds, blankets and medical supplies were successfully budgeted and delivered. New and additional wells were dug at twenty-six prisons, and sewage systems, bathhouses and latrines were constructed at 15 provincial locations.

Construction projects proliferated increasing the number of bed spaces country wide by 9,600. Con Son, Tan Hiep, An Tuc, and Can Tho were just four sites. Con Son would be able to house 15,000 prisoners within a year, and the temporary tent camps closed. Renovation of prisoner sleeping quarters was absolute in 11 provincial prisons, and funds had been requested for the rest.

Vocational programs were expanded to include embroidery, sewing, cooking, radio repair, welding, carpentry, auto repair, metal working, animal husbandry, center maintenance, center landscape gardening, barbering, nursing, cloth making, basket making, painting, fishing, turtle farming, vegetable gardening, typing and handicrafts.

We were world weary, and overworked, no doubt, but elated at our successes. Naive as it may sound, we believed our results were so substantial that the North Vietnamese couldn't ignore them. And further, that that knowledge would benefit our own POWs day to day existence. We were to do our job and phase out within five years, and it looked as if we would meet that deadline.

Total prisoners, of all civil classifications, incarcerated in newly constructed jail facilities (old local jails), and the forty-one civilian prisons, now numbered 45,000. In layman's terms, this number included unsentenced civil prisoners improperly housed in prisons, pending completion of local jails under construction. These were prisoners who would ultimately pass through the Provincial Interrogation Centers (PIC's), and District Interrogation Confinement Centers (DIOCC's) before being sentenced.

C&D had no purview within Chieu Hoi, Province Reconnaissance Units (PRU), PICs, or DIOCC's -- except to build new jails, or replace old local jails, and bring them to turnkey condition for use as detention centers. At that point, C&D was out. Administrative and financial control again belonged to the National Police Special Branch who, on a daily basis, shuffled the detainees back and forth between the PIC's, the DIOCC's and the nearest jail. This lightened our load appreciably.

Still, there were pockets of concern. The international media continued to report hundreds of prisons containing over 200,000 political prisoners were in operation in Vietnam. Over time, over drinks with sympathetic newsmen, I would ask, "Where do you people get these figures?" "Well, you know," they would say, "we got sources."

Of course, their sources couldn't be divulged. I was a source too, but was told mine were government figures and nobody trusts the government. Everything and everyone was suspect. C&D was not excepted. It was like yelling "Fore" in a hurricane.

The pressures mounted from the press, and I fought back the only way I knew how—I redoubled my oversight efforts and documented even more. I know 45,000 is correct for year end 1968--and the count for all subsequent years were correct as well--we counted each and every convict. An exercise I personally repeated on a regular basis.

The corrections program continued upgrading in the areas of health, sanitation, and security. My sphere had swelled so much I barely had time to sleep. When four military police Colonels were assigned to me as C&D Regional Advisors, I was in high clover.

LTC. Murdock was given responsibilities at Thu Duc, Tan Hiep, and Chi Hoa. The worst of all facilities were located in IV Corps-Mekong Delta. Secor went to Can Tho to focus on corrections which freed LTC. Corcoran to concentrate on jails.

Severson's police jail construction projects were moving quickly, according to plan. PICS operations were not, in any way, a responsibility of OPS, or the jail program. However, the GVN had decreed--wherever a PIC was located, a detention facility had to be constructed. These jails were for detainees being interviewed, or interrogated at the PICS prior to charging, or sentencing, by military intelligence units and the National Police Special Branch -- both advised only by the CIA.

None of us in C&D were especially happy with our position, or non position as it were, concerning jail/detention facilities. They were designed according to standards developed at the PIC centers for basic capacities of 50, 100, 200, 300 persons. PICS were administered by the Director General of the National Police (DGNP), managed by the province chiefs, and operated by his Chief of Special Branch, who was advised by provincial CIA officers.

OPS personnel, including McCann and Walton, advised the National Police at their respective levels only on civil police specialties -- traffic, communications and such. The CIA advised at its respective levels as well. Their specialty was the operation, funding, and management of the interrogation centers--the PICs and DIOCC's. All of the prison and jail construction projects, and their indicated capacities, necessarily had to be approved by the DGNP, the Police Special Branch, and the CIA. It was a functional nightmare.

It became clear, early on, that the National Police and local contractors didn't have the expertise to handle the construction. A Detention Bureau of the National Police was formally established and its head placed on the DGNP staff, answerable to the DGNP himself. Bui Do Ha was installed as the head of the new bureau. His counterpart was Swede Severson. They turned the responsibility for planning -- drawings, blueprints, and contracts -- over to the U. S. Officer in Charge of Construction (OICC).

Three-fourths of the provincial capitals required construction of a detention facility. The OICC and Adrian Wilson Associates, an architectural/engineering firm, completed necessary drawings and standards, and construction policy was prepared by Severson. Policy was adopted by the DGNP to cover all construction details regardless of size. The basic design was for semi-permanent (minimum life expectancy of five years), wood framed, aluminum roofing, galvanized siding on concrete slabs, with fence separations between housing units.

Getting land for the jails was a problem. The land had to be furnished without cost to us. If the land was not provided adjacent to the provincial Interrogation Centers, three factors had to be met in selecting other sites. The land had to be of sufficient size, must be located away from private residences, and be located in a defendable location as required by the MOI's Directive 249. (4)

Now and again, a province chief tried to make a land

sale financially advantageous to himself and his friends—like the swampland one official tried to palm off on us. My policy was to unexpectedly arrive at each potential site several times prior to final approval. Even though it was time-consuming, it paid off. Government dollars can cause people to get very creative.

Suitable building sites were hard to come by. With Walton's assistance, Severson turned up the heat on our regional and provincial advisors to scout suitable land. Special Fund (controlled by Phoenix) monies were available on a limited basis, but the major funding source was Aid In Kind (AIK) monies managed by CORDS-Pacification.

The architectural/engineering firms estimated construction costs at $275/detainee, exclusive of the contractors profit margin (roughly 30 %). The U. S. furnished all building materials, complete.

Once suitable land was found, a survey team inspected and reviewed the site, usually spending 2 to 3 days at each. The successful contractor moved on site within two weeks of the date the contract was awarded, and was normally given about 120 days to completion.

After assignment of personnel, Severson supplied the project. Weaponry and security equipment, office equipment, chairs, portable fire pumps, emergency spot lights, handcuffs, gas masks, and public address systems were shipped in and set up. Vehicles, rice bowls and cups, sleeping mats, and cooking utensils were the finishing touch. (4)

The prisoners assigned to these facilities were to be of three unsentenced categories. First, were VCI detainees in custody of the Police Special Branch, *Provincial Interrogation Confinement Centers (PIC), under the sole purview of the covert CIA.*

Second, were the judicial and ARVN Military detainees who had been convicted of civil crimes. These men were to be housed apart from the VCI detainees.

Third, were the VCI suspects and judicial (criminal) detainees held in civil province and national prisons who were unsentenced or awaiting trial. They were to be transferred from the prisons back to regional jails at the time of trial. The only prisoners housed in detention centers were to be suspects awaiting trial, sentencing, or release.

There were additional confinement spaces at the district level in the places known as DIOCC's. These were *District*

Interrogation Confinement Centers not under the control of the National Police, nor OPS. These lock-ups were under the control of the province chief and his Military Security Service (MSS), *and were also advised only by covert CIA personnel.*

This distinction is critical. It was Phoenix and these covert advised activities at the PIC's and DIOCC's that Colby would later shield from the ravages of congressional inquiry by fostering the distraction of the tiger cages.

TIGER CAGE: *An Untold Story*

Left:
Le Quang
Mai, Don
Bordenkircher
1967

Frank Walton

L to R: Randolph Berkeley, Swede Severson, Don
Bordenkircher at a jail construction site.

Michael McCann
at Con Son

L to R:
LTC. Lein, Commandant,
Chi Hoa Prison;
Commander Hau, Deputy
Director, DOC; and
Mr. Tan, Lein's Deputy
Warden

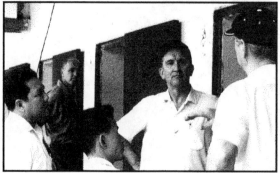

From L:
Colonel Sanh; John My-
ers, C&D Advisor; Mr.
Cam, Interpreter, OPS;
Byron Engle,
Director Public Safety;
Frank Walton, Chief,
Public Safety/Saigon at
tiger cage building.

SIX

The set-up begins as sharks gather

On a mid-January morning in 1969, Gi ushered in a tall, dark-haired man of about my age, who identified himself as Don Luce, a member of Catholic Charities and a newspaper reporter. Luce wanted me to explain, in detail, the United States advisory effort to the DOC.

There was certainly nothing to hide, but the man's odd combination of occupations put me on edge, and so did his manner. It was condescending, haughty, and demanding. My antenna shot up. In my experience, this behavior is the manifestation of a self-ordained superior. Unless my response fit his preconceived view, answering would be an exercise in futility.

As far as I knew, Catholic Charities didn't have a newspaper reporter on staff, though in Vietnam, stranger characters and combinations had come to my attention. Gi, Luce, and I sat down to coffee, and I introduced myself as a Senior Advisor, identifying Col. Sanh as my counterpart.

In 1961, William Colby was the CIA Station Chief in Vietnam. U.S. Special Forces men were attached to Colby as members of the Combined Studies Group, which was directed by a Colonel who reported to Colby.

Colby and CIA officers who directed the Special Forces often recruited and hired International Volunteer Services workers into the CIA. Through them, Colby was able to get a promising self-defense project started in Montagnard villages, using a Special Forces team to train and arm the villagers. Colby named the Montagnard units the Citizens Irregular Defense Group (CIDG) -- a viable and noteworthy group. (298)

During a taped interview with my wife in the early nineties, Luce said he first arrived in South Vietnam as a worker with the office of International Volunteer Services. "I was assigned to the Central Highlands at Ban Me Thout. I was teaching the Rhade Montagnards and refugees from North Vietnam, who had resettled there, how to plant, grow, harvest and use 25 varieties of sweet potatoes." (259)

Nonetheless, I dove in with eyes wide. When Luce inquired as to how many prisoners were confined in the forty-one centers, I told him the current count was thirty-five thousand five hundred and seventeen. Specifically, there were 5385 criminals; 22254 communist offenders; 409 armed rebels; and 7469 ARVN--military soldiers convicted of criminal activities while in uniform.

He asked what armed rebels were. I went on to define them as members of the Viet-Cong who were, at the time of their arrest, carrying arms. Indeed, they were POW's and after their cases were properly adjudicated, they would be sent to POW camps. Until adjudication, there was no place to keep them other than the provincial prisons. But, I told him, we were committed to changing that, and had, in fact, begun.

I didn't notice the shark lurking at Luce's shoulder until he said, "Rumors are that tuberculosis is wide-spread within the prison system. Is this true?" I was candid. Based on the best available information from the DOC, and also based upon my personal inspection of these centers, tuberculosis was a problem exacerbated by crowded living conditions-- which C&D was working diligently to alleviate.

Luce then pressed -- hard -- for more definitive data on the correction system and the American advisory effort to it, specifically OPS. My antenna was vibrating and my gut responded.

Since my coffee pot was always on, I suggested he stop by anytime he was in the area and have a cup. "However," I said, "the Director of Public Safety, John Manopoli, located at USAID II, first floor, second door on the left is the person to talk to about Public Safety programs."

Luce pursed his lips, but he shook my hand, and left. Luce wasn't out of the compound a hot minute when Gi and I were summoned to the Director's office.

"What did he want," barked Colonel Sanh. I related the exact conversation, which Gi corroborated. Sanh, his tail feathers up, rose to his full height to report, "Don Luce is persona-non-grata at the Directorate."

Gate security was in deep trouble for allowing Luce in the compound. Sanh was visibly upset. Luce was to be denied access if he returned to my office because, Sanh reported, "he is a Communist sympathizer and probably a Communist himself."

A for-the-record report on my conversations with Luce

and Colonel Sanh seemed in order. I never again saw Don Luce, nor did he see Manopoli, but we would have occasion to swim with his sharks several more times.

I would later find that early in 1967, Luce became disenchanted with President Johnson's policy for South Vietnam, and he openly voiced his concerns. It is not clear if he was asked to leave, or if he left of his own volition. But he left Vietnam and returned to California. (259)

On August 24, 1967, the U.S. Embassy issued passport Z7761192 in the name of Don Luce. His listed occupation was as an agricultural economist for International Volunteer Services. He first resided at 30 Huynh Quang Tien Street, Saigon, and then later moved to 146 Pasteur. August 25 he left Saigon and flew to Phom Penh, Cambodia, returning a week later. This time, however, his occupation was listed as a journalist for the World Council of Churches.

Phoenix, which was now of, by, and for Vietnamese, reverted to CIA covert advisory and funding activities to include direct involvement in operations at PIC's and DIOCC's. Their covert personas were as political attachés, agriculturists, you name it. A few were assigned to OPS.

A party of four from the International Red Cross (IRC) had made a two-day inspection of Con Son in early January. That inspection was one of a continual round of inspections they had conducted within the prison system since Public Safety Advisors entered prisons in 1965. A copy of their report had been sent to Geneva, been translated from French into English, and made available to Sanh by Jene Ott, the team leader.

The investigating team reported a generally favorable impression of the correction facilities at Con Son. They indicated more and better medical care was needed, medicine supplies should be increased, tuberculosis was present, dental care was irregular and fresh foods were in short supply. The prisoners residing in the temporary tent camp complained of the cold at night. Nothing we didn't already know; nothing we weren't working on.

Worthy of note was the team's visit to the Disciplinary Camp, referred to by the prisoners as, the tiger cages. They felt a heavy atmosphere in the camp, especially those cells where the prisoners were confined under a death sentence. Some of them had been there for two years; there had been no execution since 1966. Some prisoners, when interrogated by the delegation, answered with much emotion.

Although they are allowed outside their cells during the day, they could not leave the compound. Also, in this camp, there are, the report continued, some cells housing prisoners who have violated institutional rules and regulations. A number of prisoners are put in chains at night because, the team was told by staff and inmates, the doors to the cells were wooden and decayed. Some prisoners were a "little pale in contrast to the prisoners of the other camps and they appear to be in a worse condition." (48)

A copy of the IRC inspection, as well as, my discussion with Colonel Sanh about that report, wound its way to Colby.

Berkeley and I discussed the so-called tiger cages at some length. It seemed everyone had an interest in them just as in our country people had an insatiable interest in the details of the so-called hole. We agreed the building, dubbed the tiger cage by Con Son's prisoners, was one of the best on the island, but we also agreed, the name did not set well with the mentality of the 70's. We pledged to do something about that soon.

On February 26, I received a telephone call from Mai, the former Director of Corrections, who had been relieved of his duties pending a full investigation. Mai suggested we meet to renew our acquaintance and friendship.

A quiet lunch suited me, and we met at a local restaurant. He shared his deep embarrassment for being relieved by a corruption investigation. The investigation had been completed and he was cleared.

I wasn't surprised. I felt from the beginning Mai was a victim of the Minister of Interior's propensity for stacking the Corrections Directorate with friends the MOI trusted -- whether or not they could perform -- a practice all too common the world over.

According to Mai, MOI employees in charge of contracts had arranged for kickbacks from bids with local food vendors providing food to Con Son. He would return to the Directorate on the first of March as a chief inspector. It fit for me. MOI wanted Mai out in favor of Sanh, and this way, MOI was a good guy. Not so great for Mai, but I'd take him back any way I could get him.

Just then, Inspector Quang joined us. My antenna jerked up. Mai and Quang felt there were certain matters within the Directorate to which I would not be privy. Therefore, without knowing those matters, I would not be able to ask

pertinent questions of my counterpart, Colonel Sanh. If I knew
what was going on, and could pose the right questions to the
Director, he would truthfully answer. But the Director was not
authorized by the MOI to freely give me this information. I
would find out later it was Colonel Sanh who had sent the two
men to talk with me about "significant matters."

I went directly to USAID II and Berkeley. The new unwritten policy of the MOI was to keep the prisoner count to a
minimum at Con Son Island. The GVN legislature was very
upset about unsentenced prisoners being confined on Con Son.
They ordered prisoners be sentenced or returned to their
homes. One thousand sentenced prisoners were sentenced to
time served, and transported back to their native provinces.
Rumors persisted that a large group of fanatical women prisoners, who were communist criminals, were causing havoc in
the northern province centers. They were to go to the island
prison.

High level, closed meetings between the Ministry and Director Sanh had resulted in the firm stand -- Con Son could
capably support not more than 7000 prisoners at any one time.
They believed a higher count of prisoners would totally tax the
system, albeit a 10,000 capacity was approved and construction
in progress—via our dollars.

Additionally, province chiefs had informed the MOI they
no longer wanted to send their problem prisoners to the island.
It seemed, although the province chiefs were aware Con Son
penal facilities were totally reformed from the old tales of
"Devils' Island of the Pacific", their constituents didn't believe
it. For one to go to Con Son was to never be seen again. These
province chiefs simply feared losing the support of their constituents.

While the Minister quietly said those reports were, indeed,
rumor, he had actually authorized province chiefs to transport
the fanatical women when transportation became available,
and to house them at the new 500 man center just completed at
Tan Hiep.

Political pressures on the Prime Minister were so great
concerning the confinement of unsentenced prisoners, the Ministry was drafting new law to cover arrest and adjudication
procedures. The DOC believed if these new laws were put into
force, no more than 25,000 prisoners would be residing in the
correctional system.

Transferring prisoners from provincial prisons to Con

Son would continue, but on a very slow, and low prisoner count basis, making certain each prisoner fit the exact criteria according to the new laws. The Directorate, on the other hand, expected the prisoner count to go much higher at Chi Hoa, Tan Hiep, and Thu Duc national prisons. Province chiefs reported their citizens didn't get upset when one of their constituents was transferred to the Saigon area.

There were 4000 vacant sleeping spaces for prisoners on Con Son. According to their forecast, the GVN transfer program, if continued at the present snail's pace, could result in 8000 vacant sleeping spaces at Con Son by November— which was not what we agreed when the new 4000 man center at Con Son was complete.

None of this had been previously known to us. All of it was new, quiet, and unwritten. While we were zigging, the Vietnamese were zagging. It was in our best interest to carefully consider this new information, regroup, and develop contingency plans, should the data prove factual. While there was no reason to believe otherwise, we had learned to keep our options flexible.

A few days later, Berkeley, Manopoli, Severson and I discussed the situation in detail, but the short of it was -- if we continued with our current plans there would be too many spaces at Con Son and not enough nearly everywhere else. Time, money and resources wasted. We moved to draw up a new plan. Just in case.

Manopoli said he would be transferring to Washington in April. Frank Walton would replace him.

During March 1969, Luce was in Bangkok in direct contact with the Department of International Affairs of the National Council of Churches, and the National Program Fellowship of Reconciliation located in Nyack, New York. A U.S. Study Team on Religious and Political Freedom in Vietnam was planning to visit South Vietnam.

He told the group about allegations he said he had gathered from people claiming to be former prisoners. This information involved the alleged prisoners' detention, interrogation, imprisonment and treatment, and included a map. The map marked the location of the tiger cages and disciplinary cells. Other drawings depicted methods of torture purported to have been suffered at the hands of the National Police. (261)

After separation of fact from previous rumor, Berkeley, Severson, and I spent nearly three hours briefing Walton when he arrived. The myriad recommendations we felt in the best interest of the U.S. mission to Correction/Detention programs were specific. Walton thought we were in line, endorsed our recommendations, and asked Berk for an overview of our problems and to cite ways to overcome any, and all, deficiencies.

Frank was exceptionally adept at group management. He was a consensus builder of the finest order. And although he knew Colby when both were stationed in South Vietnam in earlier years, their jobs had been mutually exclusive — they each rowed their own boat just fine and their paths rarely crossed. This time around, the two men would be situationally positioned for cooperation, but based on their individual styles, personally positioned for conflict. (47)

Berkeley's proposal incorporated and fused specific suggestions from Swede and me. Setting background and justification to paper, in a coherent and judicious manner, was Berkeley's forte. His finished report was lengthy, corrected our problems and was an absolute breath of fresh air. Truly, a stroke of genius. If Colby bought the package and cajoled Prime Minister Khiem to accept it, we could one day go home knowing our time there was well spent.

In the next chapter I'll attempt to summarize Berk's voluminous document, adding appropriate comments for clarity in context. APPENDIX B details his recommendations.

Before it was over, this episode taught me another valuable lesson. Bureaucratic inertia is the first response of power builders and butt protectors. Creativity and genius are the enemy of bureaucracy and time its slave, so — if you want change — dream to sell the diamond; aspire to sell the emerald; hope to sell the ruby; but be ecstatic when the sapphire is purchased. Then sell many, many sapphires.

L to R:
LTC. Ve; Col. Sanh; Don
Bordenkircher in courtyard of
Camp 2, Con Son Island
Prison. 1968

L to R:
Randolph Berkeley, Chief, C&D;
LTC. Ve, Commandant, Con Son
Island Prison; Mr. Quang,
Inspector, Directorate of
Corrections

L to R:
Representative
Anderson; LTC. Ve; Repre-
sentative Hawkins on
verandah of Ve's home/of-
fice on Con Son Island.

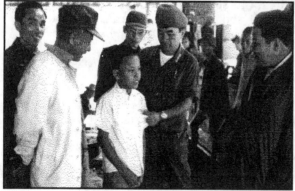

L to R: Mr. Gee,
interpreter/ administrative
aide; LTC. Ve; 13 year
old boy; Ve's Aide, Cap-
tain Cong; & Col. Sanh.
The boy is best student
in vocational carpentry;
sent to Con Son by the
Quang Ngai Security
Committee for terrorist
acts. When twelve, he
blew the top off a police-
man's head. Asked why
he did such a thing, he
replied, "I was told to."

SEVEN

HOI CAI — it's brilliance and demise

I had wings, or so it seemed. The prospect that a new GVN Ministry -- the Ministry of HOI CAI -- the centerpiece of Berkeley's proposal, was a possibility, energized all of us. It would operate under the Prime Minister, and a separate CORDS/HOI CAI advisory group, managed by Berkeley, would be directly responsible to Colby.

The justification was practical and well thought out. There was little reason for keeping the Correction/Detention advisory effort under either Phoenix or Public Safety. Both Directorates had more pressing objectives. Phoenix came into the picture as a management expediter in attacking the VCI and related matters. Emphasis was placed on the jail problem and the corrections part of OPS was asked to push needed action.

Public Safety's mission was to advise the National Police. The police had no connection with the prison system. The role of a police advisor did not normally cover corrections matters. In the U. S., the accepted practice was to separate the functions of police and corrections.

As a result, and to this day, one finds policemen have slight professional interest, or expertise in prison matters, and correctional officers little interest in police work. The correctional field, like police operations, is a professional specialty, although there are obvious areas of overlap.

The term HOI CAI suggested a psychological gambit to distinguish and dignify the return to society of former communist offenders. The present system lumped them with common criminals. This was a tactical error. We were striving to eradicate VC loyalty and build allegiance to the GVN. A HOI CAI was a citizen gone astray, who had seen the light, and returned to the fold. This approach was akin to the Chieu Hoi philosophy.

Establishing national prison and jail standards, publishing a uniform manual of standards for all confinement, processing, prisoner after care, and furnishing the central Phoung Hoang office with prisoner data were housekeeping items that either didn't exist, or needed streamlining.

Converting the thirty-seven provincial prisons to national prisons was a way to insure each got a share of the money. Making the leader of civilian prisons a Director General and giving him authority for prison operations would alleviate a lot of systemic problems, as would dropping the province chiefs as prison commanders.

The Vietnamese Air Force could provide airlift to and from Con Son and other prisons; and the Vietnamese Navy could help with logistics support to Con Son when needed, rather than when, and if, it suited some bureaucrat somewhere. Establishing Con Son Island as a penal colony would be a big step forward.

Reports periodically sent to and between the President, Minister of Justice, Minister of Interior, Department of Defense, Department of Military Justice, Director General of National Police, and other departments would really help in coordinating funding, sentencing, and the multitude of other status actions concerning detainees and prisoners.

Just empowering the Minister of HOI CAI to coordinate transfers of detainees and prisoners between prisons, based on available bed space and court status, would allow us to optimize management of spaces we already had, perhaps even reduce construction projects. There was an urgent need for specific care and treatment of juvenile offenders; and hiring an additional 2500 correctional officers was critical, if we were to properly staff the numbers we would have in prison in the next year.

Berkeley was thorough and compelling. The document was comprehensive. He had a table covering advisory man power, recommendations, and transfers. He covered liaison, and electronic data support (computers to us), and outlined all the advantages of implementing his recommendations. In short, prisons and jails would be functional, consistent, and attend to the problems created by the conflict of war without destroying, or brutalizing the civilian system.

But Berkeley's proposal that Colby, as DEPCORDS, should establish a separate CORDS Directorate for HOI CAI was probably the most meaningful change. It meant that we would no longer be CIA funded; no longer be responsible to him; no longer subject to dictates from the Pacification Committee.

"If the DEPCORDS/MACV concurs in this concept," Berkeley concluded, "implementing papers will be prepared immediately." Walton signed and shipped the paperwork off to Colby.

Organizationally and administratively, HOI CAI would be far superior to what we had. I wholeheartedly supported the concept, with only one reservation. PSYOPS. (50)

Although the PSYOPS program Berk proposed wasn't a total military type PSYOPS (short for psychological operations) program -- we would import only the Civic Affairs component -- it was one more intrusion by an outside entity into the prison system. If we had to have such a program--as Berkeley defined it, I could live with it. I just saw no need for formalization.

We had the Bang Song program and it was doing a good job. Bang Song was the theatrical troupe which traveled from prison to prison. Poetry, music, drama, and singing were inclusive and everyone joined in. It offered wholesome relief from the dreary aspects of prison life and the war itself.

The prisoners loved Bang Song. It made them happy. Happy prisoners are better behaved, security concerns are reduced. The cost was minimal - in dollars and manpower. An ideal situation.

Bang Song's drama often incorporated teaching of a political nature (re-education, if you like), and the plays had a moral, but mostly the propaganda concentrated on how to get along with others -- i.e. there's room for all kinds of thought. To me, it would be hard to improve upon either the concept, or the presentation.

My contention was we should let the Vietnamese alone. We didn't need to have ARVN and U.S. military types involved in the prison system; give the dollars to Bang Song to expand its scope; and if it ain't broke, don't fix it. I was the minority.

Two days later, Berk was summoned by Colby. Berkeley took Severson with him, and somebody's secretary gave me a call. I shot over to MACV, burning rubber all the way.

As usual, the late morning traffic in Saigon was horrendous and the fumes, noxious. When I arrived at the MACV Compound, Ambassador Colby's secretary said he was in conference, and couldn't be disturbed. After about 20 minutes, Berk and Swede exited Colby's office. They were flushed and blushed by whatever had occurred.

The three of us left without a word. Well away from the building, Berkeley suggested lunch. We piled in Berk's car and headed out of town.

Total frustration got the best of me. I snarled, "This is bull. Unless the car's bugged, I want to know what the hell happened in that meeting."

Severson laughed. "Colby told us to shove our HOI CAI recommendations up our f-----g asses, that's what happened."

I wasn't laughing.

Berkeley rotated his head and shifted gears. "Don, it's just been a very bad morning. How would you boys like a bowl of French onion soup out at the Frenchman's? I'm buying."

"Hope the son-of-a-bitch has some scotch." It was one of the few times I agreed with Swede.

About two miles shy of the prison at Thu Duc, was a rutted, dirt road leading to a rubber plantation. On plantation property was a round, thatch roofed restaurant operated by a roly-poly Frenchman, his Vietnamese wife, and daughters. Dining was al fresco—almost--the sides of the structure were open air from about waist high. Breezes whiffed through and occasionally an oxen would meander by, kicking up a puff of red dust.

The food was so good the warring factions came to a tacit agreement--Americans et al by daylight; VC and friends by night. And it worked.

My wife, on her first visit to Thu Duc, not knowing about the agreement, lunched there with several Vietnamese from the prison, remarking she felt as though she was being watched. The Chief Jailer didn't confirm or deny it when she suggested that perhaps I had surreptitiously sent guards to look out for her—something she vehemently refused—but neither did he tell her the eyes of the enemy were a more likely source. Even after she knew, the round restaurant was on her itinerary every time she visited me. They served, in our opinion, the finest French bread, the crispest salads, and the richest onion soup we've ever eaten -- before or since.

This day, we had our choice of tables, and picked a location out of ear shot of the other diners. Before Berk opened up about what had occurred at Colby's office, we ordered and had our drinks delivered. By this time, my patience, which is still in short supply, was gone. I lit another cigarette and tried to assume a pose of detached calm. I wanted the whole story.

In the same tone he would use to describe a baloney sandwich, Berk began his account. "The bottom line of the meeting was we . . . C&D Branch will remain under the management of CORDS Public Safety. DEPCORDS (Colby) and his Central Committee for Accelerated Pacification will articulate the direction of our advisory effort to us through Frank Walton. "

"The Ambassador appreciates, very much, our hard work and efforts in this ever demanding program, and he encouraged us to continue the fine work. Our recommendations for the establishment of the GVN Ministry of HOI CAI and the CORDS Directorate of HOI CAI are history, however."

"In other words, and I'm quoting exactly (expletives deleted)," Swede said, "Colby'll run his office and ours, and we'll do as we're told. If we can't live within his established organization—pack our stuff and leave. He threw his copy in the can, and wants our copies there, too."

It was our consensus the HOI CAI plan threatened the very fiber of the Accelerated Pacification Committee (APC) -- it did not fit Colby's vision for pacification. He was an autocrat who used a totalitarian approach to problem solving and program development. It was a style he had refined to an art.

A new GVN Ministry of HOI CAI and a counterpart U. S. HOI CAI advisory directorate was not in Colby's vision --therefore, it was wrong. If Colby had wanted this organizational change he would present it to his APC, and to the man, they would endorse it. They would never dare oppose him--except one member--Frank Walton. Make no mistake, Colby blamed Walton for the development of HOI CAI.

Walton had the temerity to always, in any discussion, ask the supercilious questions like who, what, when, where, why, and how much. What are the short and long term benefits and problems? If Walton didn't like the answers, he voted -- no.

We supposed every committee had a Frank Walton, and was probably better for it. Colby, however, considered Frank a disruption, and labeled him cavalier. In fact, Colby disliked and tuned out anyone who disagreed with him. He resented Frank's style to the degree there would be a time when he would lobby Engle to replace Frank. (261)

Colby's insistence that Walton be relieved only served to invoke Engle's disdain. Engle made it firmly clear he ran OPS and only he would make personnel assignments. And, further, he would relieve no one on the insistence of someone else--even Colby. To add to it, Engle trusted and exalted Walton and his style. Frank was loyal, too, and Engle plainly didn't see Frank as cavalier.

Engle and Colby did strike a middle ground eventually. Walton would serve his 18-month tour. Theo Hall, Walton's deputy, would be replaced with Mike McCann and McCann would take over Walton's job at the end of the 18 months. And that's exactly what happened. During the transition, Walton and McCann were a good team, and sat together for a time on the Accelerated Pacification Committee (APC). But, Colby never forgot the HOI CAI incident.

All copies of the HOI CAI Ministry and Directorate plan were destroyed -- except for -- mine and Walton's. Half a quart of scotch later, we returned to MACV. The day had been long enough. It was time to go home and lick our wounds. The next day we rallied in good spirit.

LTC. Murdock was left in charge in Saigon as Berk headed to Taiwan to visit his family; Severson left for Can Tho to work with Corcoran for a week; and I hopped a late flight to Con Son Island with Gi.

EIGHT

Tending details & making progress

Berkeley was, and is, a consummate diplomat. His family chronicle was in Beaufort, North Carolina, and his history, military. His slight build belied his Marine Corps training and the iron discipline of duty first. He was well-educated, politically astute, a superb writer, a good soldier, and in keeping with his heritage, a gentleman and, indeed, a gentle man.

The U.S.S. Berkeley was commissioned in San Diego, California, October of 1992, in honor of his family's illustrious military contributions. I know no other family member, but I can say it was a distinction accorded at least one deserving Berkeley.

By most accounts, Severson was an outstanding manager, a polished leader -- when he wanted to be. His prison background included a stint as Alaska's Director of Corrections. His wife and nine children stayed in Alaska during his first tour in Vietnam, but he moved them to safe haven in Manila for his second.

Swede detested leaving Saigon, and did so only when he couldn't avoid it. He liked being around the power people, the meetings, the social connections. He thrived on the cocktail circuit, and had a penchant for the luxury and comforts available in Saigon--such as they were. He was a PR kind of guy and was very good at it. I'll give him that.

Living in, or visiting the provinces wasn't always a first class experience in creature comforts, and Swede wasn't the only American advisor who dodged it when he could. Secor didn't like to go either, especially if it was an overnight trip. He'd go, but he let you know he wasn't happy about it.

Secor just liked living in Saigon. He was a retired Colonel, and liked the PX, local restaurants, and the Officer's Club atop the Rex Hotel in downtown Saigon. He didn't like the social whirl, though he enjoyed impromptu conversations over drinks. He wasn't a sports fan, or a movie goer.

I knew my profession well, and was expert in operations. But my real specialty was doing the impossible --

getting things done. I'd worked my way up quickly in the ranks of the California prison system, and cross trained as a counselor in the Parole Violator's unit. A couple of years were spent as the Lieutenant in charge of the troubleshooting squad - an early version of a S.W.A.T. team. We spent time in between crisis searching the institution for contraband - stills, weapons, drugs, escape routes, etc.

Later, I sold the department on the idea of an internal investigator liaisoning with outside law enforcement agencies. As the institution's investigator I'd made the connection between street gangs and prison gangs and was the first in the nation to put together how this underground system worked. It was a hard sell then, but now, of course, it's a basic component of a professional system.

All in all, my prison experience was balanced and intensive. When I left the California system, I was an acting Program Administrator. I was young and moving up fast. I had found my career niche. A warden's spot wasn't far off. I could have stayed at San Quentin, finished up my college degree, and probably retired at forty-five.

But the flower children proliferated and our children were approaching school age. California colleges were teeming with revolutionary types and anti-war activism. My wife, a native of California, and I agreed the climate was not one we wanted to raise our kids in, or around. The Office of Public Safety crossed our path and we went for it. We've never been sorry we did.

Severson and I shared a few things. We liked the Cirque Sportíf, though for different reasons. It was a remnant of the French -- an elite social club. The low, white, stucco building, with circular drive and a park like setting was unassuming. Though it was located in the center of Saigon, it offered a respite from the bluster of Saigon's public areas.

There was a swimming pool, but I'd go there to work out in the weight room, occasionally watch Mai play tennis - he was superb - or have dinner with Berkeley. Swede liked to sip gin and tonics on the verandah, which was gracious and inviting, and hang out with the boys, as he called them. He liked to scan the parade of notables going in and out, too, and lived to engage them in conversation.

Severson and I were also abrupt, abrasive, profane, and politically irreverent, often bringing Berkeley's heartburn to new heights. Together the three of us made a great working team, but it was Berkeley who -- always -- was the calm

96

above the storm. There was more than one time he pulled Swede and me from each other's throats.

When Berkeley left to visit his family, after the HOI CAI failure, I took his spot. I was tired, troubled (actually I was profanely angry over Hoi Cai), and needed time away from Saigon. The telephones, and the massive reporting requirements of the past weeks had taken a toll. It was definitely time to think. There were also a couple of details I needed to tend to.

Gi and I landed on Con Son at 9 a.m., the next morning. We were prepared to stay the week. The official purpose was R & R. I requested authorization to use one of the several guest houses on the beach -- a thatched hut on stilts with sleeping mats and no facilities.

Captain Tran, Ve's deputy, met us at the Loran Station and drove us to Ve's headquarters. A couple of bottles of good wine, some cheese and packaged meats from the PX were much appreciated. At the beach house, I unloaded a quart of scotch, two suitcases of miscellaneous food and snacks, and a case of soda for Gi. We jerry-rigged a campfire barbecue and spent the day relaxing.

I had a list of specific instructions for Gi. I knew about the prisoners and their problems, now was a good time to learn about the rest of the island population and their problems. Gi was to spend every day away from the prison camps. He would go to the city of Con Son, chatting with anyone he could find.

He wasn't to ask specific questions, he was to listen intently, reporting everything back to me by evening. A fist full of piasters for lunches, shop visits, and spending money, and he was on his way.

By the third day, Gi's socializing paid off. On the island lived 223 civil servants. The citizens were mechanics, jail-ers, clerks, rehabilitation cadre, and bureaucrats who supported the various administrative hats of Colonel Ve. There were 590 RF/PF troops, and 13 ARVN officers. These troops were utilized as perimeter security for the prison camps, as well as, the general security of the island.

Additionally, they were used as supervising escorts for various prisoner work details. Many, but not all, of the civil servants and troops on the island had their spouses and children living with them.

The body politic was relieved that they lived in a no-war-zone. They felt totally abandoned by the government. However, most revered Ve. He did his very best to help them, they agreed, but he received no help from anyone except the DOC and their advisors. These gentle people couldn't understand why American advisors and dignitaries of other GVN Ministries didn't visit Con Son and offer to help.

They shared their distress over living conditions. Why prisoners in the prison camps had better clothing, food, and living conditions than they did was a mystery to them. Their quarters had woven mat walls, dirt floors and thatched roofs. Prisoners, on the other hand, had the luxuries of cement floors, tin roofs, and concrete walls. During monsoons and heavy rains, they suffered while the inmates enjoyed dry dormitories and cells.

Ve came to the beach house later in the evening. By this time, I knew a lot more about Ve. He was a tough little guy. A charmer with a forceful ego and persuasive personality. You couldn't let him get his thumb on you because he'd keep you under it.

He loved everything French. Everything. He spoke French fluently and preferred it to Vietnamese. His English was passable, about as good as my Vietnamese. French Army officers trained him and he maintained their spit and polish. He was Catholic. He was considered a man's man, but woman also responded well to him. His ready smile and manly charm was hard to resist.

Ve was an extremely gracious host, and he wasn't a devious man. I've heard pilots offer to return his hospitality by bringing him a stereo, or some other large gift. His reply was always no. Nobody else had those things, so he didn't want them. He lived simply and alone with only the help of a cook and housekeeper from the village.

There was good bread on the island, but the wine, cheese, and lunch meat weren't very good. He was always thrilled when someone brought him a special cheese, or a bottle of good wine. He wouldn't accept five or six bottles, one was enough. And often he shared that with others. When he did ask for something, it was usually for someone else. He was quite selfless.

To Ve, all problems were his and he took care of everyone and everything. He was special and he knew it. He also expected others to know it. He was definitely the cock-of-the-walk, and very dashing in a palatable way. If anyone else could have been Commandant of Con Son, I never met him. Ve was perfect there. He was a highly educated and cultured leader, and would have been far too much anywhere else.

Ve kept his family in Saigon, and every ninety to 120 days he would visit them for a week. He was a very private man and rarely discussed them, or anything personal. He wasn't the inscrutable Oriental -- he was the epitome of a Vietnamese Nationalist who was nursed and mentored by the French -- food, wine, language, culture, manners.

I was lucky to have him at Con Son.

We sat on the sand in the shade of a palm, sipped scotch, and talked. We didn't talk business. Our mood was as reflective as the sea stretching before us. May in Saigon is sticky and draining. Con Son was balmy -- about as idyllic as life on earth gets really -- clean smelling sea breezes, whispering palms, lush tropical green everywhere -- the sea mirroring the brilliant blue sky, the sand's contrast stark serenity beside a man's troubled soul. It was one of those rare times when men communicate about dreams, families, and the meaning of their lives.

Later, we ambled through the small city to the prisoner's handicraft shop to buy gifts for my family. I spent more than I should have, but they needed the money and the quality and variety was excellent.

As we walked, he pointed out various historical markers -- like Franz Liszt's island hide-a-way -- and recounted a general history of the island. We agreed to write a book on its history. And we later did. I still have my copy.

When we came to the huts -- the quarters of the civil servants and troops -- we were met by a number of children, mothers, and various employees who seemed pleased to see us, especially Ve. He laughed and joked and threw a ball or two to the kids. I asked if it would be permissible for me to see inside their homes. "Of course," Ve answered.

As we toured, he described in detail how he had tried to get support for his poorest employees. No Ministry would help. He pointed out deficiencies as if they were his own. I said nothing.

What can be said about houses with walls the weight and texture of woven place mats? Walls you can see through. What can be said about dirt floors, no running water, outside latrines, and windowless windows? The poorest villager in the war torn countryside lived better than this.

We went into the village handicraft store and I pur-

99

chased more gifts than I could possibly use. The workman-
ship was excellent, and the crafts, unique. Back at the beach
hut, I poured each of us a scotch, and we sat together on the
beach with Gi, and his soda.

Sipping our drinks , we got into a serious discussion of
politics and news media. We agreed, as the war continued to
de-escalate, the political pressures on his government and
mine would intensify media coverage -- most of which
would be selective to the point of distortion. Our naive
justification was distortion sells better than truth, and we
had no power over either.

The conversation led into our inspection of employee
housing earlier in the day. I compared employee housing to
what I already knew were the housing conditions in which
his 7000 prisoners were kept. Then I compared the employee
housing to the tiger cages. Gi and Ve were emphatic -- the
tiger cages couldn't reasonably be compared to employee
housing because the tiger cages were so much better.

The discussion turned to the purpose of the tiger cages.
It seemed to me all of the prisoners kept in the tiger cage
compound were stubborn Viet Cong leadership, or their
supporters. A few had death sentences, but it had been years
since the last execution and I seriously doubted whether
there would be another. My studies of those confined in the
tiger cages indicated most were there because they refused to
attend flag raising ceremonies, stand at attention during the
playing of the national anthem, and/or salute the flag.

"It seems to me," I said, "putting these individuals in a
tiger cage only makes martyrs out of them." From all
indications, nobodies became somebodies when they lived in
tiger cages. After some hesitation, Ve agreed this was so.

A wise and courageous man, I suggested, would probably close the cages, and let the poor employees live there. It
may sound patronizing, but it wasn't. I was speaking a
language he understood. Sometime before the campfire
burned out, with the moon lowering to the west, the three of
us found sleep on mats in the hut.

As the blinding light of morning hit the shore, I saw Ve
missing from his mat. It was 6 a.m.. Gi joined me on the
beach a few minutes later, remarking on the wonderful
discussion the previous night.

At our third cup of coffee, Ve arrived dressed in full
military uniform, ribbons and all, a seldom seen grin round-
ing his angular face. "We can use your help if you will join

EIGHT

us. You can be our truck drivers," he said, explaining he had moved the prisoners out of the tiger cages and closed the camp earlier that morning.

The rest of our day, driving two old trucks with flat beds, hauling the meager belongings of jailer's families to and from their new homes in the tiger cage cells, was the high point of my week. There were smiling faces everywhere -- a sight I really needed to see.

The employees we helped move were truly happy with their new quarters. They said nothing to Gi and me, but each of them did hold Colonel Ve's hands and express their gratitude. At day's end, I asked Ve where he had put the prisoners. He informed me they were in ten large cells at Camp Two. Each cell or room had a capacity for ten people and had inside latrines. He said the prisoners were not happy about being moved to their new quarters because, as they stated, "the new cells have no significance."

We went to Camp Two to inspect the quarters there. With a flourish, Ve announced, "these are the new tiger cages." I told him his statement didn't make sense because it was clear he had just abolished the tiger cages. Perhaps this place should have a new name.

I suggested the term Segregation. This was a term we used in the United States, though inmates called segregation/ disciplinary cells the hole. Ve, in keeping with his colorful nature, blessed the suggestion and dramatically decreed "these cells shall now be known as the Segregation Unit."

Gi and I returned to the beach house to lounge in the sun a day or two more -- perhaps just a little too pleased with ourselves.

"It was a stroke of genius, Ve," I said as I shook his hand to leave. "You have my congratulations." The next time I saw the so-called tiger cage compound there were geraniums growing in pots outside every cell door, and children playing on the covered concrete colonnades. (261)

Back in Saigon, I shaved, changed clothes, and hurried to USAID II to tell Walton our Con Son success story. He grinned, saying he was expecting a telephone call from Washington, D.C., and would pass the information along. I prepared a memorandum for the record, and at the DOC told Colonel Sanh about the new segregation unit at Con Son. He, too, grinned.

Our pleasure with our accomplishment was short lived.

101

NINE

Sharks & Harpoons

In early May, 1969, a U.S. Study Team on Religious and Political Freedom in Vietnam announced a trip to Saigon. They were sent, according to their background report, by an ad hoc committee organized in late 1968—a group of well-known churchmen concerned about the war and repression of religious and political forces. They urged an end to hostilities. (51-52)

The Study Team was in Vietnam from May 25 to June 10. During that time, they were in close contact with Luce who was operating from Catholic Charity offices in Bangkok, Thailand. A week after the team left Saigon, Luce returned. (259)

The Committee described themselves as having wide national and religious representation. The team members were Bishop James Armstrong of the United Methodist Church; Mrs. John C. Benhant, Protestant Churchwomen; Ellen Brick, Associate Secretary for the National Program, Fellowship of Reconciliation; the Honorable John Conyers, Junior, U.S. Congressman, Detroit Michigan; Robert F. Drinan S.J., Dean of the Boston College of Law School (destined to be a U. S. Senator from Massachusetts; John de J. Temberton, Executive Director of the American Civil Liberties Union; Rabbi Simore Siegel, Professor of Theology at the Jewish Theological Seminary; and Rear Admiral Arnold E. True, United States Navy (retired). (52)

On May 27, all senior members of the C&D Branch were summoned to the Ambassador's office. Colby introduced us to the Study Team, and assured them they could visit any prison they wanted to inspect. Additionally, if they gave him a list of prisoners they wished to talk to, he would help them gain access. He made it clear it would be strictly a Vietnamese decision, but he would do what he could. Berkeley, Severson, and I fielded questions concerning the DOC, its centers, and the jail system.

In addition, we gave a short talk on the total C&D effort, along with fact sheets showing funding support and

103

commodities. We gave them facts on the prisoner count, and laid out VN$ piaster support to all of our programs.

Congressman Conyers voiced concern about reports of brutality in jails and prisons. Severson said he hadn't seen any cases in the detention program. I responded that I had on occasion, indeed, seen prisoners who appeared to have been mistreated and beaten, and they were residing in correctional centers.

On each of these occasions, I discussed the prisoner with the Chief Jailer. I was informed the prisoner was beaten by someone at the DIOCC or PIC during interrogation, and was returned to the center in this condition. In every case, I assisted the jailer in arranging immediate medical treatment for the convict.

I assured Conyers that, beyond these cases, I had never witnessed a prisoner being beaten or brutalized in any way in any of the 41 prisons under the purview of the DOC. However, I pointed out the DIOCC's and PIC's were not advised by C&D, and emphasized we had no control over activities at either of these facilities. No one asked who did advise these facilities, and I didn't volunteer. The reality was Colby hadn't clarified this point publicly, for whatever reason, and so we didn't either. It wasn't a big deal to C&D at the time. We were doing whatever we could to take care of our prisoners, and we had no authority within DIOCC or PIC facilities.

The team broke into groups to visit various locations throughout the country. No U. S. civilian advisors, or military escorts accompanied them. Vietnamese Ministry personnel, as appropriate, went along.

June 17, the Honorable Abraham A. Ribicoff, of Connecticut, speaking for the U. S. Senate, stated, "rumors and stories of arbitrary imprisonment of opponents of the government of South Vietnam have persisted for some time. Last week, however, the rumors were shown to be based on facts by the U.S. Study Team on Religious and Political Freedom in Vietnam." He went on to profile the team members, and charged widespread religious and political suppression in a telegraph to President Nixon just before his Midway meeting with President Thieu. (74)

Ribicoff was deeply troubled by the detailed documentation in the team's final report, a copy of which he provided the Senate. Simultaneous with the Ribicoff statement, the Honorable Ogden R. Read, New York, in the House of

Representatives, made essentially the same speech and introduced a copy of the Trip Report. (52)

The document said many thousands were arrested and denied all procedural protections under the law. Many of the prisoners remained incarcerated, without trial, in the hands of arresting authorities, while the remainder had been removed to prisons by administrative action without being charged, or adjudicated.

It was clear, team members agreed, that whatever amelioration appeared in the formal correctional institutions, it was offset by widespread torture and brutality in the arresting and interrogation process. The team visited prisons at Thu Duc, Chi Hoa, and Con Son, as well as, the detention center at National Police Headquarters in Saigon. They thanked the South Vietnamese for providing data, permitting team members to visit the prisons, and making accessible certain prisoners for interview. However, they voiced concern about being denied visitation with thirteen prisoners they had specifically requested to see.

One of the examples used in the report was a Buddhist student who stepped out of a mass of prisoners at Con Son, Camp Seven. The government translator relayed his message. ". . .refuses to be drafted. . .doesn't want to serve the United States. . .a Vietnamese citizen. . .go into the army only when have independence."

The report was critical of Operation Phoenix, and the GVN National Assembly, and detailed the earlier briefing by Colonel Sanh. "A show of hands, taken in a number of barracks, revealed that many detainees had been in prison as long as a year and a half with little hope of being released . . . the tour had been carefully orchestrated by prison officials. The only time the team deviated from the prepared pattern was when they demanded to see Camp Number Two instead of the Camp that the Prison Authorities [sic] had scheduled."

It was here, they said, they saw something of significance. "There were large dark dormitory cells (three out of about ten such cells were inspected) in which there were from seventy to ninety prisoners each, all of whom (as determined by a show of hands) were condemned to life in prison. None had lawyers or any trial other than a judgment by a military tribunal."

"The prison authorities denied the existence of tiger-cages, reputed small barred cells in which prisoners being disciplined were chained to the floor in a prone position. Although recently released prisoners referred to this practice from actual experience, the team members were unable to elicit any more from the prison officials than that the tiger-cages were no longer in existence."

Gi translated and distributed copies. Three days later, Inspector Quang came to see me. He was steaming mad. He used American curse words rank enough to make even me blush. In an effort to calm him down, I took him to lunch, returning to a summons from Colonel Sanh. Ve had sent Sanh and the MOI a blistering cable after reading the Study Team's report. He included a message for me -- we were right, he said, in reference to the abolishment of the tiger cages and adoption of a Segregation Unit.

On July 11, 1969, an article published in COMMON-WEALTH, written by a Thomas Fox, came to my attention. The article was titled DEVIL'S ISLAND OF VIETNAM-*The Price of Political Descent.* Fox wrote he flew to Con Son with two members of a U.S. Study Team -- Ellen Brick and John Conyers.

Gi recalled the report Inspector Quang made when he accompanied the Study Team to Con Son on June 3. On the manifest a Richard Dudman was listed, but no Thomas Fox appeared. I couldn't find, in any document, including the Congressional Record, anything about a team member named Thomas Fox.

Fox didn't mention a Richard Dudman as a member of this team. Further, we could never find out who Richard Dudman was, or even if such a person existed. Possibly, Dudman was a pseudonym for Fox. The need for the subterfuge would later become clear.

The Congressional Record generally followed their report. Fox told of conversations the team had with two prisoners. Certainly, they did talk with prisoners as reported by Quang. However, the prisoners Fox said he talked to were not those listed. Further, no prisoner, by any name Fox mentioned, was housed at Con Son.

Fox continued "The Major (Tran)... denied their [tiger cages] existence and told us the only disciplinary measures taken against prisoners were the segregation quarters. He proceeded to show us ten cells, each about 4 x 5 feet in area, in which stone slabs were elevated about four feet above the floor. Ankle shackles at one end of the slab kept the prisoner tied during the night hours."

Quang's report clearly indicated the Study Team did, in fact, see the segregation unit; however, the ten cells they saw were 14 feet high by 24 feet in width and 30 feet in length. Each cell had a capacity for ten prisoners. Indeed, there were concrete slabs and inmates put their bedding on these slabs to sleep. Indeed, at the end of the slab was a shackle assembly used during the night hours.

Fox went on to say that Ho Duc Thanh had been accused and found guilty of the murder of Congressman Tran Van Van. "Did you kill Tran Van Van?" Thanh snapped back, "With a gun!" According to Fox, prisoner Ngyun Xuan An lived in the next cell and said this was the first time he had seen sunlight in seven months.

Perhaps Fox forgot the prisoner they talked to, guilty of the assassination of Assemblyman Tran Van Van, was Vo Van En, #245. The team did talk with him as reported by the Inspector. Plus, Major Tran was a friend, and I knew he didn't speak English. I thought that significant. And no inmate on the island was named Ngyun Xuan An.

Again, I bought lunch for Inspector Quang. He screamed the entire time, at the top of his lungs, in his best profane English, something about the lousy American media. Couldn't blame him. I felt like screaming myself. (74)

By the end of the year, we were scheduled to lose our four Lieutenant Colonels. Leland R. McPhie arrived in country on August 1, 1969. He was hired specifically to assist Severson with jails. Another advisor would be trained and join us by mid 1970.

On August 25, Luce returned to Phnom Penh. A week later, he was back in Saigon. Coincidentally, the Viet Cong's People's Revolutionary Government (PRG) had headquarters in Phnom Penh,Cambodia and Berne, Switzerland. Their peace talk negotiators were quartered in Paris.

That same month, over three hundred female Communist criminals were transferred from the provinces to Thu Duc Correctional Center for Females. The women had been identified as the most vicious of the VC's shadow government. And they had been a busy bunch, too.

When the dust finally settled from their transfer, these females totaled 343. From the 19th of August through the 22nd the females rioted. We transferred them to the Chi Hoa National Center in Saigon by RF/PF truck. (63-4)

For the next two and half months, they absolutely drove the Chi Hoa staff crazy. I was at the center during this period working with Colonel Lein, the Commandant, and Chief Jailer Tan. To me, many of the things the women did were funny, having lived life in a U. S. prison, but Chi Hoa staff didn't see it that way. They were overwhelmed by the audacity of it all.

The ladies would take their baths and refuse to lock up. They would entice the jailers to beat them. They made faces, spit, chanted and generally kept things stirred up. No one ever laid a hand on them, but not without their trying.

When ordered to clean up their housing area, the women swatted jailers so hard with brooms they were forced to flee to the Warden's office. They organized groups and as one group rested the other would screech Viet Cong slogans, and loudly sing songs of Ho Chi Minh.

By November 5, the MOI, after pleas from Colonel Lein, gave written authorization to transfer the 343 females to Con Son. This would be the second time in the history of the island that female prisoners would be confined there. When notification of the transfer reached LTC. Ve, he hopped the first transport to the mainland. In Saigon, he spent every waking hour politicking to block the women from his island. He was successful.

But the women weren't finished yet. November 27 awoke to a demonstration by all prisoners at Chi Hoa National Prison. All four thousand eight hundred seventy-four of them. They chanted, sang, and made demands. The release of 343 Viet Cong Patriots, as the women proudly called themselves, was the primary demand. Staff moved all prisoners from the court yards to cell blocks, without incident. On this same day, the DOC's Internal Security Committee held a regular meeting.

The Deputy Director, commanders of the national prisons and members of the Inspectorate made up the membership. The committee adjourned and hurried to Chi Hoa. After their return, they recommended immediate transfer of the 343 females to Con Son. But Sanh vetoed their recommendation, telling them to go back to Chi Hoa and try to calm the prisoners.

The demonstration continued throughout the night of the 27th and finally quieted down about 10:00 a.m., the next day. During the lull, a minor confrontation took place between an alleged relative of a female prisoner, one jailer, and the prisoner. The jailer refused to allow the visitor to give the prisoner a bolt of cloth. Loud shouting among the three bounced off the walls of the institution. Finally, out of sheer frustration, the jailer allowed the prisoner to have the cloth. The ladies' win empowered them. Into the night, they chanted, encouraging others to join them.

The women were loud, and they weren't really hurting anyone. But part of a prison administrator's job is to understand the social dynamics of life inside a prison, and consider the consequences of particular actions to the entire prisoner population. The administrator must also take into account the larger issues concerned with the well being of the outside community. Possible consequences to the free community are a factor and should be considered, before deciding if, when, and how, a disturbance is to be stopped, or how far it will be allowed to go before control is lost. When control goes, safety goes as well.

The level of unrest is a factor. A competent administrator must evaluate the level, and hope he isn't mistaken. People who avoid distention of any kind shudder at an angry shout, while to others a weapon must be involved before they show concern. No matter what you call it--a commotion, disturbance, riot, brawl, revolt, or insurrection --in confinement space of any kind, it's a situation laden with the possibility of dangerous consequences.

Timing is critical. You wait too long to contain a skirmish, or ignore it, and soon you have a war. Full blown riots usually occur when a small disturbance has gone unattended, or has been ill attended. The most common mistake is to wait too long to take action, thinking the situation will defuse itself. That's an unrealistic expectation and though we might wish it, it rarely happens.

A disturbance can spread with the speed of light and engulf even unwilling participants. Fear by intimidation is very powerful reasoning when one has no place to run. It's common for prisoners who have no wish to cause trouble-- and that's close to 95% of them--to become full participants in order to avoid retribution—then and later--from the prisoner leaders and their followers.

My philosophy about disturbances is much the same today as it was then. The major difference is that I now have many more incidents behind me. Each one has solidified my belief that informed, swift, and decisive action—or inaction—is the best defense against the dangerous possibilities inherent in these situations.

When in doubt, err on the side of caution -- sooner rather

than later, harder rather than softer. There isn't much point in the waiting action if, in trying to be nice, you miss a guy with an H-bomb in his pocket.

Isolating the perpetrators, removing them entirely from a facility, or in some way separating them from each other, is a first step which often takes care of the problem. The most definitive time to act is within the first minutes of a crisis, when the perpetrators are most likely in a state of confusion trying to consolidate their support and secure their perimeters. It's also an action which Monday morning quarterbacks often fault.

I believe there is a consequence to every action, my own, as well as, a prisoner's. And each of us must take responsibility for what we do, and don't do. I'm sure it's possible that sometime, somewhere, a blameless soul has been falsely accused. But in my experience, that's rare—if— people are doing their jobs.

If you ask enough questions, and wait long enough, the truth comes out--even if the reason is simply stupidity. I've seen a lot of prison administrators do neither. It takes time and effort to gather and sort information in such a situation. Some people, then as now, are more interested in whacking notches in their gun belts than in searching for facts. Some are lazy. Others are simply afraid of law suits.

And, much as I hate to say it, there seems to me to be a proliferation of this ineptitude in recent years. I base my observation on the frequency of particular types of incidents reported from inside prisons. When prisoners run a prison, incidents are not isolated events, the apparent calm is a precursor to chaos. It is inevitable.

My belief in before-the-fact action has caused some people to fault, not my record, but my methods. Day to day structure that is firm, fair, and consistent is orderly, teaches self-discipline, helps build self esteem among participants, and creates a safer, more secure environment for everyone.

This basic dynamic, currently out of vogue and considered harsh by some, can be applied to any group setting.

Results are often dramatic and problems minimal. When a problem does occur, the decision process involves a sixth sense of the kind mothers develop about their children. Prison administrators delude themselves if they think a safe and calm prison environment just happens because they have the keys. It doesn't.

On the second day, at about 4:30 p.m., an MOI officer

informed Sanh they would have a full scale riot, at 8:00 p.m. the next day. Covert intelligence sources had picked up the information on the streets.

For more than an hour, I listened as Sanh briefed his subordinate personnel. From 10:00 p.m. to midnight, I taught a refresher course in use of a baton and riot control tactics to 300 correctional staff. And we requisitioned the Army for tear gas.

On the third day, the Chief of Cabinet wanted immediate and necessary measures taken to prevent the disturbance before it began. Sanh decided the best way to defuse things was to immediately transfer the 343 females. He was aware of minor incidents by these same prisoners over the past several months. By now, the females had the support of the majority of incarcerated males. Mostly, this was accomplished by threats from the females and about 100 hard core male Communist offenders.

Transportation to Tan San Nhut, and troop support for the aircraft was confirmed. We dispatched Mai and Secor to Con Son to forewarn Ve, and to help him to receive the ladies the next day.

At 1:00 a.m. on November 29, 110 ARVN Rangers with vehicles arrived. By 1:15 a.m., 120 National Police Field Force (NPFF) members drove through the main gate in 5-ton trucks. Five minutes later, 250 military criminal trustys, from the prison at Tan Heip, mustered in the prison courtyard. At 2:00 a.m., Col. Sanh and Col. Lein issued specific instructions.

Fifty minutes later, the entire contingent, including me, moved into the center. The women were in three large dormitories. When the doors were opened, most of the women were sleeping. Those awake began screaming. Almost in unison, each female revealed a cloth type homemade gas mask and a knife. The knives were fashioned from pieces of glass and scrap metal, wrapped and taped at one end to create a handle. Jailhouse shanks, shivs, and tools aren't fancy, but they're just as deadly as Jim Bowie's first knife.

The woman formed groups, threatening to hurt anyone who tried to move them. Tear gas was dispensed; the dorms sealed off. Within minutes the dormitories were re-opened, and the riot control group moved in.

When the tear gas was released, the women fought like banshees -- kicking, biting, screaming. They refused to walk to the vehicles. Each was restrained with a bear hug, carried to a waiting truck, and perched on a bench in the back. We didn't have enough handcuffs to handcuff everyone so guards were posted in each truck. An hour and ten minutes later, 343 women prisoners were on their way to a new home at Con Son.

Trustees from Tan Hiep cleaned up the debris under the watchful eye of correctional workers. Staff found numerous leaflets, memos and documents from the Communist Party. The information urged insurrection by all patriots. Maps of Saigon and adjacent cities, as well as, listings of safe houses and suggested contacts, were confiscated. Three hundred plus homemade gas masks and 211 pounds of homemade weaponry was also admitted to evidence.

Jailers, in subduing the prisoners, suffered fifteen casualties from multiple cuts and wounds and were relieved from duty. Numerous other support personnel had minor abrasions. Two physicians and six nurses were present throughout, and any prisoner, injured in any way, immediately received medical attention. Those male prisoners who helped the rioters went into individual cells at Chi Hoa.(63-4)

As the convoy of fifteen 5-ton trucks, with as many escort vehicles, roared through the gates of Chi Hoa, the women began to sing and chant at the highest octaves. They did this the entire distance to Tan Son Nhut. They, of course, awakened many of the personnel, bivouacked at the airport, who began following the convoy on foot.

When they arrived at the Eighth Aerial Port, the women stopped their singing and commenced to use vulgarity--in English. Some servicemen began taking photographs and mingling around the trucks. The airport security police confiscated the film and the servicemen were asked to leave. The observers withdrew only after the females threw four slop cans of urine on them.

It took another hour and a half to board the ARVN C-130's. The women refused to walk, insisting we carry them. We did -- the same way we had carried them to the trucks. The area was cordoned by security personnel, and at 5:55 a.m. the first aircraft left for Con Son. At 7:30 a.m., it landed.

Three companies of RF/PF personnel waited at the landing strip with Major Tran, Major Cong, and McPhie, the C&D advisor. There was no disturbance in flight. Once on the ground, however, the woman again demanded to be carried. We repeated the bear hug exercise and finally got them into the waiting vehicles.

At ten a. m., the sixth and final aircraft left Tan Son Nhut. Forty minutes later the vehicles and support personnel were back at Chi Hoa. Before leaving Chi Hoa, Colonel Sanh told the one hundred segregated male prisoners they would be going to Con Son on the next LST. He also cabled Ve, instructing him and his men to interview, classify, and segregate the females. They were not to be in close proximity to any male prisoner. (63)**

After the last plane, I returned to breakfast with Lein and Sanh. Meanwhile, McPhie, and his assigned USAID interpreter, Ngo Doan Khoa, assisted Ve on Con Son.

A Saigon morning newspaper carried an article by Don Luce. He reported, "the women were stripped naked, transported in the nude, and loaded on the planes naked."

In an interview with my wife, Luce would say, "Yeah, naked, parading in front of all those men. It was awful." When asked how he knew this to be true, he said he hadn't seen it, he was told by the women and he believed it because—why would they lie to him? Why, indeed.

Luce's article appeared around the world. I was witness to every move from Chi Hoa to the airplanes. McPhie reported the women arrived clothed, and were housed clothed. Sanh, Mai, Lien, Ve, Gi, indeed, all of the correctional workers deserved better for a job well done. My heart raged for them. And there wasn't a damn thing I could do about it. (63)

What was worse, no one who could, even tried.

A Florida newspaper, THE DAILY BREEZE, 11/6/69, informed the public, "Don Luce, agricultural specialist and author of a book on Vietnam will be presenting a talk and photography exhibit on . . ." The religious coalition of the Peninsula Citizens Humane Relations Council at the Rancho Vista Elementary School was his sponsor.

"Luce resigned his government position in Vietnam in 1967 and later returned under the auspices of the World Council of Churches." He would discuss the prospects of non-communist oppression in Vietnam. VIETNAM-THE UN-HEARD VOICES was mentioned, as was the foreword, written by Edward Kennedy.

** Bordenkircher was twice awarded the South Vietnamese government's highest civilian award. One was for this action. He was not allowed to keep either award per U.S. law. An acknowledgment and Job Well Done letters from the U.S. command became a permanent part of his personnel file.

The press release continued, "Luce was one of few Westerners to attend the funeral of Ho Chi Minh. He has met with North Vietnamese, and Provincial Revolutionary Government (Viet Cong) leaders in Cambodia and Paris."

Records indicate, Luce left Saigon in late September 1969 for Phnom Pehn, where he stayed until late in the month. Then on to California. In early December, he landed in Berne, Switzerland, staying there until December 16, when he arrived in Saigon. His Visa, No. 219, was good for one year. It was, of course, renewable. (61)

The Ministry of Interior's Intelligence Service reported Luce was with International Volunteer Services (IVS), Catholic Charities, and carried press credentials. He mingled with members of the Provisional Revolutionary Government in Phnom Penn, Berne and Saigon. He was the associate of left wing zealots, students and political groups in South Vietnam who were, at the least, anti Thieu and against U.S. involvement. (261)

Any other foreigner, in South Vietnam at that time, having such a profile would not have been allowed entry, let alone to live in South Vietnam. His history and profile begged me to ask Colonel Sanh how the Prime Minister could continue permitting Luce's entry back to South Vietnam. Sanh's reply was short, "Ask your friend Colby."

Could it be Luce was a CIA asset, was thought useful and necessary to the CIA, and so General Khiem tolerated his presence at the subtle insistence of Colby? Maybe. Sanh believed it and he was close to Khiem. Perhaps, Luce was just a man caught up in the thrill of the times. Perhaps.

In any event, he was an astute player. His willingness to manufacture and/or manipulate people and events to suit his own purposes--by using whatever misrepresentation necessary, and his unwillingness to tell it straight, for whatever the reason, indicts him in many quarters as a man lacking character and substance.

Whatever his reasons, I didn't care then, nor do I now. My objection was that the rockets he was firing were aimed at the wrong people, and our POW's were to suffer for it. I was incensed.

I remain incensed.

TEN

The set-up in motion — The CONDEL

Every branch of OPS was on 24 hour notice. Senate Foreign Relations Committee hearings on Pacification, and in particular the Phoenix mission, were scheduled to begin, and Colby and his pacification committee needed our input -- more briefing papers.

Colby wouldn't be going to Washington to appear before the committee. George Jacobson, his deputy (ACofS CORDS), would make the presentation instead.

LTC. Shepard, and Major John Mirola, both U.S. Army Artillery, were assigned to us early March. Shepard and Secor assisted me with national centers. Mirola was Berkeley's liaison with ARVN and PSYOPS. Later, Secor would relieve me.

My orders were to return, with my family, stateside for a long overdue home leave. After that, I'd be assigned to the International Police Academy for 90 days.

In the last week of March 1970, Harry Ellis and Raymond Keating, program evaluation officers from AID/ CORDS, were detailed to the corrections program. They were to evaluate the program since inception, and assess the current status relative to mission, goals, and objectives, in my company.

It was exhausting, but Con Son would be the final survey. I was anxious to tie up as many ends as I could before home leave.

Berkeley assembled a contingent to travel with Ellis and Keating: LTC. Shepard, C. Walstrom, U.S. Embassy Political/ Military Affairs Section, Col. Sanh, and me.

I returned from the inspection junkets expecting several letters from my wife. There were none. We were to leave for Con Son the next morning so I was disappointed, but not surprised. My mail was having a hard time finding me. I'd been on the run--moving from apartment to apartment every few days for more than a month. The VC had issued a black

115

list and I was near the top. Still, I had to admit, it was unusual not to hear from my family on a regular basis. I had a bad feeling about it.

The next morning a crumpled cable appeared under the door. My son was confined in a hospital in Yokuska, Japan for a sight threatening eye injury. My wife was with him; my daughter left behind in Taipei. I sure didn't need any more problems, and family dilemmas aren't the kind I handle well anyway. I'm a worrier and don't like feeling helpless. She gave me no details.

Shirley and I had a pact of sorts -- we shared the good and the bad news. I knew she'd handle it, but the thought didn't ease my pain much. Trying not to borrow trouble with worry, I plunged into preparation of fact sheets for Jacobson's upcoming Senate presentation and readied for home leave. Walton had scratched me from the Con Son trip to assist Jacobson, sending Secor instead.

The massive assessment report, written by Ellis, was forwarded through the maze. The summary acknowledged the advisory effort to DOC as meeting all USAID/CORDS goals and objectives. The prisons project would be terminated in June 1970. (90)

It was a grand kudos for us. We had met our mission goals. No other program had done that. But it meant my job was finished.

"It's been great working with you, Berk. Guess I won't be back after leave," I remarked, after reading the report.

My emotions were raw. I knew how rare it was for an AID program to complete its mission and be phased out. I was more than proud of our accomplishments. Lots more than proud. We'd done one hellava job.

But it was a let-down of sorts, too. I had mixed feelings about leaving Vietnam. I thrived on what I was doing, and although we'd done what we'd been tasked to do, there was a lot more we could do. Things were far from perfect, and our POWs deserved our all out best efforts. I'd miss the challenge, and maybe even the pressures. Pressure creates challenge, and spurs me to solutions.

The overpowering upside was I'd probably be posted somewhere with my family the next time around. If I kept my job. By now I knew the controversy surrounding the initial hiring of corrections people like me, and that no agency had really wanted us. It wasn't much of a stretch to deduce my staying power was dependent on a need for my

TEN

specialty--and there wasn't one anywhere else in the world.

Though things have changed some since then, with the advent of the term criminal justice, corrections remains on the low rung of the pole in law enforcement circles. Many people still think all we do is turn keys in locks. Too much Hollywood, I guess.

In any event, my reverie was broken when Berk, almost smiling, said, "Don't you believe it. Colby'll decide when we're done -- not USAID!"

Colby and his pacification committee staffed the Ellis report. The prisons project would not be considered for termination until 1975.

LTC. Ve sent a cable in April which said 340 of the 343 women prisoners sent from Chi Hoa were unsentenced. He wanted a mobile military court to come to the island to hold trials for them.

The same day another letter appeared under my door. My wife and son were still in Japan. The treatment of choice was skillful neglect, no sight had returned to the eye, surgery was scheduled, and she didn't know when they'd return to Taipei. I felt like a gnat hit by a sledgehammer. Home leave couldn't come too soon. (87)

Meanwhile, George Jacobson was before the Senate Foreign Relations Committee talking about the status of all U.S. programs. I called Berk and we caught a movie.

On April 30, 1970, I met with Shirley and the kids in Taiwan, and we returned stateside together. Our son would undergo yet another eye surgery, and I'd be working.

As a Class Counselor to forty foreign police officers from fifteen free world nations, my job was to advise, assist, and counsel them through their three-month-long International Police Academy General Course. I was elated to be with my family again, and at the same time ashamed that I counted the days until I could return to Saigon and finish what I'd started. There was so much more to do.

We spent most of May in California visiting with relatives. By June, we were in Washington, housekeeping at the Francis Scott Key, an historic hostelry, just a few blocks from State.

On June 8, the U.S. House of Representatives adopted House Resolution 976. The Resolution authorized appointment of a Select Committee on Southeast Asia. (284-9)

On June 20, that committee left for Saigon. Working in teams, members trekked to Laos, Thailand, Cambodia, Indonesia, and Singapore. Tom Harkin, now a United States Senator and a 1992 presidential candidate, was then one of the Congressional Delegation's (CONDEL) staff aides. (289)

By his own report, Harkin was interested in the tiger cages. He has said he first became aware of them after reading a U.S. study team's report. This was the same Study Team chaired by Congressman Conyers. (261)

Meanwhile, Luce continued to travel between Paris, Saigon, and Berne, and by mid June, 1970 had landed, once again, in Phnom Penh, Cambodia.

Harkin met with representatives of major news magazines, telling them of the upcoming congressional study, and of his personal agenda--the tiger cages. The only problem he forecast was his ability to find at least one Congressman who would enable his venture because Con Son was not yet on the inspection schedule. (259)

A member of the CONDEL, California Congressman Augustus Hawkins, an avid anti-war advocate, sent newsmen flying when he said he was going to Vietnam "to find a factual basis for an emotional response to end the war."

Earlier, it had been decided the committee would inspect the island of Phuc Quoc where real military prisoners of war were housed. That visit was approved and arrangements made. But once in Saigon, Harkin went to the U.S. Embassy to arrange a new flight -- to Con Son. The Embassy balked, they couldn't do it. Only the MOI, General Khiem, could approve such a visit. (254,284,289)

It appears that when Harkin couldn't get clearance to Con Son, he went to see his new friend Luce, who had returned from Cambodia, to commiserate. He couldn't believe the U.S. Embassy couldn't arrange a trip to Con Son for a high-powered congressional committee. He was amazed Vietnamese approval was required, and that only a General Khiem could give such approval, but was at a loss as to how to proceed. (259)

Luce assured him getting approval would not be a problem. He had a friend, a Harry "Buzz" Johnson, at the Ministries office, who was a Special Assistant to Ambassador Colby -- Khiem's direct counterpart.

Luce informed Harkin that Colby was CIA, relating in an interview that, "so is my friend. It's not to be mentioned, of course, but Buzz is a good friend of mine, and married to a Vietnamese lady who worked for me at IVS."

Colonel Johnson, member of the U.S. Pacification Security Council for territorial security, responsible to William Colby, was Phoenix, was CIA, and was assigned to the Minister of Interior's office. He was a friend of Don Luce, and by his own account helped him out and took care of him. Luce back-peddled, saying he knew Johnson only slightly, but that Johnson did help him with his problems with the government. (259,261)

Johnson intervened.

In 1991, Colby said, "I do not find it strange the Congressmen might have casually asked two CIA men to get them permission to visit the island . . . Certainly . . . there was no policy reason for me to be brought into the question . . ." (259)

Citing the work of Doug Valentine, again in his book, THE PHOENIX PROGRAM, page 348, "Initially, Rod Landreth advised CIA Station Chief Shackley not to allow the congressmen to visit Con Son. But, Shackley saw denial as a tacit admission of CIA responsibility (for Con Son). So, Landreth passed the buck to Buzz Johnson."

While we did not verify this with Landreth and Shackley, we have no reason to disbelieve Valentine's or Johnson's rendering.

Walton recounts George Jacobson, a member of Colby's staff, told him to accompany the CONDEL, to make necessary Air America arrangements, and to give them anything they wanted. Colonel Sanh relates that the MOI authorized the visit the previous day.

Berkeley made arrangements with Air America and prepared briefing papers, notifying James Nach, Embassy Political Officer, of the particulars: Air America leaving Tan Sha Nhut Airport at 7 a.m., on July 2, 1970. (95)

Harkin, required to produce a complete passenger list prior to departure, still didn't have such a list the day before. Further, he told Berk, he didn't intend to produce one. He also registered his displeasure with the flight schedule, grousing the hour was much too early. And besides more congressmen and staff aides might be going, but he didn't know exactly who. And what business was it of Berkeley's, in any event.

Berkeley patiently explained why it was impossible to change a flight time. The good news was Air America had assigned a C-47 in anticipation of increased numbers in the party, and the DOC had cabled the CONDEL's arrival time to Ve. Under the restraints of Con Son's communication capacity, changing times would not be acceptable. After a good bit of high pitched arrogance, Harkin terminated the conversation, commanding Berk to be sure to bring along a breakdown of U.S. expenditures to Con Son. (95)

At 6:30 a.m. on 2 July, the C-47 was ready for take off. Frank Walton, Berkeley, Major Mirola, Lt. Ronald L. Dey, and Nguyen Ngoc Cam, Walton's interpreter, gathered at the Air America terminal. At 7:30 a.m., the congressional delegation (CONDEL) sallied up. Instead of additional Congressmen and staff aides, Luce appeared. (3,95,104,259)

Congressmen Augustus F. Hawkins; Congressman William R. Anderson (a former Navy Commander in charge of the USS Nautilus), and staff aide, Tom Harkin boarded the C-47.

Walton knew Luce, and reminded him journalists were not cleared for this trip. Harkin took exception, snarling in a loud tone about how Luce's presence was required as Luce was the Congressman's guest and his interpreter. Walton and Harkin argued for a time, Walton finally allowing Luce to board the plane. Recalling Jacobson's order to give the delegation anything they wanted--Walton and Berkeley agreed to let him go rather than spark a flap neither of them could win. (104)

Berkeley remains appalled, to this day, at Harkin's behavior. In Berk's book of standards, there is no excuse for bad manners, dilettante, or artifice. It must have been some conversation to exercise him after all these years.

The plane taxied as Harkin asked questions which, in Berkeley and Walton's view, had little relevance to the Con Son visit. Copious notes were taken on Berkeley and Walton's background. And though Harkin's attitude was offensive, Berk and Walton answered easily.

Airborne now, the briefing began. Berk, a remarkably laid back and unimposing gentleman, whose conduct is absolutely professionally correct at all times, thought Harkin's frequent and abrupt interruptions more than ill-mannered. He thought Harkin impudent and antagonistic, and took rare personal offense.

It soon became apparent to Berk that the hand guiding the entourage, the one with the motivation, the one leading the charge, was Harkin. Clearly, Harkin had prepared an agenda he did not intend to share, continuing his caustic behavior for the rest of the flight. (95-104)

Walton and Berkeley put aside their displeasure to

concentrate on their job -- making sure the CONDEL had all available information at their disposal. Harkin announced he would be writing the Congressional report. In response to his incessant questioning, Berk finally called a halt, saying LTC. Ve would answer any further questions.

As the plane approached, Harkin instructed the pilot to fly about the island, so they could have a better look. The pilot complied, landing at 9:20 a.m. The only airstrip on the island was at the Loran Radar Station, a U.S. Coast Guard installation, and the island's only communications center. The flight crew cautioned the group to be back promptly at 11:30 a.m. for the return flight.

Majors Tran and Cong met the delegation. During the eleven-kilometer trip through town to the prison compound, Berkeley pointed out panoramic views of Con Son Valley, the town, the seven separate camp areas of the prison complex, and encouraged questions. There were none.

The group arrived at Ve's headquarters at approximately 9:45 a.m. where he greeted them in full dress uniform. Vietnamese fiercely believe in honoring a guest by showing one's best face. They are gracious, and polite to a fault, often spending beyond their personal means to provide for a guest. Ve was no exception, in fact, he was especially proud of the island and his part in upgrading it. He ushered everyone into his home, which was also his office, served refreshments, and invited questions.

Harkin quickly took command and asked for a map of the island showing where the camps were, by number. Berkeley recalled a map of the island hanging above Ve's desk and suggested that map might suffice, though the map was not in evidence. The wall charts were covered for security purposes.

Ve replied the map in question did not have camp numbers on it. Walton explained why Ve did not keep such information on display. South Vietnam's prisons were a favorite target for VC attacks and camp numbers were changed frequently to confuse the enemy. (104)

Harkin, incredulous, doubted this could ever happen at Con Son Island. Walton pointed out it had happened on Phuc Quoc Island, and for that reason Ve intended to do every-thing in his power to prevent such an occurrence on Con Son. Harkin remained unconvinced, stopping just short of calling them liars.

Congressman Hawkins took pains to establish the location of each camp by number. Berkeley was amazed and appalled to see guests conducting themselves as if Ve was the subject of an inquisition.

Harkin shoved a handwritten paper in front of Ve. He asked to interview the six prisoners listed. Ve was surprised. He couldn't permit individual interviews of prisoners without specific authorization of the DOC and MOI. "It is customary," Ve said, "for a DOC official to be present in such cases of prisoner interview."

"This is the common practice," Berkeley explained. "The CONDEL has been cleared to visit only the island. No request has been made, and no permission given for prisoner interviews."

Hawkins disagreed. He thought they had been given carte blanche in this regard. Berkeley stood firm, too much an old hand to ask Hawkins where he would have gotten that impression.

Harkin stood, towering over Ve with unveiled menace and said, "Do you mean to say you're refusing to let us talk to these people?"

Ve didn't flinch and calmly restated his position. Walton pointed out the party was already in a breech of GVN trust by including Luce in the delegation. Congressman Hawkins wanted to telephone the mainland. Ve, having no telephone service on the island, graciously offered to send a carrier wave message from the Coast Guard Station, but cautioned it could take some time to receive a reply. Walton suggested the message be sent. Ve complied. (94/104)

Of the six prisoners listed, Ve knew only three were on the island--Cao Lap, Nguyen Troung Con, and Ho Hung Van. The CONDEL decided they would visit camps while waiting. Ve told them to make any selection they wished.

After some discussion, the selection was made, and the retinue started off to tour, what turned out to be, several prison camps. The visit which should have ended at 11:30 a.m. continued from camp to camp with no regard for time.

The tour quickly became another inquisition. Luce acted as an interpreter as Harkin openly conducted interviews with prisoners. Harkin was definitely in charge; even the Congressmen acquiesced. He went to locked doors and asked what was beyond them. He demanded to know what buildings were "over that wall." We now know he was searching for the tiger cage area, but this objective was not made known in advance to anyone outside of the CONDEL.

As Walton and Berkeley would later recall, and as I know only too well, if the CONDEL had just asked they would have been ushered to the front, main gates of Camp Four. There was nothing to hide, and further, everyone and anyone on the island knew of the location -- that same compound had been referred to as the tiger cages since the French built it. Prisoners name every compound something, and old names die hard. There were the Cow Cages -- which housed prisoners minding dairy animals; there was the Pig Barn--where the pig farmers slept, and so on.

Harkin ordered guards to open doors, move aside, and pose for photos as he stalked the area, working his way from one prison section to another. Eventually, they came to the old French cell blocks with bars for ceilings which had traditionally been known as tiger cages--segregation cells. Ve suffered the onslaught in silence, maintaining a rear guard position. Not once did he object to the party going wherever they wished. Indeed, according to all reports, Ve was the epitome of self-restraint during the entire time.

At Camp 5, Congressman Anderson asked about taking pictures. Ve's benign response was clear, "Please, no pictures within the prison compounds. You may take pictures outside of the camps as you wish." (94/104)

Harkin continued to take pictures at will, blatantly disregarding every common courtesy. Ve noted this breech, but permitted it to continue. Neither Congressman made any move to deter their staff aide from taking pictures, interviewing prisoners, or taking notes. The tape recorder was not in evidence until later. (94/104)

In Camp 6, just before the tiger cage compound, Harkin challenged Ve for permission to take a picture. Ve refused to be goaded. "You have been taking pictures all along without my permission, why do you ask me now?"

Harkin smirked -- then took the picture. According to one observer, Harkin's continued defiant, screw-you attitude was designed to goad. Mostly, he was ignored. Recently, Berkeley said, "Short of shooting him, there was nothing we could do." (104)

Led by Harkin and Luce, the CONDEL walked along between the outer perimeter walls, bypassing vegetable gardens, until they came to a wooden door. When the two men tried to open the door, LTC. Ve suggested it would be easier for them to go to their left--around the corner of the perimeter wall--where they would find the front entry gate to

Camp 4; the route of heavy daily traffic.

The side door Harkin was interested in was kept closed for security reasons. It enabled entry from Camp 6 directly into the tiger cage sub-compound of Camp 4.

Harkin and Luce ignored Ve to peer through cracks in the patched wooden door. The two men then banged on the door while the Americans cringed anew at the uncivilized behavior displayed in clear view of their Vietnamese hosts and prisoners. A guard opened the door to check on the commotion. Luce and Harkin scrambled through the opening, grins slashing their faces, eyeball to eyeball.

This placed the party inside the compound referred to as the tiger cage area. It consisted of two barracks of 60 cells each. There were external wooden slat doors allowing access to each cell at ground level. Bars were at the tops of the cells, creating a ceiling. The entire cell block was covered by a high-peaked roof which was one story above the top of the cells. (104,284,289)

Numerous large windows provided ventilation to the area above the cells. A catwalk down the middle of the upper story gave guards a view of the prisoners in the cells below. The upper level was reached by an outdoor, covered stairwell located at one end of the building.

The prisoners kept in this area were designated as the most dangerous prisoners on the island. There were, at this time, eighty-two men and three hundred twelve women prisoners in the compound. The women were the same ones who had been moved to Con Son from Chi Hoa Prison the previous November because of their riotous conduct.

The CONDEL was absorbed in taking statements from prisoners in the building, but appeared to concentrate on several women. They lingered in the tiger cage area about an hour, interrogating prisoners through Luce, who spoke Vietnamese fluently, taking notes and photographs. (104,284)

Berkeley walked between the two barracks attempting to keep contact with the Congressmen who alternately congregated to talk to specific prisoners, or walked off on their own. As time dragged on, Berkeley suggested it was time to move along. Harkin disdainfully announced that *he* was not ready to go because *he* was not finished questioning prisoners.

As they left the compound, Harkin summoned the CONDEL for a whispered conference. Before departing, Berkeley and Walton apologized to Ve for Harkin's conduct, and Congressman Anderson specifically told Ve, "Nothing will be done to embarrass you."

Ve wanted Walton to be sure to tell the Prime Minister about Harkin's derisive behavior. Walton assured him he would pass it on to Colby with specific comment: Ve should not be held accountable for the breech of policy. (104)

The group piled into jeeps to return to the air strip, at 1:45 p.m. The Air America crew definitely was not happy. In the jeep driven by Major Tran, rode Major Mirola, Lt. Dey, Cam, Tom Harkin, and Don Luce. During the ride Mirola and Dey overheard the following conversation between Luce and Harkin, which was later recounted in a sworn affidavit.

"It looks like we put it over," said Harkin. Luce's response was a contented grunt.

"Now we can write the book," Harkin offered. Luce's exact words, lost behind the grinding gears of the jeep, were distorted, but the intonation was clear -- reproach.
Harkin's piqued response was, *"I'm* a *paid* investigator -- once *you* do the groundwork, the rest is easy."

It was, from all reports, a very quiet return flight. No one spoke to anyone. Upon return to Saigon, as a final comment, Walton assembled the delegation and said, "Contrary to some American opinions, Vietnam is still a sovereign country, and the United States is not an occupying power. Although considerable progress has been made in the processing, rehabilitation, and treatment of inmates, we all recognize the country has a long way to go." (104)

The next morning, July 3, 1970, the World Council of Churches, based in Geneva, Switzerland, published a nine page article entitled THE TIGER CAGES OF CON SON. The byline was Don Luce's.

It's probably better, all things considered, I wasn't in country when this CONDEL visit occurred. Certainly, I would have accompanied the group. Notwithstanding Jacobson's caveat, Luce wouldn't have boarded. Cameras, film and tape recorder would have been confiscated and sent to swim with the fishes.

Contemptuous, intrusive behavior would have resulted in an escort back to the airplane. I simply would not have allowed it. Captain Cong and Major Tran would have been willing supporters given the lead of an American.

The worst I'd have faced was an angry Walton, Berkeley, and Colby, and a severe chewing out. Maybe I'd have been sent back to the states. Either way would have been okay with me.

ELEVEN

Spin City & other abominations

On July 7, 1970, Shirley, my wife, and I watched the early morning news over breakfast. The lead story was quoted from the Washington Post. The commentator reported Representatives William R. Anderson and Augustus F. Hawkins toured Con Son Prison, sixty miles off the coast of Vietnam, on July 2.

They were part of a House of Representatives fact finding group, it said, which made an on the spot assessment of the island. While there, the Congressmen found tiger cages containing men and women prisoners who had been chained and beaten. Both Congressmen were shocked by what they had seen.

We stared at the screen in disbelief. She had not been to Con Son, but she had been to Thu Duc and Chi Hoa, seen numerous pictures, and heard and participated in plenty of lively discussions. She had a background with the California State Prison system, and had lived with all of my Vietnam failures and successes. The implications didn't escape her.

"Don't over-react," she said. "Everything's documented, right? Take them to see for themselves. This can't possibly be accepted as fact. "

She was wrong, and so was I. We were not only naive, we were powerless. And we were heartsick.

I made contact with Manopoli immediately. Had he seen the early morning news? He had not. I capsulized the newscast. He would get a Washington Post immediately and I should meet him at State before going to the academy. I arrived at his office, on the second floor of the State Department, within the hour.

Manopoli had been busy. "All hell's broken loose. You'll stay with me today."

By noon, the always kinetic Asian Desk swam in a sea of demands as Bunker, Harriman, Kissinger, NSC suits, and AID Deputy Secretaries lined up for answers.

In Washington D. C., on July 5, Representatives Anderson (D-Tenn) and Hawkins D-California), met with George C. Wilson, Washington Post Staff Writer. Earlier, the Congressmen told Chairman Montgomery they were disenchanted with the final report agreed to by the majority of committee members. Further, they would release their dissenting viewpoints to appropriate media, and would include comments on the prison at Con Son.

Hawkins and Anderson recounted their Con Son visit and their viewpoint, as Wilson listened intently. They asked him to hold their story until July 7 when additional information would be forth-coming. Wilson agreed to honor their request. (112)

The Anderson/Hawkins story was in more than the Washington Post--it was virtually in hundreds of newspapers, and by evening would be the lead of every newspaper in the country.

I needed to digest the Wilson article. I found a secluded office. Wilson was graphic. I was incredulous.

"A South Vietnamese prison where men and women are locked up in window-less cages and disciplined with a dusting of choking lime was described by two Congressmen yesterday. (131)

Representatives William R. Anderson and Augustus F. Hawkins provided that description on the basis of their tour of Con Son Prison. It was the most shocking treatment of human beings I have ever seen," said Anderson, a 49 year old former Submarine Officer who won the Bronze Star Combat Award.

Anderson and Hawkins were part of . . . an on-the-spot assessment of the Vietnam War. They were the only Congressmen who toured the prison, where ten thousand persons -- most of them held for political offenses -- were kept.

The formal report on the trip submitted to the House yesterday contained only one paragraph on Con Son. But Chairman G.D. Montgomery, D-Miss, of the Special House Committee said, "We do not condone the prison conditions and mentioned it briefly because we didn't want to focus the report on it."

Anderson, in an interview, said this is what he saw at Con Son in a tour that started about nine in the morning and continued until mid-afternoon, including a look at the tiger cages which (sic) South Vietnamese Prison Commandant tried to keep hidden from the Americans.

He approached a wall at one compound and looked for,

what he had been told in Saigon would be, a hidden door into the tiger cages he had heard about.

'I had been told that the South Vietnamese hide the door with a stack of wood,' Anderson said. Through an interpreter they had brought with them from Saigon to the prison, Anderson asked to see the tiger cages.

'I had been told that they were in Compound Four,' Anderson said. As I (sic) stood before an uncamouflaged door and the wall of Compound Four, Anderson pressed the issue of the cages, even asking where that door led. The Commandant said it was to another compound. But just then -- probably the guard had heard the Commandant talking -- swung the door open. The Commandant looked like a fellow who had dropped his teeth because it was obvious that the door did not lead to another compound.

The Commandant, Anderson continued, had no choice, but to let us go inside. We saw a one story foundation with no windows in it of any kind. We went up the stairs to a kind of cat walk and could look down through iron bars about three-quarters of an inch thick at prisoners inside solid concrete cages. Anderson said the concrete cages with the iron bar roofs were either side of the catwalk. Most of the tiger cages had five people in them, although a few had three. The walls stretching up to the bars were about 6 or 7 feet high, and floor space was about 5x9.

'I noticed a box standing over each cage and asked the Commandant what was in it. He said sand. I felt it and said I knew it wasn't sand. He then said it was lime for washing down the walls of the cages. But I could see lime clinging from the iron bars.'

With the help of some advance information, Anderson found the evidence compelling that the lime was thrown on the prisoners. 'Lime plays the devil with your breathing and nostrils,' Anderson said, in describing the lime punishment.

Not one of the male prisoners was able to stand, Anderson said. They (prisoners) indicated to him by both talk and pointing at their limbs that they had lost the use of their legs. Anderson figured that this was either from malnutrition or paralysis from lack of any exercise.

The only visible sanitation facility inside the cage, Anderson said, was a single wood or porcelain container about the size of a waste basket. One straw mat served as a sleeping facility for five prisoners jammed into the cage.

While he did not see anyone shackled to the wall, the

Congressman said he saw steel plates evidently designed for
ankle shackles in the cages. After walking over the double
line of the tiger cages, which Anderson estimated contained
about two hundred men in fifty cages, the congressional
party walked to the corresponding prison for the women
prisoners.

There, in a separate building in the same compound,
Anderson found a girl who spoke English. She said she was
eighteen and had been arrested while caught up in a political
demonstration. She claims she herself had not demonstrated,
but had been imprisoned for seven months with no bath in
two months. She said her sister was somewhere in the
compound, was sick, but the girl didn't know where she was,
Anderson said. She looked pitiful. Most of the prisoners
looked quite thin.

The women, too, evidently got the lime treatment as
punishment because the same boxes of it were over the iron
gratings. Some women were standing or could stand, evi-
dencing shorter periods of incarceration. Anderson estimated
there were about 150 women in the tiger cages.

The Agency for International Development's escort,
former Los Angeles Police Officer Frank Walton, told the
Congressmen that there were about 10,000 prisoners in the
whole prison complex and only about 35 of them were
former prisoners of war. Walton himself, Anderson said, had
never seen the tiger cages before. As part of Walton's job as
Head of USAID Section advising Thieu Governments National Police Force and Penal System, the former Los
Angeles Police Officer said he visited Con Son once every
three months.

The American Government through AID funds, Anderson said, had spent 100 million a year to assist the National
Police Force. 'The USAID figure is below that for this
current year,' Walton corrected. 'Since American money
links the U.S. to the prison conditions, the findings of the
Congressmen are likely to embarrass the Nixon Administration and provide Hanoi with fresh propaganda ammunition.'
The Chairmen of the Interior Committee in the South Vietnamese Assembly, Anderson said, told him that their own
efforts had not been very successful in exposing prison
treatment. The Assembly Chairman, he said, encouraged the
Americans to publicize what they had seen.

'Sickness, especially tuberculosis is rampant at Con
Son,' Anderson said. Most of the male prisoners told him

they had been in prison on the island for many years. One prisoner in part of the compound outside of the tiger cages told Anderson he had been on Con Son 17 years, received mail once a year and was bad off with TB. There's one Doctor for 10,000 prisoners. About 20% have TB.

'Some prisoners in the tiger cages claim to have been chained and beaten', Anderson said. Some of the prisoners are suspected Viet Cong while others were committed for criminal acts according to Anderson's finding."(106)

Simultaneous with the July 7 Washington Post Article, was a Saigon UPI article written by Don Luce, Secretariat for Vietnam, World Council of Churches. This article circulated mostly in Asia.

Luce said he accompanied Congressmen Hawkins and Anderson and their Congressional Aide to Con Son. He said "we saw the tiger cages despite concerted efforts by the Prison Administration and the U.S. Public Safety Advisor, Frank Walton."

Luce's reporting followed, in nearly identical form, the same ground covered by Hawkins and Anderson to the Washington Post. However, Luce described the tiger cages as "small stone compartments". "Each cage had a wooden bucket which was emptied each day. In order to see the prisoners, we climbed the stairway and looked down on the prisoners through an opening at the top which was crossed with iron bars."

He further embellished with comments he said were made by prisoners to the delegation while they were on Con Son, including a translated report of five former alleged inmates, detailing their life in a tiger cage. (92,112)

Early on the same morning, Tom Harkin held a news conference. In a special report to the New York Times, Juan M. Vasquez, reported that "a staff member of a Special House Committee that toured the War Zone in Indochina today termed its report a 'white-wash' and said that the panel had suppressed significant findings. The Committee, a bipartisan twelve-member group that visited Southeast Asia for two weeks, was 'led around by the nose' according to Thomas R. Harkin, a 34 year old former Navy pilot who now attends law school at Catholic University." (107)

Harkin attacked the U.S. House of Representatives and from the number of new stories appearing, he was in great demand. The enemy's delegates to the Paris peace talks used the media reports to exemplify their struggle, and set a clear precedent for winning the psychological and emotional sympathies of the American people.

On July 13, in the House of Representatives, Anderson (for himself and Hawkins), submitted a concurrent resolution which was referred to the Committee on Foreign Affairs. The essential elements of that resolution appear in Appendix C, but in short, it moved to correct the failure of the U. S. to demand humane treatment of thousands of political prisoners held in South Vietnamese prisons.

Every notable magazine and newspaper in the country used a lot of ink on Con Son, the tiger cages, OPS and its programs in Vietnam. The media had a field day playing Congressmen Hawkins and Anderson off against other House members who were part of the CONDEL. Harkin catapulted to hero status for what the press called telling the truth and blowing the whistle, and espousing the currently palatable and popular anti-Vietnam rhetoric. He had definitely become an item on the news circuit. (105-07,109,112,114,116-17)

Harkin was quoted extensively in NEWSWEEK, TIME, and LIFE magazines. He had covertly tape recorded conversations with the delegation, Walton, Berkeley, and prisoners. Eventually, the Moss Committee entered the tapes, and the transcription, into their record as an exhibit. It came to light that LIFE magazine paid Harkin $10,000 for the photographs he took on Con Son. And this was *before* he left the United States with the CONDEL. (102,130,135,144)

OPS in Washington D.C. and in Saigon were deluged with hundreds of press clippings pinned to letters from irate citizens blaming Walton for the horrible conditions on Con Son. But Frank wasn't the Senior Public Safety Advisor to the DOC and its 41 prisons. That advisor was me. (261)

I was deeply concerned and hurt. I was a big boy and willing to take the flak, but I suppose at the time, I believed as Frank did: we could counter the lies by simply supplying the truth—invite interested parties to see for themselves. The truth was, no one was interested. Anti war sentiment was so high stateside, the Pope could have anointed us and no one would have believed we were worthy.

I voiced my concerns to Manopoli, recalling what I had seen--prisoners in segregation units, geraniums on the tiger cage building's porches. He assured me OPS could handle the flap; to take it easy and we'd all get through it. Every now and then, there appeared a positive report in the papers about OPS and our advisory efforts. The IRC even made comment of their inspections — eight lines in the New York Times. Granted, the articles were minuscule, and often buried between public notices and classifieds, but whenever we read one, we took a few moments to thank God, and savored their every word.

On the U. S. political scene, the Speaker of the House took the matter of the subcommittee's report, which had generated division among the members amid the worldwide controversy, and placed it before a Full House Committee on Government Operations. They held an initial hearing to announce formal hearings would start on July 17. The Committee was instructed to continue until all data concerning U. S. assistance to the prison system had been accumulated. Congressman Moss was designated the Committee Chair.

OPS Washington wanted Walton back in the states to appear before the Moss Committee. I bounced back and forth from the academy to Manopoli's office, continuing to cull facts sheets, answer congressional inquiries, and expand and clarify C&D messages to the State Department.

In Saigon, Walton pleaded with Colby for authorization to develop a three or four day trip to Con Son for GVN, U. S. and Embassy officials, as well as, any and all interested members of the international media - written and visual. Walton pled the fanaticism had to stop, and proposed the way to do it was to allow the truth of Con Son to speak for itself. Frank was convinced the accurate portrayal of Con Son, OPS and C&D efforts - both successes and failures - to the public would be accepted.

But Colby put Frank under a gag order and told him Bunker was making arrangements for him to meet with the press corps at the Embassy. The media would be instructed not to identify Walton, but merely to refer to him as a knowledgeable American official. Colby made it clear Walton would not comment again publicly concerning the DOC, its centers, or any matter pertaining to the OPS effort within the Pacification Program. And neither would any of the rest of us.

Until the day he died, Frank insisted Colby never intended to fight back. He remained convinced the MOI authorized the Con Son visit only because Colby did not disapprove it. (261,276)

In those years, Colby was considered an icon. Only

a rambling heretic would give voice to such thoughts. Interestingly, Duane Clarridge in his book, A SPY FOR ALL SEASONS, confirms this trait in Colby.

Clarridge was a high-ranking officer when he retired after decades with the CIA. His comments are close-ups from someone who worked within Colby's sphere for many years. He assesses Colby in reference to a particular incident by saying, "Colby never intended to fight back . . . He betrayed his own because he didn't try," and further describes Colby as "lacking courage."

The congressional committee's report on Con Son was but a mere paragraph which, in and of itself, caused no damage to the U. S. Mission to South Vietnam, or Public Safety, or American POW's in the custody of the North Vietnamese Communists. And that was exactly the consensus intent of the committee. (276-76)

However, Harkin characterized the report as a whitewash and resigned his position. His dramatic gesture fanned passions of anti-war reactionaries, and sold lots of newspapers, magazines and TV spots. Walton and Buzz Johnson verified the entire CONDEL visit, its report on Con Son, and the subsequent spin-offs involving Harkin's resignation - ostensibly because of that report - was aired before the Central Pacification Committee. (276-288)

Our recounting of the committee action, concerning the tiger cages, dims the fire of Frank's personality, intonation, and profanity, but it is worthy of inclusion. He wrote, "When we began to draw heat from Congress and the media, the subject of our meeting was Con Son damage control." (276)

After a full discussion by the group, Colby's assessment was that all things faded in time. Walton strongly objected, wanting to take the free world press to Con Son to show Harkin's distortions for what they were -- outright lies. Walton insisted something was seriously wrong with how things were being handled. He simply couldn't believe the tiger cage incident was a fortuitous fluke, or a lucky roll of the dice, insisting ". . . this fiasco had to be planned!" Colby's response: "You're paranoid."

Frank's characterization of the committee's opinion was less than favorable. He could not believe we had been abandoned, but even that was okay, maybe even understandable, if only we had been able to fight back on our own. At the time, Walton thought it was personal. And maybe part of it was. (276)

ELEVEN

The Pacification Committee existed as a Group Think under the totalitarian control of Colby. He viewed Frank's attitude as cavalier, a veiled and patriarchal reference to a type of loud, loose cannon. He thought Frank foolishly disruptive -- without good cause. The group fell in line.

Said Buzz Johnson recently, "The whole mess was unfortunate, but the only one of us disturbed and upset was Frank."

And Frank was incensed. "Colby put a muzzle on me. He only allowed me a briefing at the Embassy. Even when I did that there were guidelines and perimeters I couldn't breach." To use Frank's vernacular - Colby was a wimp. This was the pattern which had been set between the two soon after the HOI CAI document went in the trash can.

I subscribe to Walton's later theory -- Colby decided on his own damage control—since the OPS Advisory effort was a very small part of Phoenix, it was expendable, and could be useful--a bone to toss to Congress and the media -- postulating that if both groups were busy feeding on that prize the more important and substantive programs (covert activities) of Phoenix could continue to flourish undaunted.

Representatives Hawkins and Anderson appeared on a Special Edition of the CBS Evening News anchored by Walter Cronkite. This appearance continued to fuel the outrage among various members of the government and citizens. Berkeley and his staff responded to 1400 separate questions posed by the State Department. All replies were cabled to the Secretary of State, over the signature of Ambassador Colby. (261)

On July 18, Ambassador Bunker was summoned to the White House. Walton would not appear before the Moss Committee. Rather, a seasoned State Department envoy would do it. Any and all information given the committee would be filtered through Bunker. All inquiries originating from the committee would initially be responded to by OPS, Saigon, through Colby. Bunker returned to Saigon.

On July 20, news came that Congressman Philip M. Crane would be arriving in Saigon on his way to Con Son. Crane's flight to the island, via Air America, was set for the next day. At the request of the Congressman, Walton, Berkeley, Major Mirola, Secor, and Walton's interpreter, Cam, went along. Crane also arranged for three other Americans to travel with him--two U.S. military photographers and the obligatory and customary bodyguard assigned to traveling VIPS by the Military Police.

On the afternoon of July 23, Representative Crane held a news conference in Room 1537, of the Longworth Building, Washington D.C. Crane's staff handed out copies of a news release. Numerous photographs of the alleged tiger cages, the prison complex, and prisoners housed in those camps, were prominently displayed around the room. (135)

Crane presented a capsulized briefing of his visit. He said he was on a scheduled trip to Taiwan when he read the shocking reports about Con Son Prison, and decided to attempt to see first hand if the reports were true. At his own expense, and on his own initiative, he cabled Saigon, and demanded permission to inspect the prison, and take photographs of what he observed. His demands were met.

Rumor in and around OPS offices at the time, however, was that President Nixon had asked Crane to stop off to make the visit. Who knows? Maybe he did.

The text of Crane's short statement follows:

"After inspecting Con Son Prison, and, particularly, the now infamous tiger cages, I came away with the impression that Congressman Hawkins and staff member Harkin were either blind or they deliberately misrepresented what they found there.

I cite the following points made by Hawkins and Harkin that were complete misstatements of fact based upon what I observed:

1) They stated that all the prisoners in the cages were sick with TB, open sores, eye diseases, or malnutrition. This is a complete misstatement of fact. None of the prisoners were sick except those living in the dispensaries. I saw no evidence of open sores, eye disease, or malnutrition.

2) They stated that few of the prisoners could not stand. Not true. In each cell we entered the prisoners immediately stood up. Out of hundreds of prisoners only one experienced difficulty in standing and this was due to an old injury.

3) They claim prisoners found it necessary to eat insects, lizards, etc. I found absolutely no evidence to indicate this. All prisoners appeared healthy, well-fed.

4) They stated that the air was foul and heat stupefying. This is not true. The cells in the tiger cages were well-ventilated, well lighted and relatively cool.

5) They stated that conditions were filthy. I found the cells cleaner than the average Vietnamese home.

6) They stated that prisoners were shackled to an iron

rod and lying in this position caused paralysis. This is not so. I did not see a single shackled prisoner; nor did they. The prisoners are shackled only at night to prevent escape. Not one prisoner showed any evidence of paralysis or any adverse effect from being shackled.

7) They said that several prisoners were blinded from beatings. Not one prisoner showed any evidence of beatings, nor did they complain of beatings.

8) They stated that medical care was practically non-existent. This also is untrue. Although limited, the medical care was adequate and not one prisoner complained about lack of medical care.

9) If anyone cares to investigate, I am confident that everything that I have stated will be backed up by the Inspection Teams of the International Red Cross.

In conclusion, I would like to make two observations:

1) First, I do not pretend to explain why Congressman Hawkins made such a distorted report. Only he can do that. But in his zeal to embarrass both the Vietnamese and the United States Government he has inadvertently jeopardized the safety of hundreds of American soldiers being held prisoner of war by the North Vietnamese Communist. I can well imagine the North Vietnamese will attempt to justify the mistreatment of our men as a result of such a false picture.

2) Secondly, I am convinced that the actions of Tom Harkin, the Staff Member involved, were pre-meditated and that he went to Con Son Prison for the singular purpose of obtaining pictures and information that could be used for either a book or a magazine article and that he did so without any regard for truth.

One last point...I do not mean for one minute to imply conditions at Con Son Prison were ideal and could not be improved. On the other hand, by Oriental standards, conditions at the prisons were definitely superior. In fact, Con Son would compare favorably to many of our own prisons. For anyone to portray Con Son in the way Congressman Hawkins and Harkin did is not only a complete distortion of the truth, but could well prove to be a tragedy depending upon the effect upon the treatment of our own men." (114)

The evening edition of the Chicago Tribune summed up the Crane Conference in a Willard Edwards column, Capital Views. His report is titled CHALK UP ANOTHER HARD LESSON. Edwards stated, "the temperature where Crane announced his findings, had fallen below freezing by the time he finished. Most of those present represented newspapers and networks which had played up to the Hawkins/Harkin charges. They were, frankly, incredulous about Crane's testimony." (146)

"Maybe they ran in an entire new prison population on you and cleaned up the place after Hawkins left," a questioner suggested. Crane acknowledged the possibility had occurred to him, but insisted an exhaustive investigation had revealed the impossibility of such a wholesale reform in such a brief interval. The prisoners he talked to, all hardcore Viet Cong Communists, referred to the Hawkins visit and noted two slight improvements - more water for bathing purposes and discontinuance of the use of lime to quell unruly prisoners.

"The fact," said Crane, "is that Con Son would compare quite favorably to many of our own prisons."

"Why would Hawkins lie?" demanded an irate newsman. Crane, still serving in our Congress, as unflappable today as he was then--said he would not try to explain the liberal California congressman's motives, but noted Hawkins was passionately committed to overthrowing the Thieu regime, target of the prison brutality allegations.

"Either Hawkins was lying, or you got a snow job", a TV commentator blurted. His voice betrayed a preference for the latter option. (146)

Similar leanings were evident among other press/TV listeners. Many agreed there was little news value in one congressman's rebuttal to another congressman's charges, especially when the only result would be to cast doubt on a tale of bestiality which emphasized the barbarity of war--true or not.

Their judgment was reflected on the networks that night and in the Washington-New York press the next morning. Crane's press conference and the data to back up his statements was either ignored, or given perfunctory mention--if mentioned at all. There was even a print article, or two, in which reporters bravely reasserted judgments of the blatant conjecture--presented as fact. (114)

While it shouldn't have surprised me, it did. But Shirley was far less accepting. Far less. She began clipping articles, making notes, and setting up files we would cart from post to post for the next 25 years. Neither of us bought the coincidence theory. She wanted answers. It would be years before we would get any of consequence. Everyone, including me, just wanted to put the whole issue behind them.

Crane's statement infuriated Hawkins and Anderson, and Harkin was irate, or said he was. Hawkins appeared before the Call of the House on the afternoon of July 28. His statement and numerous papers he presented are fully reiterated in the Congressional Record/House, H7231.

Representative Hawkins attacked. He strenuously objected to Crane's statements, proceeding to censure almost every statement Crane had made.

He then requested the Speaker include in the Congressional Record numerous news articles from U.S. newspapers, as well as, numerous letters sent to him since his investigation of Con Son on July 2nd. These letters were from Don Luce, numerous persons alleged to have been prisoners at Con Son, and various other individuals at one time, or another, who had been in Vietnam and expressed their views to Hawkins about the political situation in that country. After Hawkins finished, the Speaker called Representative Crane to appear the next day, on July 29.

The Speaker, Pro-tempore, under his previous order, recognized Representative Crane from Illinois. Crane's forty-five minute, restrained statement is revealing. It is printed in it's entirety in Appendix D. Suffice to say, that it judiciously refuted Hawkins, Anderson and Harkin--point by point. (135-144)

As expected, Congressman Crane's statement didn't get any ink stateside--to quote Walton--nor did Crane's statements appear in any of the international media. What did continue to be printed were the continuing comments of Harkin and Luce, and vicious attacks upon the U. S. government by North Vietnam's Premiere Pham Van Dong, and Mrs. Binh, leader of the Viet Cong Delegation to the Paris peace talks.

Premiere Dong was, at one time, himself a prisoner on Con Son Island, and Madam Binh's brother was incarcerated in Chi Hoa National Center, during the time I served in Vietnam. Quite a coincidence, I'd say.

At the time, I attributed my VC black listing to the decision to blow up a prison, rather than let the VC break out prisoners. I supplied the explosives and showed jailers how to rig them, but in retrospect I think that wasn't the only reason. There were several things I did that probably made me known to the VC and didn't endear me to them. I did my job every day, and the program was working.

When a prison perimeter force needed ammunition they could travel to the nearest ammunition dump and pick up what they needed. But they wouldn't go. I found out the VC had sent word not to go. So I embarrassed our jailers by riding on top of the ammo piled in the lead truck of the caravan, with 2 M-16's at the ready. They weren't cowards, it was war and they were just tired of it. Somehow it helped to have someone along. But the ammo got through.

Another thing I was known for, I later found out, was my strict insistence that unauthorized people not be allowed into any prison. I didn't much care who they were, if they weren't authorized, they didn't go. My experience with the worst of the worst in prisons stateside had taught me a few things about letting just anybody inside.

Weapons, money, inciteful literature, drugs, and all kinds of other problems walk in with people who have no real purpose in being there. Prison staff, and prisoners alike, have enough pressures. Most prisoners just want to do their time, and staff just wants to do their job. Issue exploitation is only one of the progeny spawned by a lax perimeter.

It has nothing to do with trying to hide something, it has everything to do with the well being and safety of those entrusted to our care. Most free people don't know what they're looking at inside a prison, comparing and measuring what they see by a free man's standard. My record before and since Vietnam is well documented and hiding things from the media, or anyone else, isn't a part of it.

Prisons have always been ripe for exploitation, and we knew early on, most especially after the RAMPARTS exposé, that our program would be prime fodder, sooner or later. That knowledge played a part in moving convicts from the tiger cage buildings and using the term segregation-- which is, after all, the purpose of secure cells.

Neither was it a secret that I didn't pass on prisoners who weren't good citizens. Once such incident involved two young Americans recently mustered out of the military who came back to Vietnam to live. They were picked up for dealing drugs and stealing and were housed, as a courtesy, in Chi Hoa prison awaiting deportation proceedings.

They raised all kinds of hell. The other prisoners were afraid of them; the staff was afraid of them. They set fires in their cell, demanded the Embassy get them out, barricaded themselves in one corner, threatened to kill people, feigned illness--you name it, they tried it.

They were so disruptive, Col. Lein cleared a 25 man cell to give them space, and the Embassy even brought them turkey dinners for Thanksgiving and Christmas celebrations.

One morning about 1 a.m., Berkeley rousts me to meet him at Chi Hoa. Embassy personnel were there standing around with Secor and Col. Lein. Lein was beside himself, he didn't know what to do with the two of them--especially since they were Americans. One was writhing on the floor, yelling as if he was dying; the other was the spokesman. To me, it was dejavú San Quentin.

Noting there was nothing to talk about, I told them they were coming out of the cell, and were going to be separated and put in one man isolation cells. They could walk out or be carried out, their choice.

I picked up a Febat -- a metal baton about 12" long loaded with tear gas -- opened the cell door and walked up to them. They couldn't believe it. They were so stunned at my audacity, it didn't take much to get them on their way to their new cell. They didn't give me any trouble. What was important is that they believed I meant what I said. Actually, I did, and they knew it. We had a doctor check them out before they went to isolation, though they had not been harmed, and were not ill—standard procedure in any well run prison.

This incident was so minor it really doesn't bear mentioning, except that the stories grew and grew until it sounded like I had single-handedly slain 3 dragons and an elephant. I need to set the record straight. The rumors created such a persona that some of the jailers would tell unruly prisoners I'd be called if they didn't straighten up--and to my chagrin, it worked.

I'm aware, as was Mai and Sanh, that Luce and a few others tried regularly to get inside one provincial prison or another. And a couple of times they succeeded. A bolt of cloth, a bottle of Jack Daniels, cigarettes--bribery worked now and again. How this helped any prisoner, I'm not sure, but I do know it caused some heartache for a few employees.

In his interview with Shirley, Luce proudly told of how he bribed his way into jails and prisons here and there across the country. She didn't tell him about the employees his actions hurt. Would he have believed it?

In the last week of July, 1970, the Prime Minister's Office in Saigon made the following press announcement: "As instructed by the Prime Minister, inter-government delegations from the Ministries of Interior, Justice, and Information, conducted a thorough investigation of Con Son Island on the so-called tiger cages at Camp Four."

LTC. Ramon Sloan, a C&D advisor newly assigned to Military Region One (I Corps) at Quang Ngai, was sent to meet with members of the American Society of Friends (Quakers). Sloan was to determine the circumstances and facts surrounding a press release (UPI) relating to conditions of brutality alleged to exist in prisons there. (133-34)

Sloan met with Lewis Kubaichn, the Society's leader, who said their team included one doctor, one nurse, three physical therapists, one prosthetic specialist, and five personnel who were Administrative. Kubaichn related, they "had been working with the dispensary in the Quang Ngai Center for two and a half years"; their present work was primarily with Maternity Care and Maternity Food Programs; the teams living quarters were located across the street from the prison.

A doctor, Marjorie Nelson, who left approximately a year before, had prepared a card file on those prisoner cases she suspected of being brutalized. Dr. Nelson's records indicated she discussed her suspicions with the U. S. Province Senior Advisor and the Vietnamese province chief. Nelson's articulate account left no doubt she suspected the injuries she saw were cases of vicious brutality, inflicted during interrogations at the PIC facility.

Further, Dr. Nelson was laudatory about the level of cooperation received from prison personnel, making it abundantly clear she had never had any indication of improper treatment by correctional personnel at the prison.

LTC. Sloan thoroughly documented his visit. His report ultimately made it to the Secretary of State, enabling responses to Congressional and press inquiry concerning Nelson's Moss Committee appearance.

During that appearance, Dr. Nelson again made it clear that in her experience with the prison, which was extensive, any suspected case of brutality upon prisoners was the result of the prisoners being interrogated at the Provincial Interrogation Center (PIC). She never saw, or had any reason to suspect, any brutality by civil prison staff in Quang Ngai province facilities. (275)

The day of Dr. Nelson's testimony was a long time coming, it seemed to me. I called Shirley to be sure she tuned in to the evening news channels, just in case I didn't make it home in time to see it.

I never knew when I'd get home. The paper blizzard at the office was worse than drowning--at least when you drown, it's over. This was more like being hungry, clawing your way through a supermarket, and knowing your money wasn't going to cover your purchase. I chased paper, wrote paper, copied paper, filed paper, found paper, and wrote answers to every conceivable question, from every conceivable source.

Backstopping the Desk Officer who was working with the envoy from State, Robert H. Nooter, wasn't the worst part; I had to interpret, clarify and expand on every piece of paper coming from C&D in Saigon. It wasn't that Berk, Walton, and the others weren't clear, or that their reporting was not accurate. It was; and they were exacting. It was simply a matter of converting prison vernacular and substance into something understandable by lay people, most of whom had never seen the inside of any prison, let alone one in rural South Vietnam. It was a lot like trying to convince a four year old milk is the product of a cow, not the supermarket. It was exhausting. (149)

I rushed home in time to take off my coat before Dr. Nelson flashed on the screen exiting the hearing room. Shirley and I held our breath. We were sure there would be some measure of vindication once her testimony became public.

We couldn't have been more wrong. It wasn't our first experience with the power of the press, but it was our first experience with the power of a sound byte. Dr. Nelson got one only. Her comments weren't even excluded with finesse -- the arbitrary cut off was messy.

Neither of us can tell you exactly what words made it to screen -- the memory is only of a realization, something akin to crashing your bike and finding you're still alive. You're not sure exactly how it happened, or even what happened, but you'll sure try to avoid doing it again.

In retrospect, I believe there was nothing we in C&D, or OPS could have done, at any point in time, that would have changed a thing. The rhetoric and tenor of the times didn't allow for painting anything about Vietnam any color but black -- Vietnam was indefensible; the guilt belonged to those who were there; all other consciences were clear, righteously clear.

It was, however, a turning point in the formation of our

personal philosophy in dealing with the press -- show them everything, explain everything; always be up front and fair; establish credibility the media representative can depend on; know to whom you speak, choosing only those whose credibility matches your own; expect like credibility from them; and the first time a breach is expected, or experienced, cut them off.

Then pray.

Still, this philosophy has, over all, served us and our media friends, long and fairly.

L to R: Frank Walton;
Mr. Cam; Berkeley; and LTC.
Ve waiting for Hawkins/An-
derson/Harkin/Luce CONDEL
visitors to complete their
tour of Con Son Prison on
July 2, 1970.

Right:
Aerial
photo of
Camps 1, 4,
5, and tiger
cage area.
Salt ware-
house is top
center.

Right:
Long view
of outside
perimeter of
Camp 4, the
so-called
tiger cage
complex.

Left:
Main gate entrance to the tiger
cage compound at Con Son Prison.
This is just around the corner from
the side door the CONDEL used to
enter the
compound.

Left: Door through wall surrounding the tiger cage buildings at Con Son Prison — the above ground, so called tiger cage buildings are visible through the opening and above the wall.

Above: Vegetable garden and alley leading to the tiger cage area. This is the "secret" door the CONDEL "found" from the directions on their map.

Left: Representative Philip Crane opens yet another door from inside the tiger cage compound to the alley shown in picture above. The above ground tiger cage buildings are again visible through the opening.

Right:
Another alley & vegetable garden surrounding the tiger cage area.

146

Left:
Another view of tiger cage compound on the well side. The door shown in the wall at left just above the X is typical inner courtyard view of doors shown in previous photos.

At Left: Frank Walton compares the cell height of a tiger cage to his own 6' 1" height. Our view is taken from the entry door as seen in the above photo on the right—under the colonnade.

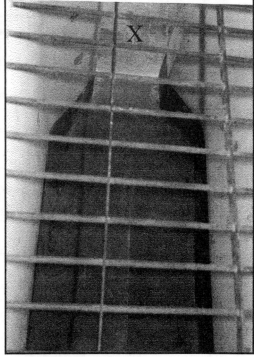

At Right:
A photo of a so-called tiger cage cell taken from above. Note the door opening at top marked by an X, leading into area shown on the cover and in picture at top of this page. Bars form the ceiling of the cell.

Right: View of tiger cage building attic area. Bars on floor are ceilings of cells. Catwalk is for jailers to walk and monitor prisoners inside cells. Note ventilation windows & air space.

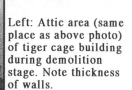

Left: Attic area (same place as above photo) of tiger cage building during demolition stage. Note thickness of walls.

Right:
Picture of a single tiger cage cell and two occupants, similar to magazine photo — without several photos staggered & layered to appear as one.

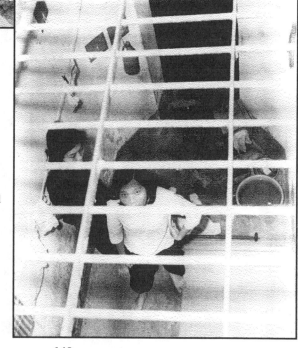

Right:
One of new segregation unit buildings which replaced the torn down tiger cage buildings.

Left:
Housing unit Ve used to house tiger cage prisoners when turning tiger cages into housing for employees.

Right: Jailer's family housing outside entrance to Camp 2. Note the tin roof.

Insert: Close-up of the woven mats used for walls.

Left:
Typical mealtime scene at all prisons. Prisoners preferred this style of dining.

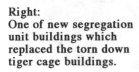

Right:
This is the indoor dining facility built with U. S. funds at Con Son Prison at the insistence of U. S. congressional visitors .

Left:
Dried fish in Con Son Prison warehouse.

Right:
Typical prison kitchen area—Foreground, cooking woks covered with pieces of heavy canvas. Wood for fires stacked against pillar.

Left:
Exterior & interior of Catholic Chapel Con Son Island Prison.

Right:
Con Son Camp 2.
L-R front:
Bordenkircher; Col. Sanh
in white shirt; LTC. Ve.

Left:
Trustee
prisoners
fishing off shore
at Con Son Island
Prison.

Right:
Entrance to Cow
Cage housing
area at Con Son
complex.

Left:
Vocational sewing &
uniform repair at Con Son.

Right:
Replacement kitchen in
Camp One at Con Son
Prison.

Left:
Con Son Camp 2
dormitory
housing unit.
Sleeping mats
rolled up on
floor. Raised
sleeping platform
at foot of back
wall.

Right:
Volleyball game in
progress—Con Son —
conducted by Civic
Education Bureau.

Left: Entrance to one of
the emergency tent camps
at Con Son Prison.

Right:
Interior of
typical tent camp
housing unit.

Right:
Gardens for prisoner consumption. Prisoners work open spaces within compounds growing food to supplement their diets.

Left:
Civic Education Branch teaching prisoners at Con Son Island.

Right:
Vocational woodworking and camp repairs.

Left:
Inside one of the five prison dispensaries at Con Son Island Prison.

TIGER CAGE: *An Untold Story*

Right:
Con Son Prison turtle farms.
Turtle meat was used for food
& crafts were made from the
distinctive shell.

Left:
Hilltop view of one of
Con Son's
agricultural & food projects.

Left:
Prisoner working at cane
making—a hobby/craft.

Right:
View of planted areas inside
prison compound. This in
Camp 1,Con Son.

TWELVE

Hanging in there

The Moss Committee was ready. Robert H. Nooter made the presentation of on behalf of Ambassador Bunker, using well over a thousand pages of material written by C&D advisors. (262,264,275)

In order to meet the massive reporting requirements, Berkeley put Severson in charge of the branch, McPhie in charge of the Detention Program, and Secor in charge of Corrections. The paper challenge was awesome, the circumstances adverse, and the pressure unyielding, but they managed to also keep up with daily duties in both corrections and detention.

On the 10th and 12th of July, 1970, the GVN sent inspection parties to Con Son to look into the tiger cage matter. This was unilateral action taken without consultation with U.S. advisors. More than once, Colonel Sanh was approached to give us either an oral briefing, or written reports on the visits in order to keep Nooter up to date.

The requests fell on deaf ears. This disturbed Berkeley. He asked Colby to intervene with General Kheim. Colby didn't reply.

Congressional inquiry necessitated more meetings with Ve. It was important to clarify the issue of shackling prisoners. Ve gave a sworn statement verifying women were never shackled. McPhie went to the tiger cage compound and observed the women mingling in the open courtyard, outside of their cells, washing their hair and clothes, and in general, socializing. (159)

Sanh testified before the Vietnamese Senate about prison conditions. Le Cong Chat, Vice-Minister of Interior, was with him. He began with the prisoner population on Con Son: that day--8000. The government wanted to close the tiger cages. However, U.S. advisors insisted on their use in spite of the government's decision to abrogate. (261)

Much progress, he continued, had been made in the past two years in the management of Con Son Prison facilities. "The prisoner population of the island cannot be compared

155

with prisoners in the U. S.--nor does the United States have a war going on in its cities. The National Liberation Front (North Vietnamese) and the Communists exploit the statements made by U.S. critics, and their propaganda is spread to prisoners of all of our centers to mount insurrections and demand freedom."

Using the most uncompromising voice he could muster, Sanh declared he, and his government, would stop the use of the tiger cages. Newsmen hurtled out the door.

Senator Bui Van Giai asked if the remarks made by U.S. Congressmen about their visit reflected the truth of the tiger cages. Sanh replied, "during our past inspections we enabled members of the Vietnamese television and newspapers to accompany us. You have seen and read their reports that clearly show that the Congressmen lied. I do not know what the U.S. Congressmen had in their minds. I can only tell you the U.S. Advisor at Con Son judged the tiger cages preferable to other housing facilities . . ."

Chalking up Sanh's comments as a last effort to save his Directorate and his own butt, I didn't challenge him. The little man had enough problems right then and no good purpose would be served. We would discuss it later.

Students at the hearing denounced the management of Con Son, and spread out numerous documents written by alleged former prisoners about their treatment on the island. Sanh's reply was rapid, "I have read these reports. Our investigations show most statements are distortions of fact. It is my opinion that you, too, are using our prison system for issue exploitation to aid and comfort our enemies."

There was now, or appeared to be, a schism between the DOC and C&D advisors. Sanh was firm and defiant — yet somewhat nervous when asked about this. (261)

"Ambassador Colby has said publicly the DOC is a GVN program, not a U.S. Program. We must have your advice and assistance on correctional matters—we will not succeed without it. But, it is our country; our system."

Berkeley surmised our partnership would end in the near future. Until then, our relationship would be strained. He made sure Colby was aware of Sanh's position. (141)

Congressional inquiries, letters from U.S. citizens, congressmen, as well as, a multitude of news stories, continued to pour into the Embassy. McPhie continuously pumped Sanh for more data. Colonel Sanh was near the end of his emotional rope, indeed, he had lost some 20 pounds, was short-tempered, and colorless. His tail feathers were definitely down.

On August 21, the Chairman of the Foreign Operations and Government Information Sub-Committee of the House Government Operations Committee authorized the General Accounting Office (GAO) to investigate OPS-Vietnam. One matter in question was the use of American air transportation to move some five hundred prisoners in early July, from Con Son to the mainland. (168-70)

It fell to C&D staff to prepare another two hundred page response, with loads of attachments, for Elwood G. Martin, of the GAO. They attacked the chore with diligence. Prisoners flown to the mainland were those who had been waiting transfer for many months. No other transportation was available. The investigative result became part of the Congressional Record, dying in the shadow of other world events, without fanfare.

Within days, the MOI announced the tiger cages were no longer in use. He acknowledged designs had been made. Bids had been taken, but no mention was made of when work would begin on the new buildings.

Immediately after the Ministry's news conference, the student leader, Cao Nguyen Loi (a friend and ally of Luce and Harkin), became the spokesman for the Saigon Student Union. He, too, held a well attended news conference. He had information, he said, from a female released from Con Son. She said political prisoners once held in tiger cages were now in secret cages, and the GVN was building a new cell house called the salt warehouse**. Leaders of various anti-government segments would be held there.

Loi also accused the GVN of not releasing the five hundred political prisoners who were airlifted from Con Son to Saigon by U.S. Air Force planes on, or about, July 13. Loi maintained the government released only thirty or forty of those prisoners and the rest were in Tan Hiep Center, a political prison near Bien Hoa. UPI and AP press wires set new fires under the DOC, and us. (261)

In truth, those five hundred were male prisoners--military men convicted of civilian crimes--and all had served their sentence. Their time was up.

At this same time, journalists were diligently reporting about prisons within U.S. borders. Typical was OUR HOPEFUL PRISONS by Harriet Van Horn, published in the San Francisco Examiner on August 20, 1970.

Oscar Wilde wrote, "All prisons are built with bricks of shame, and they're bound with bars, less God and the world discover how the men inside are broken and maimed."

In New York's ancient and vile prison called the Tombs . . . In Arkansas it was charged that guards . . . the county jail in Chicago, the worst since . . . what went on in Philadelphia's jail was stopped only when a CBS television program exposed the conditions . . . Our nation's (the U.S.) Correctional System in brief, is cruel, obsolete, insufficient and vengeful . . . Chief Justice Warren Burger . . . we need a drastic overhaul of the courts . . . Congress will have to appropriate vast sums.

And so it went, with sensationalized stories such as these provoking, ever more afield, philosophical comparisons between the U.S. and South Vietnamese prison systems, indicting every arm of the criminal justice structure. Everyone, it seemed, wanted a piece of the action. (261)

Frank Borman, a renowned astronaut, requested a visit to Con Son. He was the President's personal representative on POW's.

An aircraft was requested for a flight on 29 August, departing Air America for Phuc Quoc with a fly-over at the Can Tho POW facility en route. They were to land at Phuc Quoc at approximately 0830, which would allow a three-hour tour of that POW camp, and time for lunch there. The ETA at Con Son was 1300. (169)

Borman would visit POWS held on Con Son--military men who had killed other POWS while in the military POW camps--and return to Saigon when he was ready.

The GVN travel clearances for Borman, Walton, Berkeley, one U.S. Embassy representative, LTC. Reahrs, and LTC. Chagnon (MACV POW), came through easily. Berkeley asked for a DOC representative to go along. Sanh assigned Mai.

The next morning the party, less Le Quang Mai, left for Con Son. Mai's incoming Air America flight arrived too late to connect. On Con Son, no message had been received about Borman's visit. Thirty minutes on the beach brought belated transportation from Ve's base headquarters.

Colby's deputies, Jacobson and Mossler; two American physicians, Drs. Pharwell and Florio; and Dr. Ngoac, of the Ministry of Health also went along--at Colby's direction.

The party was greeted and then split into three groups. Mossler and Jacobson accompanied Major Tran to the tiger and cow cage areas. Drs. Pharwell, Florio and Ngoc went in company of the local Con Son doctor to inspect medical facilities. Berk, Walton, and Ve stayed behind discussing issues about what had become a titled entity--The Con Son Tiger Cage Investigation by the Moss Committee.

At about 11 a.m., Berkeley left with Major Chan to take photos of the tiger cage cell block. It was being razed and converted into a warehouse to store salt. (261)

It is noteworthy, the Prime Minister's Office did not authorize this flight, or the subsequent visit until 6:50 p.m. of the previous evening. The Prime Minister purposefully did not forewarn Ve. His reason, he later explained, was an unannounced arrival would ensure an inspection of conditions in their normal state.

Mossler, Ve and Jacobson discussed acquiring a fishing boat for Con Son. MOI had provided 2 million piasters towards the project which would ultimately improve the prisoners' protein diet. Jacobson wanted to keep up on developments concerning the boat. All agreed it was a priority item.

Candidly, Mossler and Jacobson considered the tiger cages as physically adequate cells for the confinement of recalcitrant prisoners, and cited the cow cage cells as far less desirable. They urged Ve not to modify the second tiger cage cell block until they discussed it with Colby. Ve said he would wait.

Colby's deputies specific comments were based on their observations and common sense. The cow cage cells lacked protection from the heat afforded by the thick, masonry construction of the tiger cages cells and the well ventilated second story; and the lesser number of larger cells provided less opportunity to segregate prisoners from one another.

LTC. Ve made a strong point. He urgently needed more segregation cells. Since he had been ordered to abandon the tiger cage area's 120 separate cells, he had to vacate other dormitory areas to use for disciplinary segregation. This meant increasing the prisoner count on his outside trusty program to 2000, which in turn had increased his security concerns. He emphasized he had 95 correctional personnel to control over 6000 prisoners. And none were armed.

Berkeley noted, and all agreed, by not using the tiger cage cells the GVN was publicly admitting those cells were inadequate, and this provided excellent proof for Hanoi to legitimize and validate their nefarious allegations. The position of Public Safety remained firm. The tiger cages were suitable facilities for disciplinary purposes, and this had been repeatedly brought to the attention of the DOC.

Unfortunately, a higher level of the GVN appeared to have been stampeded into a hasty retreat from the controversy. Worldwide attention and an avalanche of allegations based upon testimony from Communist prisoners, eighty percent women who had twice been moved for riotous conduct, was too much for them. Berk encouraged Jacobson to regain the initiative, forcefully and as soon as possible, with intercession at the Prime Minister's level.

The medical team made a list of medical supplies on hand for immediate and future needs. They ordered delivery to Public Health, and eventual shipment to Con Son. (169-261)

Mirola and Gi made a scheduled visit to the National Women's Correctional Center at Thu Duc on August 24. When they arrived, a disturbance was in progress. Approximately 900 Communist prisoners had attacked workers, trustys, and common criminals assigned to the general population. They barricaded themselves in the prison proper, threatening continued violence. Their weapons were clubs, bricks, and available debris. The Major saw one wounded male prison official with a head wound and blood all over his shirt, and several females attempting to stem the flow of their own blood. (172)

Deputy Director Hau was in the Commandant's office. The Communist prisoners chanted at deafening levels, causing a platoon of National Police Field Force (NPFF) personnel to shoot rifles in the air to quell the noise. This only encouraged the prisoners to continue.

As Commander Hau recounted the situation: At about 9 a.m., female prisoners housed in the isolation block had forced their way into the main prison compound to join other Communist prisoners. National Police were securing the outer exits of the institution, but had not yet entered the main compound. On hand tear gas grenades were out of date and corroded by the weather, and could not be used. (Two excellent reasons why non-toxic lime is used in this part of the world in place of U.S. type tear gas. Aside from the extra cost involved in procuring and shipping it, there is even greater cost in maintaining proper temperatures to store it in tropical climates such as Vietnam.)

Berkeley arrived at 11:45 a.m., immediately arranging with the National Police to deliver 200 tear gas grenades in case they were needed. Berkeley, McPhie, Commander Hau and the Province Chief met in the Commandant's office. Ten female trusty prisoners and two male jailers had been injured, but the extent of all injuries was not yet known.

The National Police were in control of the exterior of the prison. Prisoners were loose in the central courtyard. Apparently, the interior doors to many of the prison dormitories had been shattered. A Ministry of Justice official arrived and conducted discussions with the communist, female, ring leader. The official said the forty-seven Viet Cong females wanted to be housed together as they were before the riot, instead of being split into three groups.

The VC women involved in this disturbance were a part of the same group creating the August, 1969 disturbance at Thu Duc, and the scheduled riot at Chi Hoa in November, 1969. One hundred eight women were returned to the mainland by ship on 4 August 1970. Forty-seven went to Thu Duc. There were, on that day, 1200 prisoners at Thu Duc--900 were Communist criminals.

At 1:30 p.m. Colonel Sanh arrived. It was learned the riot began on the 21st, when 43 women burst out of their isolation building's small recreation yard to join other prisoners. They broke down a wooden door to effect this. The guards made a tactical error in allowing all 43 to congregate in the recreation yard at the same time. Four of the 43 were from Con Son. Carbines were fired into the air and it quieted the situation somewhat. However, skirmishes continued. (176)

The Director decided to humor the VC ring leaders by allowing them to see the twenty-eight other women to prove they were unharmed. Colonel Sanh and the province chief agreed the prison commandant should proceed cautiously, use loud speaker music to overplay the chanting, and not feed the unruly elements until they decided to quiet down and return to their housing areas. By early next morning the situation was under control, all prisoners were eating breakfast, and the institution was back to a normal routine. (176)

Soon after, OPS was notified Vice-President Agnew might visit Vietnam. Berkeley decided a memorandum to was in order.

Berkeley said one of the most disgraceful news items to come out of the war was the infamous tiger cage incident created by the congressional group . . . visiting Con Son on 2 July 1970. He went on to suggest the Vice-President visit with international media along to see conditions first hand. This was a perfect example of the power of the press to destroy on the basis of irresponsible allegations.

Berkeley's restraint was laudable, but the letter never cleared Colby's desk. It, too, was relegated to his waste can. This time without comment. (173-261)

Frank Borman issued a press release. He found conditions at Con Son to be reasonable, and the furor over the tiger cages there dramatically overplayed. (180)

On September 2, a new, one hundred page report titled PRISONS IN SOUTH VIETNAM was distributed by the Student Anti-Oppression Committee, one of several organizations operating under the umbrella of the Saigon Student Union (SSU). The report had no publication date, but was widely distributed to press agencies. (263)

The booklet contained a number of articles on the arrest, interrogation, and imprisonment of students. It was written by thirty students who professed to have been released from various prisons, most in early 1970.

Included in the compilation was the complete text of articles written by Luce, and the Congressional Reports of Congressmen Hawkins and Anderson. A student representative delivered a copy to the American Embassy requesting it be given to the President. The Embassy reported the document was sent to the Secretary of State, and subsequently shared with the White House.

Colonel Borman appeared before a joint session of Congress in late September. Excerpts from his brief speech address his Con Son visit.

"I've recently returned from a 25 day trip around the globe," Borman began, "in furtherance of the cause of our prisoners of war, and I must tell you that I can only report American anguish and human tragedy."

"Although it had no direct relationship to our Prisoners of War, due to the huge amount of publicity that was accorded to the Con Son conditions I thought it imperative that I stopped there and report back to the President on the conditions that I found. I was very disturbed by some of the reaction in this Country which essentially said how can we be concerned about our prisoners when we are treating, or the South Vietnamese are treating, the prisoners of war from the other side so badly?

"I can tell you that there were only 29 POWS in the Con Son Prison. They had been convicted of murder or other felonies upon other prisoners while in POW camps. They had then been transferred as criminals to Con Son, where they were receiving the privileges of the Geneva Convention. None of these 29 men were in the so-called tiger cages. Though I visited the tiger cages at the time, they were not occupied. In all candor, I found a much less disturbed situation than I had been lead to believe by the publicity that was accorded them by the media throughout the world.

"I found for instance, that the tiger cages were not pits, but, part of a two-story building that instead of a ceiling, had bars. It is true that the cells were small, as I said, there were no people in them at the time. I could see overcrowding and long incarceration in these cells would be very undesirable.

"Nevertheless, I submit to you that this was a very much misrepresented case in the Press of the Free World. I can also tell you that one of the blocks has now been destroyed and the other is unoccupied.

"I request that all of you in someway [sic], everyday [sic], remember the people, the U.S. citizens, who are prisoners, and I strongly beg you not to forsake your countrymen who have given so much." (191)

Actually, it didn't take much ink to print the selected comments the press dutifully reported. One column, one inch. Borman, after all, was of some national credibility. Apparently, he just wasn't credible enough.

** Ve writes in his draft of Ve & Bordenkircher's, their, Con Son history, "Con Son Archipeligo": "On the Hon-Cau island, the French authority had built a lepers camp and had confined there a number of lepers. Afterward, the prisoners who committed contagious diseases were transferred there. They were rather free to circulate the island and were called upon by a physician once a week. Today the Tuberculosis Section was transferred to the municipal area, at the Salt Field, in order to enable more regular care.

THIRTEEN

Going home

I returned to Vietnam ahead of schedule, and by the second week of September, overworked and stressed out, we were beginning to get on each others nerves. Walton summoned Berkeley to castigate him over failure to meet deadlines. This was the first time any of us had seen Berkeley visibly upset. And it was the one and only time I observed. Loosing one's cool just wasn't in Berkeley's bible. (188,261)

By way of explanation, not excuse, Berkeley barked that some of the reasons deadlines were not met was because his time was being expended on congressional inquiries, briefings of VIP's, flight planning, congressional pressure, riots in prisons, logistic support problems at Con Son, and a continual flow of rumors and press stories about atrocities that had not occurred, but which had to be translated, responded to and filed, and unrealistic deadlines imposed by MACV without regard to the complexities of research and staff coordination among disparate civilian offices--none of whom marched to the beat of General Abrahm's drum.

Berkeley wasn't finished yet. He took another breath to add it was difficult, indeed, to cope with the unrealistic number of priorities assigned to him over the past three months--most of which were conveyed by word of mouth within Public Safety.

Additionally, he was constantly called on matters deemed urgent and that he, Berkeley, had promptly placed Walton's requests on the top of the list, and accomplished them as quickly as he could, but, however, there had been so many top priorities it was inevitable some of the original, urgent problems would fall into second, third, seventh, or thirteenth place, as the case may be.

With some rare exceptions, Berkeley raged (with barely a blink in between) he and his staff had worked every day and night since June without a day off, and everything that had happened since then had been one constant and continuing crisis.

Everything Berkeley said was true, and Walton knew it

was true; as did we all. Walton had suffered the same problems during the same time frame, but to hear Berkeley fire back to him what he already knew, only incited him. Walton was on the verge of an assault when McCann, with his always good judgment, left the sidelines to intervene.

Mike McCann was notable for the wisdom he consistently displayed, but in this instance he excelled. Berkeley and Walton were ready to snap. They each needed someone to kick, and each was available to the other. It was a perfectly understandable explosion.

McCann had been busy, too. While Walton focused on the tiger cage debacle, he took over all other duties. But he took the time to soothe the situation between the two men, and after wounds were licked and bruised feelings massaged, everyone got back to work. However, relations between the two men were never again quite the same.

It was a hostile and traumatic exchange. And one none of us were soon to forget. It brought, to me at least, the reality we were living. This situation wasn't going to get better no matter what we did, nor was it ever going to be truly over. Perhaps it's not possible to understand the depth of such a frustration unless one has experienced it.

The injustice to everything we believed in and had been working for, wasn't the worst part. The worst part was being abandoned by those who led us. Being expendable is one thing, bleeding to death in sight of a lazy doctor is another. Either way, the mark is indelible. Dead is dead.

One morning in September, Berk had occasion to talk at length with Margaret Elwood, a U.S. psychologist, working with the Department of Public Health. Public Health had a ward at Cho Quon Hospital for treatment of prisoners from the Saigon area. (193)

Elwood said Luce had a large, official looking book of photographs of conditions at the mental and prison wards at Cho Quon. In her opinion the photographs were gruesome and the Tiger Cage story paled in contrast.

Miss Elwood, who had attended many meetings at the University where Luce was a speaker, depicted his statements as anti-United States. She was so concerned she had communicated her sentiments to the Embassy.

According to her, Luce was a close friend of a Mr. Miller of the Vietnam Christian Service Committee (CSC) who had endorsed the idea of Luce visiting Cho Quon and taking pictures. Elwood knew the CSC instructed its members not to assist Americans, at any time, with medical care, even in emergencies, but they did and would provide medical care to known members of the Viet Cong. The CSC, she said, was under investigation because of a complaint by a U. S. minister who had visited in 1969.

Berkeley immediately told McCann and Walton of the critique. I picked Berk up and we drove to Cho Quon where we were joined by Inspectors Mai and Quang.

The four of us toured the psychiatric ward and found a very sad and deplorable situation. However, no corrections prisoners were housed there. We next went to the regular prison ward where there were 22 prisoners from Chi Hoa and Tan Hiep. Our short tour was enough for Mai. Quang notified Sanh to remove the prisoners--immediately.

Shortly, Quang returned saying ambulances were en-route to take prisoners back to the dispensary units of those institutions. In view of Elwood's information, we agreed not to take any prisoners, for any reason, to Cho Quon.

By the lunch hour, all prisoners had been removed. Quang and Mai returned to the Directorate, while Berk and I opted to go to the Frenchman's in Thu Duc. I called Secor and asked him to meet us at the restaurant.

During lunch, I cleansed my soul of the guilt I felt over being in D. C. while my friends and colleagues were going through the hell and heartache of a congressional inquiry. I reminded them Ve had closed the tiger cages before I left for Washington. He had opened up a new segregation unit, freeing the tiger cage cells for use as housing for jailers and their families. Gi and I saw it happen.

I'd helped move staff families into the building, and on a return visit some weeks later observed pots of geraniums decorating the covered porch area. The staff families had definitely made the place their home. I just couldn't understand what had happened.

Secor filled me in. When the riot at Chi Hoa was broken up and those three hundred women were transported to Con Son, Ve panicked. He could have put the women all together in one housing unit, but he was afraid they'd continue to rebel and get support from other communists on the island. So, Secor continued, Ve kicked the jailers out, and put the women in the tiger cages.

McPhie helped Ve transport the women from the airstrip, Secor explained, and McPhie thought the cells were okay, cool, well ventilated, and all. He didn't know anything about tiger cages. He sure didn't know they were staff housing.

At the time, I had no reason to question Secor's veracity, and it was true--McPhie was new to Con Son and a new hire. We discussed the past three and a half months in detail before I addressed my immediate concern. How were we faring with our GVN counterparts at the Directorate? Again, Secor had an answer.

"Don, relationships are *very* strained." I was aware everybody--U.S. and GVN--had busted their butts putting out fires created by the formal inquiry and the news media, not to mention the panic Washington laid on the Embassy and MACV. Concurrently, the Vietnamese news corps, Ministry of Interior, Ministry of Justice, and the Prime Minister's office were making Colonel Sanh's life miserable. Everyone was still at full stress level.

Secor believed Colonel Sanh, LTC. Ve, and their staffs blamed the Americans for all of the pressure placed on them. We were Americans, and therefore, responsible.

But he was pleased to say the construction, renovation, and rejuvenation projects were either on schedule or ahead of it. Various rehabilitation programs were still expanding. The only real problem, he emphasized, was the same damn 343 female prisoners who had everyone on edge.

Severson went on home leave as soon as I returned, and McPhie took charge of Detention. I strongly urged Berkeley to take a couple of weeks off -- the time was right. His confrontation with Walton was the result of overwork and stress more than anything else, he admitted, and I was probably correct. A trip might be just the thing.

Before leaving the Frenchman's, Berkeley told me to assume his duties. Secor took my place with the DOC.

After a week with his family, Berk returned refreshed and ready to plunge in again. That same afternoon, McCann, Berkeley, McPhie, and Major Mirola joined Walton and me to work out Con Son's immediate action program.

The consensus was that there were sufficient isolation (disciplinary) cells existing at Con Son. This excluded the tiger cage cells. However, a program had to be designed to improve the behavior of the disciplinary and recalcitrant prisoners. We could use an existing camp, but the entire group had to be isolated from other prisoners. Colby called it a reformation unit. A layman would call it a rehabilitation program, and I would call it Administrative Segregation. We used Colby's language, of course. Due process had to be a part of any procedure and protocol recommended, and it had to be done soon. (195)

The meeting concluded with Walton's directive: 1. Construction of new prison sections would be expedited; and; 2. Ve would be urged to establish a reformation unit using one of the existing camps, in its entirety. We would also assist him in the design and development of a humane program; 3. I would take Mirola with me to Con Son for as long as it took to thoroughly survey and update our knowledge of prison operations there, and; 4. Scott Napier, Marine Police Advisor, would survey the existing fishing industry and examine its maximum potential. Construction of isolation cells and acquisition of a new fishing boat would wait for our full reports and recommendations.

Twenty days later, the three of us returned to Saigon. Our reports were brief. The most urgent priority was a fishing vessel of sufficient size to enable off shore fishing. The concurrent priority was the program I devised for reformation units at all national prisons.

The proposal was inclusive. The establishment of an inter-institution disciplinary court which authorized the court officer to provide sentences to incorrigible prisoners. The sentences ranged from warning and reprimand to sentencing in the reformation unit of one day to, not more than, thirty days. All such action required thorough documentation by using information from staff disciplinary reports and court dispositions.

The minimum acceptable requirements I outlined for the physical plant, included a table of organization for staffing; prisoner treatment and control; a system of identification; and an orientation program. Plans for food service, definitive programs for health, sanitation, education, vocational training, recreation, religious worship, work programs, inmate accounts, key and tool control, visiting, mail, proper search, and contraband control were also delineated.

Appended was a comprehensive emergency plan to include riot control and hostage taking. And there was a complete standard operating procedure manual. These procedures were inclusive of processing, security and control, required physical examination before unit confinement, assignment to quarters, orientation, continuance counseling, and a proposed inmate daily schedule from 6:30 a.m. to 9 p.m. -- lights out.

By the end of October, the reformation unit proposal was adopted in toto by the Prime Minister and given the highest priority for implementation. John Myers, our latest addition to the advisory staff, was assigned to Con Son full time to assist Ve with the project. (195)

On November 2, I gave a think piece to Berkeley titled PRISONERS IN TURMOIL — *a Personal Viewpoint.* After reading the paper, Berkeley sent it to the American Embassy, Ambassador Colby, Frank Walton, OPS Washington, and the Department of State. He liked it. (204)

It wasn't the first time I had presented such comment, nor would it be the last. Throughout history, and into what was then my future, prisons have suffered from lack of funds and training, arcane mind sets and mechanisms, skewed public perceptions, and legislation totally irrelevant to the problem. And, in one form or another, the disadvantages of being incarcerated have also remained the same. My assessment is as real today, and as valid, as it was then.

The litanies are familiar. Free world prison administrators are bewildered . . . citizens and government representatives are crying inhumane treatment . . . politically motivated leftist radicals point their fingers . . . to proclaim, those prisoners are not criminals -- they are political offenders . . . the convict hears the rhetoric and sees those actions as the perfect justification to commence riot and chaos. The prison guard, as fearful as the convict, implements force. Chaos begets chaos.

In response, government appoints citizens and officials to Blue Ribbon teams to investigate. Reports continue to indicate the causes of the chaos to be:

a. Brutality during detention, and interrogation by police.

b. Prolonged detention.

c. Lack of proper medical care, inadequate rations, and inactivity during detention.

d. Overcrowded conditions.

e. Malady of the con boss system.

f. Brutality by convict trustees upon other inmates.

g. Non-existent or ineffective assistance to inmates families during incarceration.

h. Ineffective system of parole.

i. Halfway, work furlough, and work release programs non-existent or ineffective.

j. State or government inspection of facilities lacking

or non-existent.

  k. Follow up and/or interview with discharged convicts lacking or non-existent.

  l. Uneducated, untrained, uninformed and low-paid correctional workers.

Mao Tse Tung decreed murder, mayhem, kidnap, subversion and terrorism not to be criminal acts when performed as a method to overthrow the established government of a capitalist and/or imperialistic republic. The literary work of Mao is the policy from which Che Guevara, Abby Hoffman, Jerry Rubin, and in Vietnam, Phan Van Dong, and Madam Nguyen Thi Binh formulated the rationalization, rhetoric, and action requirements for implementation by the radical left.

Around the world, terrorism fosters stringent anti-crime, no-bail, and war condition prerogatives invoked on the premise of preventing crime and protecting life and property. These laws and their methods of enforcement bring about a significant increase in prison/jail populations. This peculiar category of civil offender became commonly known as a political prisoner by a news media seeking sensationalism; by the radical left seeking a cause; and by the necessity of a sound byte. The term has come to be a catchall for any dissident actions or views.

As a practical matter of prison classification, the term political prisoner should be defined as someone on either side of an issue, who philosophically disagrees with anyone on the opposite side of that issue, and who is unfortunate enough to be on the side not in control of the government at that time.

In most cases, the degree of disagreement is at issue as well. Any disagreement tantamount to insurrection, or fomenting of such, to impair the ability of a duly elected government to govern would, in most cultures, constitute a civilian crime.

The status of the individual political prisoner changes to a criminal classification when acts are validated by behavior in violation of the civil criminal code -- such as murder, rape, treason, robbery, burglary, mayhem, and other such behavior which would land any citizen in prison, once convicted.

Insurrection and sedition are elements of treason. Therefore, it could be said, political prisoners are those people whose behavior has been just shy of treason. The person so incarcerated as a political prisoner may yet be waiting final investigation, indictment, and conviction for the crime of treason.

The real problem is the definition of treason, and the interpretation of a particular country's law as concerns treason -- what specific acts constitute the crime of treason?

In August, 1970, 3,000 riotous inmates at a California prison demanded the release of all political prisoners. The Warden said, "What the hell is a political prisoner? "

Our order of battle in Vietnam was to assist the GVN corrections and National Police jail system during the war. Those systems were tasked to provide incarceration of a Viet Cong shadow government (infrastructure) who had committed criminal acts designed to assist enemy fighting forces, and aid in the fall of an elected government.

The GVN confined about 23,000 of those communist criminals, but some members of the U.S. and GVN Congresses referred to them as political prisoners, as does the International Committee of the Red Cross, without really knowing what constitutes the category in prison vernacular. Nor did the Geneva Convention define category criteria.

Without a lawful definition — where does one segregate the political prisoner? Prisons, jails, mental hospitals, islands, hotels, a villa in St. Tropez? At what point does the benign political prisoner become a destroyer of governmental power? Can a political prisoner be benign?

History and current events demanded a swift and specific course of action by the GVN DOC and the National Police Detention Bureau to deal effectively with the communist criminal. And they did that. Then the problem became how to make his life more bearable during incarceration, and promote his reintegration into society.

That job required our specific action recommendations to the GVN and meticulous follow-up by the U.S. advisory counterparts. Should any one action appear doomed at GVN operations level, it had to be pursued at the highest levels of government. To do less is not an option. (204)

To this, I attached 38 separate and specific recommendations I believed should be followed in our efforts to assist the DOC and NPD facilities.

Today, I could employ the same overview, with very little change, and I would be correct in theory with segments of today's prison environment. The difference is merely one of degree on both sides of the issue. We've come a hell of a long way in my 38 year tenure in corrections and law enforcement. We've evolved into a criminal justice system; educated and trained prisoners and even most employees; instituted programs for educational and vocational training; and changed with the times, insofar as our funding has allowed us to do so.

But the world has changed, too. And the type, quality, and level of sophistication of convicts with it. We educate convicts through college but can't find funds for on-going training/education of correctional workers. Common sense has been replaced by a social work philosophy, and master's degrees in just about anything.

Some examples of the irrationality of our times: It's a little hard to come up with a vocational training program which can provide the income selling angel dust can provide, or convince a prisoner to buy into learning to make license plates or furniture as a viable alternative to selling crack.

Poorly paid correctional workers and the public are expected to applaud the use of tax dollars for reconstructive surgery, top medical specialists, college degrees, and the services of a dietitian for convict meals—all in the name of self-esteem and societal acceptance—when they can't even dream of meeting those needs for their own families.

But there are certainly basics to humane treatment. Every prisoner must be safe from other prisoners, be fed, be clothed, be warm in winter, and cooled should the heat of summer become oppressive and life threatening, be allowed and encouraged to worship, and be provided activities and work to keep busy the mind, body and spirit. In short, the prisoner should be treated as a human being, and be expected to behave like one.

If there is a problem, in managing today's prison systems in our own country, it is in the last expectation cited above. The permissive attitudes encompassed by the treatment programs of the past twenty to twenty-five years do not expect anything from the convict.

The attitude -- abdicating responsibility for our own actions, and not holding others responsible for that which they choose to do -- has spread to our larger society. This philosophy holds we, society, are the responsible parties, en toto, and therefore the individual is not to blame. Society, environment, circumstance created the problem, and therefore, should fix it--with or without commitment from the individual.

An outgrowth of this victim philosophy is that the concept of security has become secondary to all treatment considerations. Truly a concept of well meaning dreamers. In the short term one might meet some expectations—in the long term, never. Like it or not, real change is internal.

My experience and conviction is that security can exist without treatment programs, but it's an impossibility for treatment programs to be effective without security. In short, excellent security begets excellent treatment.

When people live in fear, in prison or out, survival is the priority. In order to direct energies toward behavioral change, i.e. treatment, prisoners must be able to traverse the confines of their world in safety. Treatment programs can only flourish in a secure surrounding. In truth, all things flourish in secure surroundings.

The prisoner is as responsible for his incarceration, as we on the outside are responsible for our lot in life, and like us, should be held responsible for his actions. If he or she was your blood you would, and should, expect no less in terms of humane treatment.

Beyond that, I can only say firm, fair, and consistent administration and management are the foremost tools in dealing with prisoners. Prisons aren't perfect, and never will be. Nor are the convicts. Nor are managers and administrators of prisons. Yet there are many in each category dedicated to improving the prison environment for prisoners and staff alike.

A prison isn't a place to hang out, to have fun, or to flex muscles, under the shadow of a white hat. Confinement wasn't intended, nor should it be, a place to which you would like to return. And while most prisons are historically underfunded for necessities, it has also been shown money isn't the answer to every problem. Improvement takes many forms.

Three days after I submitted my composition, the MACV Surgeon General, accompanied by physicians from the Ministry of Public Health, was at Con Son to examine 110 prisoners.

Of the 110, 109 complained of some form of paralysis of the lower extremities. There were no signs of malnutrition, no skin problems, no major health problems with the prisoners--only the paralysis. Another team would study the paralysis problem. For the MACV Surgeon General to have made this visit, he had to have been activated by General

Abrahms. Things were again looking up.

A few weeks later, another medical team returned with neurologists. They examined the 109 prisoners alleging paralysis. Ve and his staff insisted the prisoners could walk and their complaints were for use as propaganda only.

The official report of the neurologist, and accompanying physicians, was clear--there was no medical or physical reason the inmates could not walk. Their opinion—the prisoners were feigning illness. The GVN should eliminate the remote possibility of hysteria as causing the paralysis by sending the prisoners to the mainland where facilities and psychiatrists were available to investigate hysteria.

The media continued to print articles of torture, brutality, and inhumane prison conditions. By the end of September, it appeared the tirade was slowing.

In the October issue of the PROGRESSIVE was an article by Thomas R. Harkin, VIETNAM WHITEWASH--*The Congressional Jury That Convicted Itself.* The article reviewed the CONDEL's Con Son visit. However, it contained a new and unusual twist--one designed to revalue the old hash of Con Son and concoct a timely hero. (200)

Harkin turned his attack toward members of the House of Representatives. In his seven page story, Harkin had not a kind word for anyone, except Representatives Hawkins and Anderson. He referred to them as true statesmen.

Viciously attacking his one time political mentor, colleague, close friend, and recent employer, Representative Neil Smith of Iowa, Harkin said he gave his surreptitious tape recording made during the Con Son visitation, as well as, his photographs, to Smith.

Harkin didn't want Smith to turn the photographs over to the committee. When Smith asked what he intended to do with the pictures and tape recording, Harkin said he wanted them before the public, so pressure might be brought to bear on the government to change conditions.

Harkin neglected to mention truthfulness helps. To my mind a free public becomes informed by presentation of facts, not perspectives. Debate on perspectives is open to a public informed enough to thoughtfully choose a perspective. Perhaps I misunderstand the concept. Perhaps this does not apply to issues decided by emotion where values, experience, education, reputation, and a history of credibility are of little consequence.

Blasting Smith, Harkin outlined his worry over the

materials; how he couldn't sleep and how he couldn't forgive himself if something happened to the pictures; and how his meaning escaped Smith's understanding.

According to Harkin, the now immoral Congressman laid open the suitcase, taking out the three canisters of film and the box containing the tape. Harkin reached over, grabbed the film and tape, and kept them. His dramatic conclusion alleges Smith to have angrily thrown the suitcase into the car, berating Harkin all the while. (200)

Tom Harkin, in his rote article, did not, at any time, mention LIFE paid him $10,000 for photos of Con Son, and a copy of his surreptitiously made tape recording. Nor did he note the deal was made before he landed in Vietnam.

Harkin's revelations prompted journalists to renewed interrogation of CONDEL members. Another media frenzy ensued and Harkin was again a fair-haired boy. At that time, few people knew Harkin was setting the stage to propel himself into Congress. He had learned his political lessons well, and in 1974, in Iowa, defeated Rep. William Scherle in a race for the U.S. House of Representatives.

In every exposé there is the possibility of repercussions. Witness the case of Don Luce. The Director of the Vietnamese Press Center, Nguyen Ngop Huyen, admits on November 16, 1970, Luce's press credentials won't be renewed, and the reason is the tiger cage story. The GVN pro-government Saigon Post, an English language newspaper, cheered the decision, "The mills of the Gods have finally caught up with Don Luce."

This remark was inadvertently ? omitted from stateside published reports—rather the tone painted Luce as a victim of harsh and unwarranted action.

Representative Hawkins entered into record before the House that Luce lost press privileges, and wants Congressional assistance to get back his credentials. Congress denies Luce, and he isn't allowed to return to Vietnam again until after the U.S. withdrawal.

Luce revealed his version of why he was kicked out of Vietnam in an interview with Shirley, my wife, "It was a combination of the exposé on the Tiger Cages. . . the Saigon government wanted to do all sorts of things to me. Some of them were ridiculous, like the World Council of Churches had brought in dried milk and those things like that. At the time, they decided that I owed back taxes, import taxes, on all the relief goods that the World Council had brought in...

. so I said, 'Well, send me to jail.'"

Luce continued, ". . . that attitude wasn't in the best interests of the Embassy so Buzz Johnson told me he cleared my name of the back taxes on dried milk, and cooking oil, and whatever else." (261)

Meanwhile, in Geneva the peace talks continued and the Viet Cong Delegation demanded a new series of investigations. They said comrades reported numerous caves and dungeons housing prisoners were spread throughout the island of Con Son. The White House, Congress, and the Embassy inquired about the alleged caves.

As a precautionary measure, O. Gordon Young was assigned to assist Myers. Gordon was born in Yunnan, China, in 1927, the son of a missionary; and spent thirty years in Southeast Asia, notably in Burma, Thailand, and India. He was assigned to our advisory team and rumor had it he was CIA. He was an educated naturalist-hunter-ethnologist -- a graduate agriculturist of California State Polytechnic College. And he had the same name as my father-in-law. Which is irrelevant, but an affable aside. I liked my father-in-law, and I liked Gordon.

I introduced Gordon to Ve and Myers, citing his credentials and confirming his special assignment to C&D branch as an agriculturist. My hope was Gordon could, after a survey of the island, assist in the development of a modern agricultural program to improve yields at Con Son.

Gordon could assist Napier and Myers with the fishing vessel, the fishing program, and the turtle ponds. There was no reason for Young to visit the prisons as they were under the advisory purview of Myers.

I told no one the real reason behind Young's assignment. He was to go over every inch of Con Son to verify the existence or non-existence of caves, pits, dungeons, tunnels, or any other clandestine lockups of prisoners which might be unknown to us. If he found none, as I suspected, his reports would assist our team in Paris. If it was true, well, we were in deep you know what. (261)

When I returned to Saigon, I was dispatched to the Saigon Zoo. Fresh from Paris was another VC allegation--thousands of political prisoners being held in the Saigon Zoo. I spent a full day combing every inch of zoo property, camera in hand, concluding the zoo was, indeed, a zoo.

Hundreds of Vietnamese families were visiting, but the only prisoners I saw were exotic animals. In spite of my findings, the media continued to print speculations initiated by the VC delegation charging the zoo was a detention camp for political prisoners. Too bad none saw fit to verify the claim by sending a correspondent there. (211)

On December 1, Gordon returned to Saigon. In summary, his report was an intensive natural science survey of the island. He made numerous recommendations to upgrade existing agricultural programs, as well as, suggested new and innovative approaches to increase production of animals and yields of vegetables.

He had traveled, by foot, every inch of terrain on Con Son and its adjoining smaller islands. There were no covert lockups found anywhere. None. Nada. Zip.

Young also made a progress report on the fishing industry. The prisoners would have a supply of fresh fish. The U.S. government supplied a LCM-8 fishing vessel in November of 1970. US$1,695* was set aside to buy spare parts; and US$20,034* to purchase fishing equipment--nets, hooks, and the like. Petroleum was extremely scarce on the island, so US$21,525* was allocated to buy gas to run the boat for one year. *(In 1970 dollars)

Napier was dispatched to train inmate boat crews, advise on advanced fishing techniques, and assist Myers in setting up a system to get fresh fish to the prisoners' mess. All of Young's data found its way to Colby's desk, and ultimately to Mr. Nooter who presented it at congressional inquiry. (207)

Soon after, the Prime Minister announced the formal investigation into allegations by the Vietnamese press against Con Son, Commandant Ve, and Colonel Sanh, had been concluded. All charges against Colonel Sanh were dismissed as not supportable. However, Ve was refused public exoneration. Reasons for that maneuver would not be released by the Prime Minister's office.

Ve became depressed. His deep dissatisfaction stemmed from the lack of support he received from the GVN and his superiors during the investigation. He felt his family, future, and military career had been maligned, and no one was helping to clear him.

Sanh was distressed when he told me the U.S. and GVN press reports concerning Con Son had demoralized DOC employees to the point thirty-one personnel resigned, twenty-eight requested transfer to other ministries, and fifteen requested retirement. There were three hundred forty-eight personnel positions vacant and no applications had been received for several months.

One thousand one hundred sixty-two inmates housed in Camp 2 were shackled. Prisoners and staff each presented different views, causes, reasons for utilization of the shackles. Documented facts did not exist concerning the prisoners' condition, or the reason for the shackling. Myers was told by Major Trang, Deputy Commandant, "Too damn busy with American VIPS and inmate disturbances and do not have time to do documentation."

And to keep things from getting dull, the 29 POW's confined in Camp 5 went on a hunger strike. In a separate section of Camp 5, 184 women had been restricted to quarters for demonstrating and refusal to lockup after their exercise period. Because they refused to work, 360 inmates were restricted to their cells in Section 2-Camp 6.

The picture was bleak and personally disheartening. I discussed the deteriorating circumstances with Ve and Myers. Ve put the shackles on the hard-core prisoners because they intimidated other prisoners in the compound. Further, they refused to work, chanted and disobeyed regulations. He simply took the trouble makers out to Camp 5, segregated, and shackled them.

New isolation cells were under construction, and when complete, Ve would establish a classification team to interview each inmate at Camp 5, releasing those who wanted to work. Those inmates who still refused to work, and/or were leaders who pressured weaker inmates, would be transferred to the reformation unit. (215)

During the last week of December, 1970, the Ministry of Labor, and Ministry of Public Health, in company of their U.S. advisors, traveled to Con Son to develop education, vocational training, industry, and medical programs for the inmates. We would have to run very fast to regain any semblance of the order, trust, and momentum we had enjoyed a year earlier. All in all, 1970 was one hell of a year in the annals of South Vietnamese prisons.

Robert Bernstein, MD, Brigadier General, Command Surgeon, reported in January, 1971, about his assignment of three physicians to examine one hundred sixteen male prisoners at Con Son. LTC. Robert Young, Majors Leon Menzer, and Richard Pulson, were neurologists.

These same 116 prisoners had been previously examined and their complaints of paralysis had been sensationalized from statements made by Representatives of the Provincial

Revolutionary Government of South Vietnam (Viet Cong) via news reports written by Luce. (255)

The inmates complained of a loss of sensation in both legs. The alleged average duration of their paralysis was two years. All prisoners attributed their condition to the combination of being shackled, beaten, and an inadequate diet of rice and spoiled or salty fish. None complained of loss of bowel or bladder control.

The neurologists' physical examination revealed no evidence of malnutrition. All had normal musculature without atrophy or fasciculation. The skin, mucous membranes and hair distribution were all normal, as were pulses in the legs. All patients had normal ankle and knee deep tendon reflexes with no pathologic reflexes.

The prisoner patients exhibited diagnostic findings of malingering or hysteria. For example, when a patient was asked to flex the knee or ankle, the limb would not move, but the muscles used to extend the knee or ankle were held to contract. Patients who complained of total paralysis were observed to move their legs when asked to roll over, slide back on the examination table or remove their clothing.

The report concluded there was no objective evidence of organic and neurologic disease. It appeared the complaints did, indeed, represent either malingering or hysteria. Differentiation between the two would require extensive evaluation of each patient by a Vietnamese speaking Psychiatrist. There was no known psychiatric medical treatment for hysteria. There was no indication further studies, or medical evaluation, was needed.

Walton dispatched a copy to Sanh, telling him there was no basis for further study. Additional treatment should be handled through normal Vietnamese medical channels.

Shortly, David V. Brown, MD, was assigned to the Correction/Detention Division, and the MOI attached Pham Tan Touc, a Vietnamese physician to the DOC. Walton recommended Brown work in counterpart with Touc in developing programs for improvement of prisoner diet, sanitation, training medical personnel, and implementing medical programs at all national and provincial prisons.

When the media received copies of the medical report on the 116 paralyzed prisoners, there was minor reporting. However, in response to the scant press given the medical examinations, Luce began pumping letters to the media signed by prisoners and family members portraying the examinations as contrived. At the exact same time, copies of the same letters were sent by the Provincial Revolutionary Government (PRG) membership to the American delegation in Paris. (255,271)

On January 14, 1971, Colonel Sanh asked to meet with me. My manual of Correctional Standards for the Directorate was approved by the MOI. Additionally, a one thousand bed National Juvenile Reformatory at Dalat had been completed, and staff assigned. He invited me to the opening ceremonies scheduled for February 2nd. By the day of dedication all juveniles held at various DOC facilities would be transferred to the Dalat Center. It would be administered by the Ministry of Justice.

He appeared pleased, and a feeble smile lit up his eyes a bit. When he handed me a copy of the Prime Minister's Directive, Communication 38-97Th/Bdpt/ubp, which established for the first time in South Vietnam, a system of conditional parole for prisoners, he stood tall, like a rooster should. The Prime Minister expected provincial and Judicial authorities to release suspects or prisoners who met criteria for conditional parole. Immediate release of selected, low-level Communist offenders who were found non-threatening to national security was a priority. (222)

When the province chief, or mayor, approved the prisoner was to be released immediately and the Ministry of Justice, and MOI were to be advised. Additionally, any sentenced offender who demonstrated good behavior and attitude would also be released. It was a huge step forward.

Appended were definitive procedures for the operational mechanics of the program. Colby responded by telling advisors to work with the DOC on making a computerized reporting system a reality. (222)(224)

Meanwhile, Engle recapped his meeting with Congressman Montgomery in Washington. Montgomery wanted to be remembered to us. He said he was very much impressed with the OPS program and its advisors, and he apologized for the conduct of two committee members and their aide. Nice, but it didn't change a dime.

In furtherance of the extreme heat being generated in Paris by the PRG concerning prisoners, Luce continued to write about mistreated prisoners, and Congress continued to pressure the White House.

Despite our objections, work was now under way to destroy the tiger cage buildings. Construction of three blocks of isolation cells to replace them had begun. We had voiced our objections--strongly, but were overruled. These new cells were about the same as the former cells, but were designed to hold two prisoners each, as compared to the three to five inmates once held in the French built cells.

With the total blessing of the U.S. Congress, US$ 400,000 built this new disciplinary section. In an attempt to quell the hue and cry emanating from the congressional hearings, the SV government had closed the tiger cages. One cell block was demolished, and the other used for housing the families of prison guards. (231)

When the media learned of the money expended to replace the old tiger cages, the frenzy began anew. In order to expedite the construction of these new cell blocks, the contractors arranged for paid, inmate laborers.

And inmates were, indeed, paid for their labor. However, the media, notably Luce, reported the prisoners were forced to build the 288 isolation cells. These news reports were replete with convicts written accounts of beatings and brutalization during their forced labor on this project. (226)

Construction of the isolation cells moved slowly. One hundred twenty laborers refused to work and other inmate laborers from other camps volunteered to take their place. The day before, a Camp 6 laborer had passed under a scaffold and a dribble of cement landed on his head. The laborer threw a can of water in the contractor's face while ranting and raving. The Camp 6 prisoners decided they would no longer work. (231)

In early March, Manopoli appeared for a short visit and long discussions. On March 14, Berkeley arranged for a flight to Con Son. Mr. Arthur, Assistant Administrator USAID, Washington, D.C.; Mr. Seigal, Deputy Director USAID/V; Mr. Chambers, Executive Officer Civil Operations/CORDS; Mr. Elliot, Community Development Director/CORDS; Mr. Sheldon and Mr. Pesacreta, of OPS; Commander Tran Cong Hau, Deputy DOC; and Manopoli were members of a special survey team. (233)

The dignitaries were briefed by corrections advisors living on the island. In February, Ve had been promoted to full Colonel and was transferred from Con Son to Military Region Three (Bien Hoa). His replacement was LTC. Tiep. Advisors reported he was a welcome change. Gordon Young was especially pleased. Whereas I thought Ve a presence, Gordon perceived him as arrogant.

But the honeymoon was soon over. Tiep instructed the advisors to vacate the beach house where they were housed because he said, he needed it for VIP visitors. This left the advisors on the street. The Coast Guard Station on the island had room for only one person, and we had three advisors-- Young, Myers, and Delgar Wells, who was then supervising the fishing program.

Relations between Americans on Con Son and the Commandant deteriorated. Tiep made the town of Con Son off limits to members of Loran Coast Guard Station. We agreed Tiep's unreasonable and unrealistic demands were his way of letting everyone know he was in charge at Con Son, and not the Americans.

The fishing industry was floundering. As long as Wells was there to insist the boat go out to fish every day, there was an adequate catch. If, for one reason or another, he wasn't available, the boat simply didn't go out.

Since his first day, Tiep had played host to clusters of demanding Americans all wanting everything done immediately. After just thirty days on the island, he was near the breaking point. Colonel Sanh had visited on March 4. Our relationship with Tiep ended shortly after their meeting.

The entire group, with Colonel Tiep, tromped all seven prison camps and the agricultural areas. Every member was impressed with the adequacy of the old tiger cage cells, and thoroughly depressed by the new isolation cell blocks. The consensus: anyone seeing the new construction would conclude the U.S. was party to building substandard facilities. The old tiger cage buildings were definitely better.

Modifications had to be made to the buildings. They trapped heat like an oven. Heavy duty exhaust fans would be installed at each end to provide air flow, and the access doors, at the end and center of each building, required installation of louvers for low level ventilation.

Tiep displayed propaganda materials brought in by visitors and demanded construction be completed as soon as possible. He was justifiably concerned. The material was mostly summarized news reports by Luce and the PRG in Paris, encouraging prisoners to revolt.

Just that day, Tiep had 2302 prisoners who refused to work. Because they insisted on chanting and causing disruption in the camps, he had them shackled. The shackling took the breath of the visitors who immediately saw visions of a new frenzy and Congress pounding on their backs. Tiep, although strained, tried to be diplomatic while making it very clear his problems were the fault of Americans and their media.

The delegation, who were all substantive members of USAID/CORDS, discussed the various problems brought to their attention. They framed recommendations which they later articulated to Ambassador Colby in great detail.

Two of the three advisors would be reassigned and rotate back to Con Son as needed. One would remain, housed at the Coast Guard facility. Every effort would be made to speed construction of the disciplinary section.

Colonel Sanh and I had been in session at the DOC that day. He was seriously concerned and deeply hurt when he overheard his bureau chiefs concluding he was my lap dog. We both knew it wasn't true, but it was apparently the perception of his staff. Sanh, his superiors at the Ministry of Interior, and Commander Hau truly believed every problem in the past year and a half had been caused by the Americans. (233)

Sanh was the first to admit fantastic strides had been made in the civilian prison system, and much more needed to be done. But -- they all found it very difficult to excuse the terrible behavior of the American Congress, the news media, and the pressure advisors were exerting on them to do things overnight. (261)

Tears welled as he continued. "The sickness is all problems were generated by lies of two American Congressmen and their aide. Why did you not denounce them and repute their distortions? Even the American Embassy allowed them to continue their lies."

Both of us were very aware of our lack of power at our level, and knew all we could do was our best under the circumstances. I sensed Sanh's feeling of betrayal no less than my own.

"But we have done something," he continued, tail feathers rising. "Luce will no longer be troublesome. He is to be thrown out of my country with no press pass renewal." (219)

Sanh predicted LTC. Tiep would be a hard man to deal with at Con Son, not only in relationship to Americans, but also in his own relationship. He believed Con Son would deteriorate under Tiep's leadership.

Sanh handed me a letter written to the MOI by Col. Ve. He encouraged me to read it very closely, adding Mai would be reassigned by the end of the week. Without any hint of rancor, he added, "Mai has become expendable."

Before I could ask what happened, Sanh, struggling now to keep his tail feathers up, said, "Just read."(236)

Later that afternoon, I read the letter. Ve apologized for the heavy burdens Con Son had placed on the Minister during the last year and a half. He discussed the visit by the CONDEL, and could not understand why his country did not support him. He felt he had been personally and professionally denigrated by his country's refusal to demand an apology from the two Representatives and their aide. His country, his Ministry, and he, had been hurt beyond repair.

The remainder of Ve's letter is worth recounting.

"They came to Con Son with one purpose in mind, to find the tiger cages, and to exploit them to the world. Their tongues told only lies, and we did not repute them.

"Before I go, Sir," Ve continued, "we must remember it was the Minister who approved the trip. We must all remember once before, in our history, women were housed on Con Son island and it, too, was a disaster. But, this time, because the women caused many problems at the province centers, they were transferred to Thu Duc. At Thu Duc, they rioted and . . . sent to Chi Hoa. At Chi Hoa, they destructed the center and were planning a huge riot.

"Mr. Le Quang Mai, Inspector (former Director) and Mr. William Secor, U.S. Advisor, came to the island at the insistence of the MOI and the DOC. They told me the security situation at Chi Hoa Center and I was ordered to accept 343 female prisoners. I protested loudly -- but, no one would listen -- the Ministry had made up its mind.

"Many months earlier I emptied the tiger cages of prisoners. I opened a new segregation dormitory for those prisoners and authorized the poor correctional jailers and their families to use the tiger cages as apartments--and they were happy and thanked me.

"Then I was forced to take the female prisoners from Chi Hoa. Where could I put them? I couldn't have them in camps where they would encourage other prisoners to cause trouble. So, I told Mai and Secor I had no choice but to put the females in the old tiger cages. They both approved my choice and we moved the jailers back to their old huts to live in and put the women in the disciplinary section.

"On the day the female prisoners flew to Con Son, Lee McPhie and Mr. Khoa were here on the island. They assisted us in transferring the females to the tiger cage compound.

There were no secrets. There was no subterfuge.

"There was no malnutrition, there were no beatings. The females were never shackled at any time. Males who are disciplinary problems were shackled. But, they are only shackled at night when very little staff is on duty.

"There were no paralyzed prisoners. They were paralyzed only when Americans were here. When the Americans left, they could walk. I told everybody that, but nobody listened!"

Now, I had tears. And I was beyond anger.

At USAID II, I passed copies of Ve's letter around. Berkeley and I were discussing it when Secor came in. I abruptly interrupted our discussion, asking him to step to a vacant office down the corridor.

Secor took Ve's letter and read it. "So?"

"So? Ve says you and Mai approved his putting the 343 women prisoners from Chi Hoa in the tiger cages. True?"

"So what? The women had to go somewhere. It's his God damn island, and his stinking prison, so what's the problem?"

No doubt whatsoever -- Bill's bulldog face and gravel voice, six foot plus frame, and 250 pound body suited him and had served him well as a career Army officer, and for five years at San Quentin as the Death Row Sergeant. But I had developed a bulldog quality of my own. My voice lowered an octave.

"Well, Bill, here's the problem -- do you remember when you, Berkeley and I met at the Frenchman's for lunch and I asked you how the women ended up in the tiger cages? Those cells had jailers in them when I last visited them. You said McPhie was there the day the women were flown in, and he didn't know any better."

"I believed you. McPhie was new. So I chalked it up to damn poor communications and original sin. But you--you lied to me. You screwed up, and you knew it."

"Bullshit," Secor spat. "I didn't lie to you, I just forgot. We've been f____g busy. I forgot. All right? Con Son's not my island. Those damn prison camps aren't mine either. Ve was the boss. I couldn't tell him where to put prisoners."

If I had wanted to spend the rest of my life in prison, now was the time to assure it. My eyes felt like firecrackers waiting to go off. Instead, I lowered my voice another octave, spewing a speech with my finger nearly up his nose.

"We've spent millions of dollars. Millions of hours,

blood, and sweat on this, and you tell me, you couldn't tell Ve where to put his prisoners! There're other places he could've housed those females. You *controlled the purse strings!* You could've got off your fat ass and taken the time to look. You should have found an appropriate place, arranged for transformation of the unit to accept female prisoners, and insisted, if necessary, demanded, Ve house *those* females in *those* quarters.

"But, you didn't do that. And *do not* tell me you could not have done it! For God's sake, you could have stayed to help him!"

Secor's response was for me to lighten up. He did recognize if he could do it again, he'd do it differently. I wasn't in the mood.

"Mai's no longer with the Directorate," I said, "he's been reassigned. You're going to have a change of scenery, too. You'll assume responsibilities as Regional Advisor in Can Tho by noon Monday. Advise me when you're at post."

I was nearly out the door when Secor's skeptical protest came blasting past me. "You doing this just because I let them put them females in the tiger cages?"

All I could do was stare.

Bill hated living in the provinces -- no PX, no nice apartment, few Americans -- cramped his style. I knew he'd try to have me overruled, but he wasted no time at all. He beat me back to Berk's office.

I walked in just in time to see Berkeley look up from his desk, squarely at Secor, and quietly say, "Don is the Senior Advisor to Corrections. If he has decided to transfer you to IV Corps, I'm certain he has good reason. I'll advise Walton to contact the chief Public Safety officer in that Region to tell him you will be reporting."

That's the last time I saw Secor.

A few weeks later, I was summoned to Frank's office. Mike McCann intercepted me. There was an urgent cable from Bangkok where my wife and children were living. My family needed me. There were no other details.

I left the office and telephoned my wife. Our son's earlier eye injury had caused traumatic glaucoma. He was in a Thai hospital scheduled for emergency surgery the next morning. I left for Bangkok the next day, too late to keep my promise to my boy of being there should he be hospitalized again. My hope was he would understand. I tried to remember what it was like to appreciate and be appreciated. My heart was in my shoes.

Four days later, I returned to Saigon. Ambassador Colby had returned stateside because his daughter was seriously ill. His deputy replaced him. Walton had also returned stateside and Mike McCann stepped up to Chief.

I was very pleased. We worked well together, and I respected him enormously.

Long after his retirement, Frank would tell me his version of his unstable relationship with Colby. And why he was assigned permanently to Washington.

Ambassador Colby was fed up with Walton, especially his inability to follow the Group Think format of the Pacification Committee. Colby hadn't forgotten the embarrassment of the HOI CAI document either. He collared his old OSS colleague, Byron Engle, who refused to fire Frank, and also refused to transfer him out of Vietnam. But Colby didn't let up. Finally, after some time had passed, Engle gave Colby an option. Walton would finish his tour in Vietnam, wouldn't return, but he wouldn't be fired. Mike McCann would replace Theo Hall, immediately, and later Walton.

And that's what happened. Walton served in Washington until his retirement, but Colby never forgot Engle turned him down on Frank's dismissal. A couple of years later, when Colby was confirmed as Director of the CIA, he would make Engle, still on the CIA payroll, one of his first orders of business.

Early in 1973, Engle elected retirement. Two minor heart attacks helped him decide.

Over the next few months, health, sanitation, security, and programs for prisoners continued to improve. Of course, we were simultaneously responding to Congressional inquiries and news reports, most of which were simply fabrications.

Nooter was still in Washington, testifying before the House. We continued to prepare daily responses for him. In early December, I wrote the end of year report on the program. It would be the last one I would do in Vietnam.

My son's visual problems were becoming worse and additional surgery would be required. The worry and guilt I felt over the family situation was taking its toll. A decision was made for me. At the request of the Aid Mission, Engle ordered my return to the United States to be with my family and insure the necessary medical assistance for our son. I would not return to Vietnam. I was assigned the post of

Assistant Director Administration at the International Police Academy (IPA) in Washington, and would also be an instructor and class counselor to foreign participants.

On January 6, 1972, I reported to the Academy in the Georgetown section of Washington. If our country ever needed an enema I know the hose would be inserted in our nation's capitol. But we did the best we could to tolerate living there. By end of our first year, Shirley and I decided to build a small home in Charles Town, West Virginia. It was fifty-three miles from our country lane to the Academy, and in spite of the one hundred and six mile round trip I drove daily, it was less expensive, quieter, and more real than the suburbs of D.C.

My administrative work and classes were often supplemented with rush assignments. At State, I continued to assist the Vietnam Back Stop Officer with responses to congressional inquiry and news stories. It seemed evident, as long as there was an Office of Public Safety and we were in Vietnam, I would be, in one way or another, assisting in the tiger cage fall-out.

Frank Walton, on June 20, 1972, wrote for the record about his meeting with David Marsh of NEWSWEEK. Over lunch, Marsh confided, "Harkin planned to set up a visit to Con Son Island prior to his trip to Vietnam, and was communicating with a close source in Saigon. He preconceived the exploitation of the tiger cages and their prisoners. He met with the right people. You were set up." More confirmation but no surprise. (238)

In mid 1972, the congressional hearings slowed down. Nooter did a splendid job rebutting the awesome number of questions thrown at him. Apparently, Congressman Hawkins and his former congressional aide felt it an appropriate time for a new attack. This time, the attack focused on Walton.

Hawkins, from California, boosted a large Afro-American constituency. He considered Frank a racist and bigot while assigned to the Los Angeles Police Department, and he brought this to the attention of the media. This new issue infuriated Walton and was, for Frank, the final blow. It prompted his decision to quietly retire, leave the mainland, and spend his remaining years swimming in the waters off Hawaii. In retirement, Frank found time to pen and publish a book about the Black Sheep Squadron of W.W.II, with whom he served.

But this maligning of Frank was too much for John

Monopoli and Johnson F. Munroe, also of OPS. They contacted their sources in Los Angeles. They took some time to thoroughly investigate Walton's career with L.A.P.D. and the Sheriffs' Office. Additionally, they called their friends, who called their friends, to summon support for Walton. Information surfaced about a testimonial dinner held for Frank when he was transferred from Commander of the Los Angeles Police 77th Street Division, in December 1948.

The police division included the Watts District of Los Angeles. At that dinner, Walton was presented a plaque by the honorary mayor, Evan Moseby. Munroe talked with Moseby, who then resided at 3930 West Side Avenue, Los Angeles, and operated a clothing store at 3121 South Vermont. Moseby vividly recalled the occasion of the testimonial dinner and that he did, indeed, present a plaque to Walton. He said, "at that time I operated a dinner club known as The Last Word and the dinner was held there."

Moseby also said he was known, during that period, as the Mayor of Central Avenue. He held the dinner to express his appreciation, as well as, that of the community, which was largely black, for Walton's two years of service there. Moseby provided a photograph of he and Walton taken at the testimonial. (261)

Every person in attendance on that December evening escaped Moseby's recall, but he did remember Captain Earl Sensing, who was at that time, Commander of the adjoining Newton Street Division, and Joe Harris, a reporter for the Los Angeles Sentinel. Munroe mentioned the recent publicity describing Walton as prejudiced, bigoted, and one who oppressed minorities.

Moseby disagreed. On the contrary, Walton's record was superior in relationships with the black community. Other citizens on the committee agreed with him. The committee had, after all, planned the dinner to honor Walton.

Munroe talked with Captain Sensing, then a Personnel Officer for the Los Angeles Police Department. Sensing recalled the dinner very well, stating he, too, had a copy of the photograph. Sensing's assessment was that such statements proved Hawkins a liar.

Munroe, Monopoli, and friends of Walton in Los Angeles arranged for this information to be passed to California media and their stories resulted in a backlash on Hawkins. Hawkins attack died. "Better than nothing," growled Walton, but it was empty acceptance.

THIRTEEN

On January 27, 1973, a cease fire agreement in Vietnam was signed. It put two restrictions on assistance to South Vietnam's National Police, and the DOC. Article 5 of the agreement required advisors to the National Police leave the country within 60 days. Article 7 limited the replacement of armaments, ammunition, and war material to a 1-for-1 basis. Since the goals of the OPS Projects had been largely attained, all advisory dollar support was terminated on those programs on June 30, 1973. By April 1973, all USAID OPS Police Advisors were out of Vietnam. The loss of funding was anticipated.

In late January 1973, the Indochina Mobile Education Project completed its first printing of the book, HOSTAGES OF WAR, about Saigon's political prisoners, written by Holmes Brown and Luce. Copies were distributed worldwide. By March, the first printing was exhausted. The second printing was completed in April. I understand there have been several printings since then.

On September 13, 1973, at a hearing before the Subcommittee on Asian and Pacific Affairs of the Committee on Foreign Affairs-House of Representatives-93rd Congress, Bella S. Abzug, Representative from the State of New York, appeared with Luce.

Abzug told the committee there were a lot of American citizens interested in the fate of political prisoners confined in South Vietnam. Her view was whether the number of prisoners was 200,000, or 100,000, or less, the essential question centered on when the release of prisoners would occur. She alleged new arrests of political prisoners since the cease fire agreement; charged the GVN with refusing to release those arrested before the cease fire; and said the staff of the U.S. Senate Subcommittee on Refugees, the International Red Cross, and numerous journalists were refused permission to visit prisons at will, or to talk privately with prisoners. Abzug presented documents, said to be written by people previously incarcerated in DOC prisons, all of which charged brutality, repression, and pain. It was a great story.

Representative Abzug's assertion brings to mind a comment Luce made to Shirley at their interview in 1992. When asked if he knew the difference between a jail and a prison, a PIC and, or, a DIOCC detention center--Luce responded, "No. It's not important."

Perhaps she asked the wrong question. She should have asked if there are important differences between the varieties of sweet potatoes he brought to Vietnam.

Luce appeared next before the Committee. He, too, presented a myriad of documents, most of which were reprints from his book. After outlining the articles of the cease fire agreement, he noted USAID's assistance for our programs was terminated. But he had a complaint. Public Safety was abolished -- but its programs and funding continued, he asserted, saying another $3.3 million of U.S. tax money was being spent on prisons, police and police telecommunications under USAID programs. Luce's facts were, again, skewed.

In fiscal year 1974 -- calendar year 1973-- USAID requested $600,000 to train 200 personnel from the National Police Command in computer system management and technology. Another $196,000 was requested to finance the training of 60 police officers in other aspects of police management. All of this training would be conducted outside Vietnam and was in keeping with the terms of the cease fire agreement.

USAID obligated $172,000 for advisory support of the Correction Center Project during FY1973. Additional funding was not requested, and the program was thereafter terminated.

In FY1973, USAID obligated $848,000 for advisory support and commodities under the telecommunications project. In FY1974, USAID requested $520,000 for replacement commodities under the Public Works General Support Project.

By the end of April 1973, there was no Office of Public Safety and there were no Public Safety Advisors to the National Police in Vietnam. Nine telecommunications advisors, previously working under the aegis of Public Safety in Cords, continued to provide advisory telecommunications assistance, and worked for the Public Works General Support Project. The combined telecommunications Directorate was a non-police, civilian directorate furnishing country wide communications to civilian agencies of the Vietnamese government.

Five logistics technicians, previously with OPS, were assigned to new positions in the USAID logistics general support project. Two other technicians who advised the personnel of the MOI's computer center, and one technician assigned as an assistant program officer with the Office of the Associate Director for Commercial and Capital Assistance, were formerly assigned to OPS.

USAID reported none of these changes violated the cease fire agreement. Further, Congress approved every one.

By early May 1975, the Viet Cong won their first United Nations recognition. Press releases revealed the new communist government had released all prisoners from Con Son Prison where inmates were held in the notorious tiger cage cells.

Before terminating his appearance before the committee, Luce charged money used to build the new tiger cages came from Food for Peace commodities. Public Safety supposedly took Food For Peace money, sold it on the local market, and paid Raymond, Larson, Knutsen, Brown, Root, and Jones (a U.S. contractor) to construct the isolation cells. His most acrimonious accusation was to cite two stockholders in the company as Mrs. Lyndon Johnson and John Connolly. Indeed, the company was a large contributor to President's Johnson's election campaigns. (261)

Luce's rhetoric—true and untrue—was widely reported.

The Provincial Revolutionary Government (PRG) ordered all officials of the former government to report to communist headquarters by Thursday May 31, in Saigon. They were then confined at Con Son for an unspecified period for political reorientation.

A few of my Vietnamese friends and professional colleagues were fortunate to extract themselves and their families from Vietnam. However, most of them did not. They were required to report to communist authorities under threat of death. They, like those above, were shipped to Con Son for punishment, and mending of their twisted ideology.

Gi's fate is particularly significant to me. Early in my tenure, after Benson's tearful farewell, I was a bit more than surprised at the large contingent of Vietnamese on hand to welcome me aboard. Benson, the man they all loved, was gone and the attitude was -- you're now the advisor and that's life -- so let's get started. I would come to view this amazing oriental ability as a personal lesson to learn; explained later by my dear friend Gi, as strive to be a willow.

Years later, the day in 1975, when rumors of Gi's fate as an American collaborator reached me--when Gi, forced to watch his two beautiful daughters and his wife hung up-side-down in their village square, and gutted like pigs before his eyes, accepted his own torture** and death with the courage of the oak -- I cried real tears for him, and for the wisdom to mimic the willow. A stance I've yet to achieve.

It was, to me, ultimate and cruel irony that our friends were now doing time in prisons I helped build. They did not carry arms. They were anti-communist. Anti-North Vietnam. Pro United States. And they were declared enemies of the state and the people by the new government in power. They were categorized as the infrastructure of the former Thieu government.

The United States government, nor the world media voiced protest to the atrocities of the new communist regime.

** We cannot verify this beyond any doubt. Later, other of our Vietnamese sources said they had also heard these rumors but tell us they lean to the belief Le Duc Gi died of cancer. Either way, my trusted and loyal friend is dead.

FOURTEEN

Faclusions

In Frank Walton's view, Luce wasn't expendable by Colby, or the Saigon CIA Station. He had a door to the enemy which was to the CIA's advantage. Their cost was minimal--keep the Saigon government off Luce's back.

Luce's visa was pulled by South Vietnam in 1971. Today, Luce is the Executive Director of International Volunteer Services, Inc., with offices in an unassuming structure not too far out Connecticut Avenue in S. W., Washington, D. C. Among other things, he earns his living arranging tours to Vietnam. He reports he often travels to troubled countries. (261-276)

And, Tom Harkin...well...Harkin had the advantage. He was able to capitalize on the free and lavish media coverage of the tiger cage incident, and propel himself into Iowa's congressional delegation in 1974.

In 1984, he was elected by Iowans to the United States Senate, where he serves today. The man who would be President, ran unsuccessfully as a Democrat contender for that office in 1992. His oft repeated philosophy, "attack don't defend", typifies his manner, and is an appropriate summation.

William Colby, after returning to the United States, was assigned the number three position at the Central Intelligence Agency. Before the demise of Public Safety, he was elevated to the position of Director. One of his first orders of business was to arrange the retirement of Byron Engle, Director of Public Safety. Our sources are vehement Colby gave Engle an offer he couldn't refuse. Elephant's aren't the only ones with long memories.

Colby had long been fed up with Walton's unwillingness to let the tiger cage flap die, and his inability to follow the herd mentality of the Pacification Council. Further, he never forgot Frank's audacity in referring Berkeley's HOI CAI program to him. Frank's administrative gall was too disgusting to swallow.

In reply to Shirley's letter of October 9, 1991, Colby

wrote, "I do not find it strange that the Congressmen might have casually asked two CIA men to get them permission to visit the island and that the CIA men passed the question to the American pacification advisors to ask the Vietnamese authorities. Certainly, before the frenzy occurred after the visit, there was no policy reason for me to be brought into the question, as our policy was to let Congressmen see what they wanted to and not to stage manage their visits." (259)

Ralph McGehee, a veteran CIA paramilitary officer, is quoted by Doug Valentine in his book, THE PHOENIX PROGRAM, page 274. "I have watched him (Colby) when I knew he was lying, and not a flicker of emotion crosses his face. But what made Colby even more dangerous was his manipulation of language. He regarded word usage as an art form. He was a master of it."

I would agree--he had the verbal expertise to talk a puppy off a meat wagon. Masterful. And, hey, that worked for Colby.

William Colby died in 1996. His death was attributed to a heart attack while canoeing.

Guenter Lewy, in his book, AMERICA IN VIETNAM, recognizes the dubious tiger cage tale influenced Congress. Lewy nails the World Council of Churches, Congressmen Anderson and Hawkins, Tom Harkin, and Don Luce with creating the impression of subterranean dungeons, by use of the word pit.

"It should be finally noted", said Lewy, "that many of those who accepted the allegations of a paralysis suffered at Con Son also bought the hoax of underground tiger cages." Lewy cites Tiziano Terzani, in his book THE FALL AND LIBERATION OF SAIGON, 'the cages were small pits dug in the earth covered with iron gratings . . . prisoners could not move. . . their legs atrophied. . . frightful sticks of skin and bone.'

James Cary, reporter for the San Diego Union, recounted his February 3, 1974 visit to Con Son. Cary said, he "found the VC prisoners there well-organized . . . also reported by two American political scientists who visited the same prison later . . . It was evident each cell had its internal infrastructure, well-organized, and with internally designated spokesman . . . This suggests the Con Son prisoners . . . had the organization capabilities to stage the paralysis as a propaganda effort."

The AMERICAN LEGION MAGAZINE, in an article

by Philip C. Clarke, February, 1979, relates, "of all the horror stories emanating from the Vietnam War, few received wider play and greater attention than the tale of the tiger cages. . . Even today, post-war books cite the tiger cages as proof of the brutality of the wartime Saigon Regime (sic)."

"Exploited to the hilt by propagandists anxious to discredit the Saigon Government and push a U.S. withdrawal, the accounts served to convince millions of Americans that Saigon was unworthy of continued U.S. support. The examples of misinformation, distortion, and down right prevarication fed to Americans about the tiger cages are numerous and shocking.

A widely circulated leaflet charged the Thieu regime with holding 202,000 political prisoners. The American Security Council Fact-Finding Team traced the report to a Paris educated, left-wing cleric named Chan Tin. Tin claimed to head up an investigation of mistreatment of political prisoners.

An official U.S. Embassy investigation found, as of December 31, 1972, the total number of prisoners in South Vietnam, including war prisoners, was 43,717. Yet, the phony figure of 202,000 political prisoners actually found its way into the Congressional Record!

Clarke's article concludes, "The tiger cage story put out in 1970, served as one of the most successful propaganda operations ever undertaken by Hanoi's Psychological War Department."

And on June 27, 1995, early advocate, Mary McCrory editorialized in the Washington Post to "Put down Tom Harkin's reunion as packing the seasons biggest punch . . . 25 years ago he discovered the infamous tiger cages and put another nail in the coffin of Richard M. Nixon's doomed Vietnam policy."

Harkin would lead a congressional delegation to diplomatically recognize the current Vietnam regime.

As McCrory reports, "Harkin would be joined on Con Son by former Congressmen Gus Hawkins and William Anderson; Don Luce, . . ., and Cao Nguyon Loi who . . . is now a prosperous businessman."

July 3, 1995: an AP photo of U. S. Senator Tom Harkin gifting General Vo Nguyen Giap at the Presidential Palace in Hanoi appears as front page news.

On Wednesday, July 11, 1995, President Clinton holds

a press conference to legitimize relations with the country of Vietnam. CNN's cameras capture Senator Tom Harkin standing behind the President.

On November 5, 1996, Iowans again elected Harkin to the United States Senate.

And yes, we advisors made mistakes. None, however, were worthy of front page coverage, condemnation, or crucifixion. And none were illegal. Even with mistakes, our effort was top notch and so was what we accomplished there. The years I spent in South Vietnam were, despite the hell of wartime, and the havoc wrought by distortions, lies, political inquiries, and smoke and mirrors, full of achievement -- personally and professionally. The C&D Branch performed admirably under the most horrendous conditions and fulfilled their assignment with distinction.

The advisory effort to South Vietnam's corrections system began in 1962 with one single advisor. Americans were not permitted in the prisons. In 1970, the number of advisors working on prison matters totaled fifteen. The Red Cross, U.S./GVN medical teams, and USAID/Cords inspections were frequent.

A total of 20,000 new sleeping spaces were a reality. We had sleeping space for 48,366, and the total population was 36,129.

There was sufficient bed space, however, there were still unsentenced prisoners being housed in prisons. Once the GVN began to transfer unsentenced prisoners to jails until trial, the problem of overcrowding was over in the prisons. And the new parole system would substantially reduce the numbers in jails and prisons.

Segregation of prisoners by sex and crime category was a reality. Cooking, dining, water wells, and bathing facilities had been renovated and upgraded. Dispensaries were in every prison and each clinic was supported by Public Health professionals.

Our advisory effort included a medical program directed by a U.S. physician, who was counterpart to a medical doctor on the Staff of the DOC. Every prison facility encouraged religious worship, and many had separate facilities for Buddhists and Christians. And we spent money in support of it.

Formal, fairly sophisticated, occupational skills training programs were established at the four national centers. While there were a few visible signs of an industrial program, most prisoners made simple items to sell in neighboring villages.

At provincial prisons, prisoners were typically engaged in every-day living, plus a variety of activities which had to do with improving or maintaining the centers. There were no cell blocks. Prisoners lived in long, segregated dormitories.

Guards were conspicuous by their absence, except at the entrances. Literacy training and academic instruction was at every prison. Daily food allowances were increased. The prisoner death rate dropped from 48 a month, in 1966, to 11 a month, in 1971. The Con Son death rate dropped from 4 to 1.5. And there were twice the number of prisoners in 1971. No small feat.

Vietnam had a relatively satisfactory system of jail and penal facilities by this time. Appropriate shelter and care was a reality and improvements came as fast as resources of the government would permit. We were pleased the flow process of civilian suspects and prisoners was finally working--moving prisoners through the legal process as it was designed to do. The key to this accomplishment was Mike McCann. He insisted his advisors ramrod the process, and held them responsible if failure occurred.

USAID funds in the amount of $1,711,000 were spent for C&D programs from January 1963 through January 1972. Of that, $1,487,000 was spent for commodities, equipment, materials and supplies for province prisons and Thu Duc, Tan Hiep and Chi Hoa national prisons. Advisors salaries came to $216,000, and participant training in the United States was a low $8,000.

Additionally, $1,026,000 of Special Funds (CIA money) was spent on the priority -- Con Son. These funds purchased a fishing vessel, fishing poles and nets, construction of new disciplinary cells to replace the tiger cage block, dispensaries, sanitation, and equipment, material and supplies for farming, animal husbandry, and vocational training programs. Another $220,000 from the Special Fund constructed detention centers and provided materials and commodities.

Con Son had 2,000 trusty inmates living in small houses throughout the island, with little or no supervision. An additional 1,500 inmates returned to the camps at night after working at the piggery, goat ranch, landscape gardening, and at a 200-hectare truck farm. Twelve vocational training courses taught 1,100 inmates each day; and handicraft programs were available to all, except those in maximum security cells.

Housing for jailers and their families, however, was not improved. The Ministry of Rural Development was responsible for upgrading employee housing, but their priorities were elsewhere. The logic was: no war damage at Con Son--no upgrading needed.

The nine year period of the program (1963-1972) accounted for $2,957,000. To me that was a lot of money, and still is, but if the funds are paralleled to a war time perspective, the entire money spent would not have purchased one jet fighter plane.

These were not small accomplishments. At least to us, they weren't. And hey, that's good enough for me.

On the Internet, 1997, someone named Howard Ryan writes in Chapter 5 of his CRITIQUE OF NON-VIOLENT POLITICS, about human rights issues and uses a quote from, THE WASHINGTON CONNECTION AND THIRD WORLD FASCISM, to make his point -- "The United States supplied funds and technology for Tiger Cages, interrogation centers, and electronic and other equipment used for torture. . ."

In what is now Ho Chi Minh City, at 28 Vo Van Tan, is the War Crimes Museum, a popular tourist attraction. For a small admission fee, a visitor can see a model of the infamous tiger cages which purport to give an inkling of the atrocities some people went through while housed there.

And in another cyberspace article titled NOTES FROM VIETNAM, Vivian Rothstein revisits Hanoi to relive, she says, her activism of the '60's when she was recruited for a trip to Hanoi, by Hanoi, from the ranks of Students for a Democratic Society in Chicago.

On Rothstein's return trip in the early 1990's, she and her fellow activist visitors requested Mrs. Trung My Hoa, the only female member of the Communist Party Secretariat, recount her story of struggle.

"I was sentenced to 18 months . . . but in fact I was in prison 11 years. In 1969, I was put in the Tiger Cage (a rectangular hole dug into the dirt with steel grating overhead) when I met Congressman Tom Harkin who exposed the existence of the Tiger Cages to the American people, in 1970. For a year about five women were kept in one very small cage. "

"Even the five women couldn't speak to each other. So we survived like beasts, not like human beings. Whenever they heard our voices or whispers they threw lye on us and used thorn stick [sic] to beat us and after the lye they poured water on us. Our hair turned into a strange thing and the lye turned our skin brittle. We were treated and tortured like some wild animals."

And so it continues.

While I'm amazed, I'm not surprised. And I am, of course, deeply saddened the tiger cages seem to have become a symbol of evil. There's nothing I can change about that. What I can do is what I've done by writing this book. I've told my story.

That the United States eventually and officially recognized the Vietnam conflict as a mistake does not, in my opinion, elevate Harkin and Luce, vindicate them, nor validate their deed.

But then, each of us must live with our history. And that, too, is good enough for me.

My life is my message.
- Mahatmas Ghandi

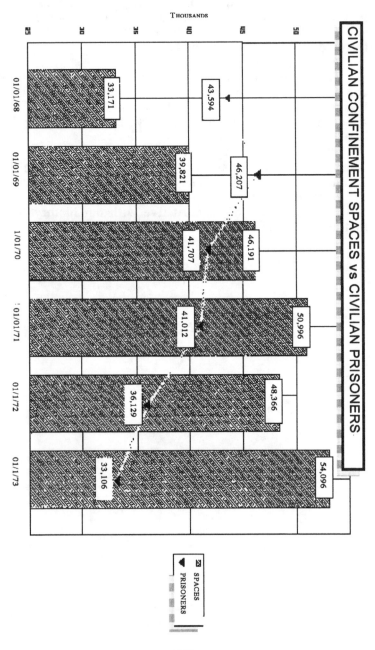

CIVILIAN CONFINEMENT SPACES vs CIVILIAN PRISONERS

THOUSANDS

Date	Spaces	Prisoners
01/01/68	33,171	43,594
01/01/69	39,821	46,207
1/01/70	41,707	46,191
01/01/71	41,012	50,996
01/1/72	36,129	48,366
01/1/73	33,106	54,096

Legend:
SPACES
PRISONERS

DIRECTOR
Office of Public Safety

EXECUTIVE OFFICE

INSPECTION & REPORT BRANCH

- **Field Operations Division**
  - Marine Police Branch
  - Saigon Metro Police Branch
  - I CTZ
  - II CTZ
  - III CTZ
  - IV CTZ

- **Technical Support Division**
  - Budget & Programs Branch
  - Logistics Branch
  - Training Branch
  - Manpower Branch

- **NPFF Division**
  - Logistics Branch
  - Plans/Operations Branch
  - Admin/Personnel Branch
  - Dalat Training Center

- **Police Staff Operations Division**
  - ID Branch
  - Investigation Traffic/Order Branch
  - Research Legal Branch
  - Central Record Branch

- **Corrections & Detention Division**
  - Corrections Branch
  - Detention Branch
  - Operations Branch

- **Telecom Division**
  - Administrative Branch
  - Technical Services Branch

NATIONAL & PROVINCIAL
CORRECTION CENTERS

**NATIONAL
CENTERS**
—

Tan Hiep
Thu Duc
Chi Hoa
Con Son

**PROVINCIAL
CENTERS**
—

Binh Long
Tay Ninh
Binh Duong
Gia Dinh
Kien Tuong
Chau Doc
Kien Phong
An Giang
Kien Giang
Thong Dinh
An Xuyen
Back Lieu

**PROVINCIAL
CENTERS**
—

Quang Tri
Thua Thien
Danang City
Quang Nam
Quang Tin
Quang Ngai
Dontum
Pleiku
Binh Dinh
Phu Yen
Darlac
Khanh Hoa
Tuyen Duc
Ninh Thuan
Dien Hoa
Binh Thuan
Long An
Binh Tuy
Go Cong
Dinh Thong
Kien Hoa
Vinh Long
Vinh Binh
Da Xyen

SOUTH VIETNAM

Gulf of
Siam

Con Son Island

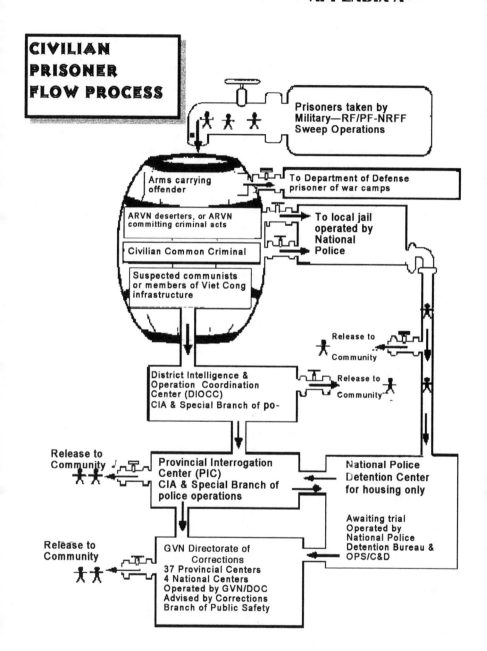

CIVILIAN PRISONER FLOW PROCESS

Prisoners taken by Military—RF/PF-NRFF Sweep Operations

Arms carrying offender

To Department of Defense prisoner of war camps

ARVN deserters, or ARVN committing criminal acts

Civilian Common Criminal

To local jail operated by National Police

Suspected communists or members of Viet Cong infrastructure

District Intelligence & Operation Coordination Center (DIOCC) CIA & Special Branch of po-

Release to Community

Release to Community

Provincial Interrogation Center (PIC) CIA & Special Branch of police operations

National Police Detention Center for housing only

Release to Community

Awaiting trial Operated by National Police Detention Bureau & OPS/C&D

GVN Directorate of Corrections 37 Provincial Centers 4 National Centers Operated by GVN/DOC Advised by Corrections Branch of Public Safety

Release to Community

SPECIAL FUNDS (Phoenix)
To Con Son Correctional Center 1/1/67 to 1/1/72

A. CONSTRUCTION MATERIALS	YEAR	QUANTITY	COST In US Dollars
Cement, 50kg bags	1968	41,286	$49,543
	1969	3,920	4,604
	1970	18,900	21,600
SUBTOTAL		**63,200**	**$75,747**
Aluminum Roofing (sheets)	1968	1,260	$2,998
	1969	1,056	2,513
SUB TOTAL		**2,316**	**$5,511**
Rebar (various sizes)	1968	mt 475.44	$56,101
	1969	5.00	590
SUBTOTAL		**mt 480.44**	**$56,691**

B. BARRIER MATERIALS	YEAR	QUANTITY	COST
Barbed Wire	1968	spls 1,930	$20,651
Lumber	1968	bf 600	50
Tie Wire	1968	lbs. 21,000	2,310
Steel Stake	1968	ea. 2,500	3,000
SUBTOTAL			**$26,011**
Sewing Machine	1967	10	700
Motor (boat,35hp)	1968	2	650
Sawmill, portablee	1968	1	18,000
Filing cabinet	1968	7	420
24 volt battery charger	1971	1	120
1 1/2" self joinn bilge & wash down pump	1971	1	225
8" compas	1971	1	300
12 volt HD batteries	1971	2	120
battery acid	1971	drum 1	250
small fishing boat	1971	10	1,000
insect spray, repellant	1971	N/A	300
Field jacket	1971	1	30
FM 5 radio	1971	5	6,000
Plywood	1971	sheets 12	142
8" pipe	1971	4	77
Manila rope	1971	spls 3	161
4" pipe	1971	1	12
cable wire	1971	rolls 2	81
Stainless steel rod 10"	1971	65	77
Generator	1968	2	4,000
Prefab House	1969	10	18,500
Truck, Kaiser 1 1/2 ton	1969	2	5,018

A. CONSTRUCTION MATERIALS, Cont	YEAR	QUANTITY	COST
Truck, Gladitor 1 1/2 ton	1968	2	5,986
Forklift	1969	1	96618,500
Generator, 100kw	1969	1	9,6425
Generator, 100kw	1969	1	9,000
Generator, 100kw	1969	1	9,000
Generator, 100kw	1970	1	9,000
Generator, 5 kw	1071	2	1,000
Truck, 5 ton	1970	1	4,735
Forklift	1971	1	8,300
Camera	1970	1	469
Jeep CJ5	1970	2	6,000
Water Pump	1970	3	759
Floodlight, electric	1969	10	1,400
Connector, Plug, Electric	1969	10	11
Cord, assembly, electric	1969	ft 100	12
Lamp Incandescent	1969	40	30
Lanter, heavy duty	1969	22	608
Battery, replacement	1969	22	342
Charger, AUt 115 volts	1969	10	204
Tent, Medium	1970	20	8,280
Tent, Large	1970	19	11,400
Fishing boat (LCM-8)	1971		210,000
Fishing Supplies & Equipment	1971		1,695
Petroleum Products	1971		22,034
Disciplinary Cell Block	1972		485,000
SUBTOTAL			$833,391
GRAND TOTAL			$1,026,016

*37% of the $2,739,000 total 10 year support to the Directorate of Corrections

MINISTRY OF INTERIOR
DIRECTORATE OF CORRECTIONS
REPUBLIC OF SOUTH VIETNAM
ADVISORY SUPPORT BY OFFICE OF PUBLIC SAFETY
CORRECTION & DETENTION BRANCH
Total Annual Costs

Fiscal Year	C&D $SUPPORT	GVN/DOC BUDGET	VN$ to US$[1] CONVERSION	TOTAL VN$ $US BUDGET
1963	$37,000	$ 198,300	$1,680.51	$ 38,680.51
1964	34,000	217,708	1,884.98	35,844.98
1965	41,000	202,972	1,720.10	42,720.10
1966	75,000	200,000	1,694.92	76,694.92
1967	78,000	306,277	2,595.57	80,595.57
1968	729,000	487,687	4,132.94	733,132.94
1969	743,000	467,000	3,957.63	746,957.63
1970	223,000	672,007	5,694.97	28,964.97
1971	196,000	1,300,000	11,016.95	207,016.95
1972	416,000	847,000	7,177.97	423,177.97
1973	167,000	1,286,000	10,898.31	177,898.31

TOTALS

VN$6,184,951 US/VN$2,791,414.85[2]

US$2,739,000 [3] US$52,414.85 [4]

[1] VN$118=US$1
[2] Grand Total 10 year Project Cost in US Dollars = $2,791,414.855
[3] US Dollar Support was 98% of the Total US/GVN Budget
[4] Vietnamese Dollar Support Does Not Include Salaries

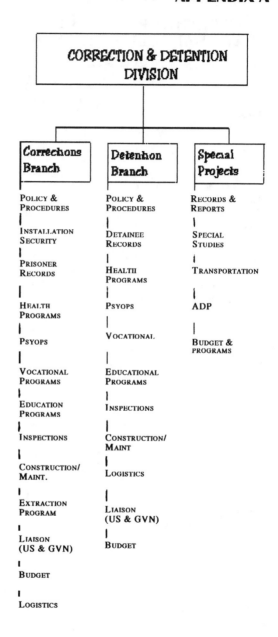

CORRECTION & DETENTION DIVISION

Corrections Branch	Detention Branch	Special Projects
POLICY & PROCEDURES	POLICY & PROCEDURES	RECORDS & REPORTS
INSTALLATION SECURITY	DETAINEE RECORDS	SPECIAL STUDIES
PRISONER RECORDS	HEALTH PROGRAMS	TRANSPORTATION
HEALTH PROGRAMS	PSYOPS	ADP
PSYOPS	VOCATIONAL	BUDGET & PROGRAMS
VOCATIONAL PROGRAMS	EDUCATIONAL PROGRAMS	
EDUCATION PROGRAMS	INSPECTIONS	
INSPECTIONS	CONSTRUCTION/ MAINT	
CONSTRUCTION/ MAINT.	LOGISTICS	
EXTRACTION PROGRAM	LIAISON (US & GVN)	
LIAISON (US & GVN)	BUDGET	
BUDGET		
LOGISTICS		

VN DIRECTORATE OF CORRECTIONS
& NATIONAL POLICE DETENTION CENTERS
January 1, 1972
Total Civilian Prisoner Sleeping Spaces (10 sq meters per person)
versus Total Civilian Prisoner Count

	ACTUAL COUNT	ACTUAL SPACES
NATIONAL CENTERS		
Chi Hoa & Saigon	5,586	5,995
Con Son Island	8,071	10,750
Tan Hiep	1,183	*1,140
Tu Duc	853	1,700
SUB TOTAL	15,693	19,585
I CORP- MILITARY REGION I		
Quang Tri	172	440
Thua Thien	646	1,450
Quang Nam	1,595	*550
Quang Tin	548	950
Quan Ngai	1,313	1,600
Danang	1,757	*1,170
SUB TOTAL	6,031	6,160
II CORPS - MILITARY REGION II		
Kontom	115	300
Binh Dinh	1,439	1,325
Pleiku	301	680
Phu Bon	9	1,350
Phu Yen	512	*400
Darlac	277	300
Khanh Hoa	753	*495
Ninh Thuan	153	350
Tuyen Duc	287	460
Quang Duc	2	115
Lam Dong	12	130
Binh Thuan	386	1,050
Cam Ranh	57	50
SUB TOTAL	4,293	7,005
III CORPS-MILITARY REGION III		
Binh Tuy	49	155
Long Khanh	37	400
Phoc Long	12	75
Binh Long	213	*190
Binh Duong	274	750
Jay Ninh	501	525
Hau Nghia	90	300
Bien Hoa	487	*470
Phuoc Tuy	333	805

APPENDIX A

	ACTUAL COUNT	ACTUAL SPACES
Gia Dinh	351	550
Vung Tau	118	*50
Long An	314	350
SUB TOTAL	**2,779**	**4,620**

IV CORPS-MILITARY REGION IV

Go Cong	244	1225
Kien Tuong	78	410
Kien Phong	138	500
Dinh Tuong	629	*515
Kien Hoa	667	*610
Vinh Binh	411	560
Vinh Long	614	940
An Giang	343	476
Kien Giang	542	*300
Choung Thein	98	600
Phong Dinh	1636	2840
Ba Xuyen	482	770
An Xuyen	363	510
Back Lieu	611	*480
Chan Doc	418	*240
Sa Doc	59	20
SUB TOTAL	**7333**	**40996**
GRAND TOTAL	**36129**	**48366**

* Overcrowding at centers. Province Chiefs wouldn't transfer prisoners to other vacant space within their region, fearing contempt of citizens & negative reports from media.

NOTE: This was the last report of space vs prisoners by Senior Advisor Bordenkircher

INMATE TRAINING PROGRAM
GVN DIRECTORATE OF CORRECTIONS

National Correction Centers (4)

Vocational Activities Skills Training

Cloth Weaving
Basket Weaving
Mat Weaving (Plastic)
*Carpentry
Masonry
*Welding
*Cabinet Making
*Auto Mechanics
*Machine Shop
Blacksmithing

Culinary
Wood Crews
#Typing
Deep Sea Fishing
#Center Maintenance
#Landscape Gardening
#Inside Construction
#Outside Construction

Handicraft

#Carving
#Painting
#Sculpture
#Theatre Arts

Correctional Industries

*Electrical Appliance Repair
*Tailoring
Fowl Raising
Lime Kiln Materials
Animal Husbandry
Mosquito Net Production
#Barbering
#ARVN Uniform Production

*Radio Repair
Rabbitry
Paint
Fruit Crops
#Embroidering
Tile Production
#Basic Sewing
Inmate Clothing Production

Bean Sauce Production
#Mechanical Drawing
Truck Farming
Fish-Net Making
Brick Making
Roofing

Province Correction Centers (37)

Vocational Activities Skills Training

Mat Weaving (Rice straw)
*Electric Shop
*Center Maintenance
*Masonry
*Plumbing
*Brick Making
*Embroidering
*Blacksmithing
*Sewing (Treadle machines)
*Barbering
*Paint Shop

*Culinary
*Wood Crews
*Inside Construction
*Landscape Gardening
*Outside Construction

Handicraft
*Carving
*Painting
*Sculpture

Industries

Rabbitry
*Carpentry
Fowl
Raising
*Vegetable
Gardening

*U.S. provided hand tools, accessories, materials, supplies, & power tools by American Aid Chapter Budget.
#Vietnam supplied equipment and supplies.

APPENDIX B
HOI CAI PROPOSAL
shortened version

Establish a GVN HOI CAI Ministry. The term HOI CAI is suggested as a psychological gambit to distinguish and dignify the return to society of former communist offenders. The present system lumps them with common criminals. This is a tactical error when we were striving to eradicate VC loyalty and build allegiance to the GVN.

Construe a HOI CAI as a citizen that had gone astray, but had seen the light and was returning to the fold. An approach similar to the Chieu Hoi philosophy.

Establish national prison and jail standards.

Report periodically to the President with appropriate recommendations for any corrective action.

Elevate the GVN Directorate of Corrections to a Director General and give authority for the operation of all civilian prisons in Vietnam.

Convert the thirty-seven Provincial Correctional Centers National Corrections Centers.

Establish Con Son Island as a penal colony.

Terminate the practice of assigning Province Chiefs as prison Commanders.

Draft in place the personnel employed by the Directorate of Corrections and the National Police Detention Service.

Charge Vietnamese Air Force to provide airlift to and from Con Son and other prisons; and the Vietnamese Navy with logistics support to Con Son.

Empower the Minister of HOI CAI to coordinate transfers of detainees and prisoners to insure optimum utilization of facilities.

Direct the Minister of Justice to make periodic status reports to the Ministry of HOI CAI on all persons awaiting legal action and the results of such action.

Direct the Department of Defense to have the Department of Military Justice furnish the Minister of HOI CAI with data on all persons held for military court actions, under trial, and the resulting sentences.

Direct the Minister of Interior to report to the Ministry of HOI CAI the results of actions of all Provincial Security Committees; and the Director General of National Police and the Director General of Corrections to render such reports on persons under their control.

Publish a uniform manual of standards for all confinement, processing, and after care of prisoners, and furnish the central Phung Hoang Office with prisoner data as required.

Respond to the urgent requirement for specific care and treatment of juvenile offenders.

Order the Director General of the Budget and Fiscal Affairs to fund an additional 2500 cadre for the remainder of calendar year 69 and year 1970, and recognize other budget requirements after presentation of justification.

APPENDIX C
SHORTENED VERSION
ANDERSON/HAWKINS RESOLUTION BEFORE THE HOUSE

Resolved...that the Congress (1) condemn the cruel and inhumane treatment and conditions of confinement of large numbers of political prisoners held in South Vietnam; (2) urge the Government of South Vietnam immediately to (a) cease cruel and inhuman treatment of prisoners, (b) take all steps practical to adequately cope with widespread malnutrition and disease within its civilian prisons. (c) reexamine and reform its system and practice of justice, (d) bring all prisoners, political and otherwise, who have not been tried to a prompt and fair trial, and (e) release the innocent, including those whose only offenses have been to peaceably speak out against the current government of South Vietnam on behalf of peace in Vietnam: (3) Characterizes the civilian prison assistance program carried out in South Vietnam by the United States Agency for International Development as (a) ineffectual, (b) counterproductive of the goals the United States seeks in Southeast Asia, and (c) in need of an immediate investigation;(4) and urges the President to initiate...such action...(a) impress upon the Government of South Vietnam that the United States does not and will not condone cruel and inhuman treatment of prisoners nor the system of justice being carried out under the 1968 An Tri Administrative Decree and that satisfactory and early resolution of these matters will be a strong factor in the determination of future United States Assistance to that Government (b) create emergency task forces...to meet crucial need for better living facilities for large numbers of civilian prisoners, and the dietary and health care of thousands of civilian prisoners, (c) cause prisons containing political prisoners in South Vietnam to be opened, no areas containing prisoners excluded, to impartial inspections by an appropriate independent international body, (d) emphasize to the Government of North Vietnam the forgoing action as additional clear proof of the concern of the United States for humane and fair treatment of all prisoners, (e) reiterates the demand of the Government of North Vietnam similarly demonstrate its concern by immediately conforming to all tenants of the Geneva Convention of 1949, which that Government signed in 1958, relative to the treatment of American and ally prisoners of War, including provisions for immediate impartial international inspection of all prisoner of war facilities, humane care, attendance to dietary and health care needs, free exchange of mail and packages between families and prisoners, and the prompt exchange of American and allied Prisoners of War held by North Vietnam and its allies with prisoners of War held in South Vietnam with priority release given to sick or injured prisoners and those who have endured long periods of confinements."

APPENDIX D
Representative Phillip Crane before House of Representatives
(*complete text*)

"Mr. Speaker, let me begin this discussion by disposing of two questions which were alluded to by several of my colleagues in yesterdays proceedings.

First, that I violated the standards of the House of Representatives and that I questioned the integrity of the distinguished gentlemen from California (Mr. Hawkins), I will simply and humbly repeat what I told that gentleman personally—there was certainly no personal affront intended, and that I do not question the motives or the integrity of the distinguished gentleman from California.

Second, that I singled out the distinguished gentleman from California for particularly harsh treatment, and that the gentleman from Tennessee (Mr. Anderson) was somehow -- intentionally or inadvertently -- ignored. My simple response is contained in the report of the Select Committee on U.S. involvement in Southeast Asia. In his supplementary views to that document, the gentleman from Tennessee notes that a detailed report of conditions is contained in the supplementary views of Congressman Hawkins. In the effort by members of Congress to investigate the question of possible inhumane or brutal treatment of prisoners in the prison at Con Son Island, it is virtually important for all of us that our attention is focused on that problem rather than personalities.

In this connection, we have previously heard the testimony of two of our colleagues who visited the prison on July 2. I visited the same prison twenty days later, and I can only report what I saw.

Permit me to focus for a moment on the attitude with which I embarked upon my visit to Con Son. My expectations were to a large extent based on what I had read in the Media (sic) that I now know to have been somewhat less than accurate. For example, I had read in the Economist that the tiger cages were "pits dug by the French." Imagine my surprise when the tiger cages turned out to be two story above-ground buildings -- not pits at all.

I had also seen photographs like the pair on page 27 of Life Magazine of July 17, 1970. Let me emphasize that this is a pair of photos -- virtually everyone with whom I have discussed this article had assumed them to be a single picture of a single cell housing seven inmates. In fact, they are 2 photos of separate cells with three and four inmates, respectively.

Another example is my distinguished colleague (Mr. Hawkins) has described the island as "remote." Actually, Con

TIGER CAGE: *An Untold Story*

Son is a weekend retreat from Saigon for both Vietnamese and American citizens who fish and swim off its lush, tropical shoreline, a mere fifty miles from the mainland.

The charges that have been made regarding conditions at Con Son Prison can be considered in two groups: those pertaining to physical conditions and those that have to do with the treatment of the prisoners. Let us examine them in turn. The "tiger-cages" had been reported to be cells of inadequate, filthy, stupefyingly hot, and lacking ventilation. The report of the five students who had been in the tiger cages at Con Son indicated rainwater poured into the cages through the tile roof.

According to Life Magazine, the July 2 visitors gained the impression that "all the prisoners were sick: with TB, open sores, eye diseases, and malnutrition."

It was reported that lime dust was used to quell rebellion on the part of prisoners. "The report of the Five Students" further tells us that they regularly sustained beatings, and were fed rice containing sand and pebbles. It has been further charged the prisoners were so paralyzed from being shackled few of them could stand. LIFE states they were forced to eat insects and the like.

It is extraordinary how different (sic) the conditions that I observed on my visit only 20 days later. I had the opportunity to inspect the tiger cages and "cow cages" which the earlier did not see. Permit me to describe what I saw.

The tiger cages measure five and one half feet in width, ten and a half feet in length, and ten feet from floor to ceiling. One enters each cell through a door at the ground level. There are no windows in the walls, but the bars are at the ceiling of the cell. Two-thirds of the cell at ground level is elevated approximately one foot.

It is on this platform that the prisoners sleep on straw mats. At the ground level in each cell is a small wooden box which serves as a latrine and is covered and emptied once a day. Anchored in the cement of the elevated platform is a metal bar almost flush with the platform. This is for manacling prisoners between the hours of 5 p.m. and 6:00 a.m. Col. Ve indicated that this is necessary for security reasons. After inspecting the doors to most cells, I concluded his concern for security was valid since a solid kick on most would open them.

It should be noted that none of the guards at Con Son Prison are armed and the prisoner/guard ratio is 100 to 1, in contrast to the Cook County, Illinois jail where the ratio is 7 to 1. The escape of these hard core Viet Cong prisoners from their cells could prove to be a real security threat.

Each cell, in addition, contains a bucket of water for laundering articles and for bathing. Clothes lines were strung in the cells where prisoners had laundered articles and they were hung to dry. Each prisoner had a flight bag containing personal belongings hanging from the walls, and there were other personal articles such as eating utensils, bowls, an embroidery work which is done by prisoners to sell to acquire money to buy special articles periodically from the Prison Canteen.

The walls of the prison are concrete, approximately one and half feet in thickness. Con Son Island is at 9 degrees North latitude. It is hot and humid most of the year. There is one rather large window at the second floor level for every two cells, and there are air spaces in the doors to the cells. At no place in the tiger cages does the sun hit the prisoners directly, although, there is ample diffused light throughout. Since the concrete walls, one and a half feet thick, would act as insulation against the heat, one can readily see that for the cells to be "stupefyingly hot" it would have to be more "stupefyingly hot" outside. I saw no evidence of filth on the floors of the cells. The walls had not been freshly repainted, but they were not particularly dirty, and there was even less foul odor than a Westerner detects in the rice fields of the mainland.

As for the condition of the prisoners themselves, I saw no evidence of malnutrition, no evidence of eye infection, no evidence of open sores with exception of one male prisoner with a small band aid on his cheek bone, and no paralysis of limbs except for one young girl who explained to me that her inability to use her limbs traced back to an incident antedating her arrival on the island of Con Son by six months. I saw all the women prisoners -- over 300 of the them -- and approximately fifty of the men. The later are now all housed in the "cow cages." I saw no prisoners with any evidence of beatings, and none of the prisoners I spoke to mentioned anything about physical beatings. I saw no prisoners with evidence of bruises or abrasions on ankles or wrists from manacles.

The cow cages are so called because they are in close proximity to a cattle feeding shed. They are square rooms measuring 12 x 12. There are no ceilings on these rooms, but the ceilings space is covered with a taut barbed wire at the elevation of approximately 8 feet. This is to permit maximum ventilation between ceiling level and the rafters of the roof. Each cell has one window near the ceiling measuring approximately 3 x 2 feet that is boarded and looks out upon the yard in front of the building. These buildings were also of concrete.

There were eight prisoners in each of the cow cages cells I visited. All of the prisoners appeared to be in good health and not undernourished. In fact, clad as most of them were in undershorts, it was apparent that some of them carried excess weight. I have photos available taken inside the cells of prisoners that will verify this point. I am in no more position to comment on the alleged mistreatment of prisoners based upon hearsay then are those that visited the prison on July 2nd of this year. I can, however, comment on both the condition of the cells and the condition of the prisoners, of course, observable to me.

A question arose in my mind during my visit as to the possibility that a different set of prisoners had been moved into the cells than those who had been there on July 2nd. There are approximately 9500 prisoners on the island, slightly over 300 of whom are women.

Since the U.S. Navy patrols the waterways between Con Son Island and the mainland, a distance of approximately fifty miles; and since the island is dependent upon the U.S. government for air transportation; and since the transportation of the 300 hundred odd women from Chi Hoa Prison to Con Son eight months ago represented a rather major logistical problem; I cannot conceive there has been a switch of the 300 odd women who were there on July 2nd with 300 others during the time that elapsed between July 2 and July 22.

In addition our Aid Officials, Mr. Frank Walton and Mr. Randolph Berkeley, who accompanied my colleagues on their visit on July 2 and myself on July 22, and in the interim made other visits to the island to inspect the tiger cages and cow cages, testified to the fact that they recognized prisoners who were there during all of their visits.

Donald Luce, the journalist who acted as translator to the two members of the Select Committee, has since written to my distinguished colleague from California. He accurately states why it would have been very difficult for the South Vietnamese government to change prisoners: I think we can be sure the press here will carefully watch prison conditions.

With a vigilant press, and a large logistic problem involved, and with the eye witness accounts of various officials, I believe it highly unlikely that a change of prisoners could have taken place. If any suggestion is made that a change did take place, the burden of proof should fall on those who maintain that a switch was made. Permit me to call to the attention of my colleagues the distinguished backgrounds of the two gentlemen who direct the U.S. activity in this area:

Mr. Frank E. Walton is serving his second tour of duty as Chief Public Safety Advisor to Vietnam and the Agency for International Development, having served in that capacity from 1959 to 1964 and having returned to that post in April of 1969, after an interim assignment as Chief of the Vietnam Division of the Office of Public Safety, AID, Washington, D.C.

Mr. Walton came to Federal Government Service after serving 23 years with the Los Angeles Police Department and the Los Angeles County Sheriffs' Office as a Law Enforcement Officer (sic) in all phases of police operations, training, supervision, administration, and corrections. He holds a B.S. in Police

Science and Administration and an M.S. in Government. His experience included two years in command of the Los Angeles Police Training Academy with time as Deputy Chief for Corrections for Los Angeles County.

Randolph C. Berkeley, Junior., The Chief of the Correction and Detention Branch, Public Safety Directorate, of the Agency for International Development in Saigon, is a retired career Marine Corps Colonel who entered on active duty with the Marines directly upon his graduation from the United States Naval Academy in 1938. He served in increasingly responsible posts, being assigned to Cherry Point and Camp Lajune, N.C., as Chief of Staff and Commanding Officer in 1958 and rising to the top intelligence position at Marine Corps Headquarters, Washington, D.C., in 1961, which post he held at the time of his retirement from active duty in 1965. His varied experience throughout his Marine Corps career including command and intelligence and counterintelligence assignments in the early 1960's, and command aviation assignments throughout the 1950's, makes him uniquely qualified for the Administrative Duties (sic) involved in overseeing The Prisoner Detention and Correction Program in South Vietnam.

A part of the debate on this issue apparently centers on the credibility of their testimony. It strikes me as not all together proper to draw conclusions as to the conditions of Con Son Island without having had the advantage of talking to these two gentlemen who were eye witnesses during the July 2nd visit as well as the July 22nd visit. In addition to these gentlemen, three other Americans accompanied me on my visit to the prison: Mr. James Nach, Embassy Political Officer, Lieutenant Carl Mallet, US Navy, and Specialist Hill, who took photographs of the prison during my entire visit. These are unusually clear and detailed pictures of both the "tiger" and "cow" cages, and of other parts of the prison.

The prisoners in these cells at Con Son are there, according to the testimony of Lieutenant Colonel Nguyen Van Ve, and by the admission of thirty-two whom I interviewed, for two reasons: first, they were imprisoned under the An Tri Law of the Vietnamese Government, which enables the Government of Saigon, working through provincial Security Committees at the local level, to jail Vietnamese citizens suspected of Viet Cong-National Liberation Front-Associations for a period of two years and reserves to the Government the power to secure extensions at the convenience of the Government.

Second, there is rule at Con Son Prison that all prisoners must salute the flag of the Government of South Vietnam. The prisoners in the tiger cages and "cow cages" had refused to do this. There is a third point that should be mentioned about the women prisoners at Con Son: They had instigated a riot in the

Prison of Chi Hoa in Saigon eight months earlier, which was the immediate cause for their transfer to Con Son.

I think it is important to realize in this context that I spent approximately two and a half hours talking to prisoners in the tiger cages and cow cages in contrast to the one-half hour spent by the earlier delegation. This means I had five times a greater period in which to interrogate prisoners. I indicated to the prisoners that I was not a representative of the American military, but rather a representative of the U.S. Government. I encouraged them to talk, but I did not ask specific questions that might be considered loaded.

I had the services of three interpreters -- one American and two Vietnamese Nationals -- rather than a single source. All of those to whom I spoke acknowledged membership in the National Liberation Front and were proud of that fact. The major preoccupation of each of the thirty-two prisoners to whom I spoke was politics. All of them indicated their opposition to the Government of South Vietnam. They were also critical of the United States for providing Military Support to South Vietnam against both National Liberation Front and the Government of North Vietnam. Several prisoners, indicated their loyalty to the Government of North Vietnam.

On the second point, one may reasonably question Col. Ve's insistence all prisoners on Con Son salute the flag. Still, all prisons have their rules, and non- conformity to this rule by any prisoner would result in his transfer out of either the tiger cages or the cow cages. The action of defiance of this particular regulation at Con Son by prisoners in the isolation cells was a voluntary one. In the interviews I had with 20 women and 12 male prisoners, they took pride in their refusal to honor the flag representing a Government they view as iniquitous.

Specifically regarding the women prisoners, their attempts to generate a prison riot at Chi Hoa -- near Saigon -- provide yet another evidence of their commitment to offer as much resistance as a prisoner can to his captor. Resistance, of course, is the prerogative of any prisoner. But, as I said, it was for this action the women were transferred to Con Son Island.

Some of the prisoners indicated their displeasure with the prison diet. The eighteen-year old English-speaking girl showed me some dried fish she had in a small plastic bag as proof of the unpalatably of the prison fare. However, the dried fish she produced was the same type of dried fish I saw prisoners in Camp Four, outside the tiger cage and cow cage areas, eating with their rice. Some prisoners indicated that prior to two weeks before my visit they did not have enough water for bathing, this had been corrected. None of the prisoners mentioned insufficiency of drinking water.

Quite sufficiently, I believe, not a single prisoner raised the question of the use of lime dust to quell unruly prisoners. The use of lime dust, I have been informed, is not novel in that area of the world. It is in fact, apparently a cheap substitute for tear gas as we use in the United States and is considered preferable because it can be localized more effectively than tear gas.

When I spoke to the attractive eighteen-year-old-English-speaking woman previously mentioned, a self admitted member of the National Liberation Front, she explained to me that she was an idealist, which she viewed the Government in Saigon as oppressive, and that she had been jailed without trial by that Government, and therefore, would not honor the flag of that Government. I explained to her that one must pay a price for such idealism and, in this instance, the price was confinement in her isolation cell. She acknowledged to me that she had obeyed certain rules as a Member of the National Liberation Front. I pointed out to her that we all live under rules, and that now she was in a position that she had to obey the rules of Con Son Prison or else continue her defiance within the confines of her isolation cell. She indicated to me that she preferred to carry on her private war in this manner, which is her choice.

The question legitimately arises as to whether there was not an attempt by the prison authorities to clean conditions up between July 2 and July 22 when I visited. In response to that suggestion, let me offer the following:

First, virtually the only physical change in the cells that could have occurred in that interim was that the floors could have been swept. There was no evidence, as I indicated earlier, of fresh paint or white wash on the walls.   The cells could not have been made noticeably cooler. Regarding the condition of the prisoners, their reported malnutrition could not be cured in less than three weeks. Open sores cannot be healed in less than three weeks and paralysis of limbs can not me remedied in less than three weeks.

As for the reported TB cases, I saw approximately sixteen women in the Dispensary across the yard from the barracks containing the tiger cages, all of whom were suffering from TB, all of whom are under treatment, and all of whom are seen by a Doctor on a weekly basis. I examined the records of the Orderly in charge of requisitioning and dispensing medicine for the tiger cages. His books are well kept and entries made every ten days. I inspected entries for the last eight months. He indicated that there are some shortages of medicines, especially streptomycin and penicillin, but examinations of his books revealed that approximately 90% of needed supplies was routinely filled and that the 10% shortage, I suspect, is true throughout most of South Vietnam.

The An Tri (sic) Law offends the sensibility of most Americans. But it must be recognized that every government reserves onto itself the right to protect itself against destruction. In our own Constitution, under Article One, Section Nine, the denial of writ of habeas corpus is permitted in times of internal insurrection or external aggression. Under this provision of the United States Constitution, President Abraham Lincoln made thousands of political arrests without benefit of counsel and without benefit of trial during the Civil War.

More recently, in the memory of most of those here present, during a time of emergency, we arrested the entire Japanese population of our Nation not because of any suspension of individuals, but simply because they were Japanese.

This is not to say that Americans look back on either one of these examples with pride; it does, however, suggest that during times of National Emergency, when the Nation has been under attack, we have resorted to the exercise of this prerogative, which governments have always claimed, and we are not in a very good position to describe actions of this sort (as) characteristic of totalitarian dictatorships, not democratic societies.

No one denies that there are any number of innocent individuals who suffered in the United States by these actions, and there are undoubtedly instances in South Vietnam today where innocents have been jailed under the An Tri Law. But when one considers that the government of South Vietnam has been under constant attack since 1956, and when one considers further the people of South Vietnam have had fourteen years experience at self government instead of several centuries, it is not reasonable to condemn the South Vietnamese Government for an action in our own recent past exercised by a government "of the people, by the people, for the people."

I will publicly state that if LIFE MAGAZINE is so inclined, it can pay me $10,000, the sum reportedly paid to Mr. Tom Harkin, for my more distinct and superior photographs taken on July 22, and that I will in turn contribute that $10,000 to the purchase of streptomycin and penicillin for the prisoners on Con Son Island.

Mr. Harkin informed the Congressional Committee when they requested the photographs he took of the tiger cages that he would not give them up because he had a "higher obligation to those five hundred human beings who are in jammed into those cages."

I submit that Mr. Harkin's humanitarian instincts would find their greatest gratification in joining with me in this worthy effort by contributing his $10,000 to the purchase of medicine and food for the prisoners. Surely, considering the fact that there is always suffering in any prison system, Con Son not excluded, no one would want to make pecuniary gain from the misfortune of others.

In conclusion, Mr. Speaker, permit me to make the following observations:

First, the An Tri (sic) Law may be a serious restriction on individual rights as we in America know them, but the war in Vietnam is serious too. Clearly, this law has precedence throughout the history of democracies including our own.

Second. If conditions at the South Vietnamese prisons need improving, and I believe they do, let us constructively suggest how they might best be performed without indicting a whole government and a whole people who are trying, under very adverse circumstances, to build a viable democracy.

Third. Those who would encourage the United States to exercise still more influence over the South Vietnamese Governments' (sic) action--such as my distinguished colleague from Tennessee does--should realize they cannot have it both ways. If the United States is to disengage and "Vietnamize" the war-- as I believe it should--it will have less and less influence over the actions of the South Vietnamese Government.

In other words, we cannot have a disengagement and a "puppet" government in Saigon -- at the same time.

I have not attempted to white wash conditions at Con Son Prison. I went there, after hearing the reports made by earlier visitors, expecting the worst. I was most surprised at what I saw. In fact, it made me -- caused me to consider the possibility of a rotation of prisoners for show.

It was only after realizing this would have been impossible with the female prisoners and at least unlikely with the men that I felt compelled to elaborate on the conditions I found. I do not presume to do so in any official capacity. I went to Con Son, and I have reported what I saw at Con Son Prison, as an American citizen concerned with the cause of full information and of the truth be served."

TIGER CAGE: *An Untold Story*

BIBLIOGRAPHY

The following letters, memos, talking papers, fact sheets, news clippings, reports, and original documents are the chronological map of several thousand pages used by the authors in researching this book. Most of this data is one-of-a-kind, originals and/or official copies of original writings.

The U.S. Government shredded, or the Vietnamese Communist Government destroyed, other copies of these documents at war's end, except for those materials and documents which were forwarded to the United States Naval Academy Archives. The completeness or content of material housed at that facility is not known to us.

The information listed here is part of the Bordenkircher Family Collection which has been catalogued by and is maintained by West Liberty State College Library, West Liberty, West Virginia. The Bordenkircher's retain ownership & proprietary interest in all materials of the family collection currently housed at the college.

1. OPS/V, "Talking Papers," 5 pages, Frank Walton, 1966.
2. OPS Program Assessment," Letter to Charles Mann from Sir Robert Thompson, 3/8/66, 14 pages.
3. "Province Names With Literal English Translations," USAID, 5/16/66, 2 pages.
4. "A Report On The Manner In Which Political Prisoners are Processed in the Field," R. Lowe to USAID, 5 pgs 7/13/66
5. National Review, James Burnham, "Hanoi's Special Weapons System," 9/9/66, page 75.
6. Department of State Bulletin, "Harriman to Supervise U. S. Actions on POWS in Vietnam, Pg 88.
7. Newsweek, 8/15/66, Page 32, Prisoners of War," Kenneth Crawford.
8. National Observer, 5/1/67, "The Situation in Vietnam-Changing the Old Guard at a Fortress Embassy," Wesley Pruden
9. "Text of Ambassador Bunker's Statement at Press Conference," 4 pages, 5/11/67.
10. Information Notes, "Prisoners of War," Department of State, 8 pg, US Government Printing Office
11. "Berkeley's Analysis of Ambassador Locke's Memo on ICEX," 27 pgs, 8/17/67.
12. Evan J. Parker to Chief of CORDS, "Crash Screening and Detention Systems Proposal," 2 pages, September 25, 1967
13. L. Wade Lathram to Randolph Berkeley, "Plan for Restraint Facilities for Civilian Detainees in Vietnam, 3 pgs, 10/26/67
14. Berkeley Memo, "Listing of SIDE Conference Attendees," 11/28/67.
15. Berkeley, "Brief Resume of SIDE Activities in November," 12/5/67.
16. Berkeley, "Key Issues of SIDE and Dates of Occurrence 12/67," 17. "Office of Public Safety Casualty Summary," 12/67.
18. "South Vietnamese Life tables for 1967," Saigon 1967 Demographic Survey.
19. Photograph-General Loan Executes Viet Cong Officer, 2/1/68
20. Berkeley to Director ICEX, "Confusion In American Effort in Saigon," 2/5/68.
21. Information Notes "Basic Data-South Vietnam," Department of State, 4 pages, U. S. Government Printing Office, 4/1/68
22. General Cao Van Vien Memo to Each Corps -"Counter Attack on Correction Centers," 4/12/68.
23. Randolph Berkeley Memo to William Colby, "Correction and Detention Matters W/Monthly Report," 4/23/68, 8 pages.
24. Bordenkircher to Berkeley, "Correction's Budget Matters," 2 pgs, 4/23/68.
25. Washington Post, Stanley Karnow, 6/11/68, "Attacks on Saigon Called a Threat to Peace Talks."
26. News articles, "Political Bill Gains In Saigon," Nguyen Ngoc Rao, "Westmoreland Leaves Vietnam for New Port," UPI, 6/11/68.

27. "Handbook on Legal Processing of National Security Offenders," D. E. Bordenkircher, C&D/PSD, 7/1/68.
28. Presidential Decree, #280-a/TT/SL, 7/1/68, Establishment of Phoung Hoang
29. Ministry of Interior Circular #757-BNV/CT/13-A/M, 3/21/69, "Classification and Rehabilitation of Offenders."
30. Ministry of Interior Circular #2212-BNV/CT/13-A/M, 8/20/69, Improvements of the Methods of Resolving the Status of Offenders
31. Directorate General National Police Service #1229/TCSQG DTTTU/CG, 1/12/70, "Preparation and Processing of Arrest Report, Police Disposition Report, Name Index Cards, & Fingerprint Cards for Persons Detained by National Police."
32. Central PHUNG HOANG Permanent Office Circular #00401/ UBPH/TU/ UPTT/NK, April 21, 1970, "To Give Village Authorities Information on the Situation of the Persons Arrested by PHOUNG HOANG Operations"
33. Central Pacification and Development Council Circular #1206-PThT/BDPT/ HC, 4/24/70, "Phases of Interrogation and Procedures Applied to Arrested Cadres"
34. Central Pacification and Development Council Circular #1440/PThT/BDPT/ KH, 5/13/70, "The Public Prosecutor's Role in Pacification and Development"
35. Prime Ministerial Circular #105-TT/ThT/PCI/1, 5 June 1970, "Handling of Persons Captured During Operations"
36. Central Pacification & Development Council Circular #1082/UBPH/ TU/ VPTT/NH/K, 10 August 1970, "Utilization of VCI Target Folder"
37. Ministry of Interior Circular #2238-BNV/ANNCT/I/A/M, 24 August 1970, "Processing of Communist Offenders"
38. "PHOUNG HOANG SOP 3," 1 February 1970.
39. Handbook, "Current Breakout of VCI Executive and Significant Cadre," (Short title: "Green Book").
40. USAID Briefing Paper "Police Assistance as an Instrument of Foreign Police," 10 pgs, Nov. 1968
41. P. L. Severson to ACOFS/CORDS, "Police Detention Program," 4 pgs, 1/23/69.
42. Bordenkircher Memo to Berkeley, RE: Saigon Daily News Article "Con Son Sinking Into Oblivion," 4 pages, 1/24/69
43. OPS Fact Sheet, 1 page, 1/28/69,"Public Safety Program-Vietnam".
44. Berkeley Memo to ACOFS/CORDS & Chief of Staff, "Recommending DEPCORDS visit to Con Son, 3 pages, 2/10/69
45. Colby to Berkeley, "Concern of LTC. Ve's Press Briefing," 2/14/65, 18 pgs
46. The Christian Century, Don Luce, "Behind Vietnam's Prison Walls", 3 pgs 2/19/69.
47. Bordenkircher to Berkeley, "A View of the RVN Correction System," 10 pgs, 2/24/69
48. Berkeley to Gen. Long for Chief of Staff, "Transmitting International Red Cross Report on Con Son", 8 pgs, 3/13/69.
49. Manopoli to Bordenkircher transmits "Vietnam Civilian Award," 3/24/69.
50. Berkeley to Colby, "Proposal for Establishment of Ministry of HOI CAI & HOI CAI Directorate," 21 pgs, 5/1/69.
51. Inspector Quang to DOC, Nguyen Phu Sanh, "Congressional/ Religious Delegation visit to Con Son," 4 pgs, 6/3/69.
52. U. S. Study Team on Religious and Political Freedom In Vietnam -"Findings on Trip to Vietnam 5/5/69-6/10/69, for the Congressional Record," 16 pages.
53. Bordenkircher performance evaluation report. July 1969.
54. Washington Post, "Viet Experts Think the Unthinkable", Murray Marder, 7/13/69.
55. Berkeley Memo to C&D Branch, "Thanks for a Job Well Done," 7/22/69.
56. Gen. Long to Colby, "Trip to Hong Kong & Taiwan by MACV/CORDS Psychological Operations Research Group," 3 pgs, 8/3/69
57. List of Chinese Officers Who Organized PSYOPS Conferences, 8/3/69.
58. Bordenkircher to Berkeley, "Reference Materials on Status of SVN DOC, 5 pgs, 8/7/69.
59. General Long to Colby, "Hau Nghia Detention Facility Construction,"

9/25/69.

60. Berkeley to Walton, "Problems with Colonel Ve and Colonel Sanh," 10/28/69.

61. News Release, UPI, "Vietnam Expert (Don Luce) to Speak", 11/6/69.

62. DOC Prisoner Population Count, 11/26/69, Bordenkircher.

63. McPhie to Berkeley, "Transfer of 342 Female Prisoners to Con Son," 12/28/69.

64. Berkeley to Colby, "Movement of Female Prisoners to Con Son," 11/28/69.

65. Colby to Bordenkircher, 12/19/69, "Appreciation for a Job Well Done".

66. Walton to Engle, "1969 A Year of Progress," 12/11/69.

67. Los Angeles Juries RE: Walton; "Viet Police Developing High Skills," by Arthur Dommer, 12/15/69.

68. Bordenkircher's performance evaluation report, 1970.

69. Engle to Bordenkircher, "Thanks for Job Well Done," December 25, 1969

70. List of all OPS advisors assigned to Vietnam, 1/1/70.

71. OPS/VN Fact Sheet, 1/1/70, "SVN Internal Security Capabilities.

72. OPS Fact Sheet "Public Safety Program Vietnam," 1/8/70.

73. OPS Fact Sheet, "Indicators of Progress," 1/9/70.

74. Bordenkircher to Colby, "Study Team on Religious and Political Freedom in Vietnam," 1/17/70.

75. OPS "Correction Program Fact Sheet," 1/21/70.

76. Walton OPS Reporting Fact Sheets to Colby for use before the Senate Foreign Relations Committee, 1/22/70, 96 pgs.

77. French Press Agency, "Con Son Island Prison Report," 1/23/70.

78. Missions and Tasks Report, C&D Division, OPS, 1/3/70.

79. Monthly Report of the Detention Branch, G&D/OPS, 1/5/70,

80. Bordenkircher Fact Sheet, "Correction Center Space," 1/5/70,

81. "Projects Status and Accomplishment Reports," OPS to Colby, 2/1/70. (DSAR).

82. Bordenkircher Memo to Walton, "Con Son Civic Education Program," 2/12/70.

83. USAID, "Field Trip to Con Son Island Report," 3/27/70, 5 pgs, Program Review.

84. OPS Fact Sheet, "Corrections & Jail Administration Program," 4/24/70.

85. Berkeley to Colby, "Progress Report on Con San Civic Education Program," 5 pgs, 4/29/70.

86. Seniority Listing of OPS/VN Personnel, 5/1/70.

87. Col. Sanh to Ministry of Justice, "Request for Mobile Court to go to Con Son; RE: Unsentenced Women," 5/4/70.

88. Berkeley to Bordenkircher, "Exemplary Performance of Duty and South Vietnamese Administration Medal, First Class," 5/5/70.

89. Major Ellis report on visit to Tay Ninh Correctional Center. 5/17/70.

90. "Project Appraisal Report for the Correction Center Project," USAID, 120 pgs, 6/15/70.

91. Berkeley to Colby (DEPCORDS) transmits names & written allegations of five students, & CONDEL visit to Con Son on 7/2/70, assisted by Don Luce, 7 pages.

92. "The Tiger Cages of Con Son," Don Luce, Publisher, World Council of Churches, Geneva, Switzerland, 9 pages, 7/3/70.

93. Berkeley Memo, "Passenger list for CONDEL Con Son Flight of 2 July 70," 7/3/70.

94. To Ministry of Interior No. 369/TTCH/CS/VPK/HT, 1430 hours, 7/2/70, (Permission CONDEL to talk to 6 prisoners).

95. Berkeley Fact Sheet, 7/4/70, "Chronological Sequence of Events-CONDEL Visit to Con Son on 7/2/70." Sent to Colby.

96. Berkeley Memo to Vice President Spiro Agnew Suggesting His Visit to Con Son Island, 7/7/70

97. Secor to Colonel Sanh "Maximum Security Areas on Con Son," 2 pages, 7/6/70.

98. Berkeley to Secor "Tiger Cage Problem Areas", 4 pgs, 7/6/70.

99. Berkeley's Working Papers on Con Son, 8 pages, 7/6/70.

100. New York Times, 7/7/70, Gloria Emerson , "Americans Find Brutality in South Vietnamese Jail."
101. William J. Burns to Frank Walton about Con Son, 7/7/70.
102. Transcript tape-recorded visit 7/2/70 of CONDEL to Con Son, U. S. House of Representatives, 22 pages, 7/7/70.
103. Minister of Interior Press Release, 7/8/70, "Re: Rehabilitation Policy of South Vietnam," 4 pgs.
104. Berkeley Fact Sheet to W. Colby, "Con Son National ... Center," 43 pgs, 7/7/70.
105. Washington Evening Star, 7/7/70, "House Aide Quits," by Robert Walters
106. Washington Post, 7/7/70, George C. Wilson, "S. Viet Prison Found Shocking."
107. New York Times, Juan M. Vasquez, "House Units Report On Vietnam Termed `Washed' by Aide.," 9/8/70.
108. Frank E. Walton, "Backgrounder for Embassy Press Conference on Con Son," 7/9/70.
109. Washington Evening Star, 7/9/70, "Tiger Cage Horror Related," Raymond Coffey.
110. Washington Post, 7/9/70, "Tiger Cages at Con Son," Unknown.
111. Arthur Hargrave letter to Congressman Hawkins, 7/8/70.
112. Compilation of news items regarding Con Son, 7/9/70-7/13/70.
113. Letter sent from Dr. Marjorie Nelson to Rep. Hawkins, 7/10/70, 3 pgs
114. Berkeley Memo, 7 pgs, "Partial compilation of allegations From Official statements & press releases about Con Son," 7/11/70.
115. Secor to Colby, "Movement of Prisoners from Con Son to Saigon," 7/13/70.
116. Concurrent Resolution, U.S. House, No. 677, 7/13/70, "Condemns Treatment of Civilian Prisoners in South Vietnam."
117. Concurrent Resolution, U.S. Senate No. 74, 7/14/70, "Condemns Treatment of Civilian Prisoners in South Vietnam."
118. New York Times, 7/15/70, "500 from Con Son Flown to Saigon."
119. Washington Evening Star, 7/15/70, "Muskie Hits Con Son Prison."
120. Berkeley Memo, "Con Son Events," 7/15/70, 3 pgs.
121. Secor Memo to Berkeley, "Tiger Cages on Con Son Island," 7/16/70
122. Joint Report of MOI/DOC "Inspection of Con Son" to GVN MOI, 7/17/70.
123. New York Times, 7/17/70, UPI, "Letter Charges Torture at Second Vietnamese Prison."
124. Life, 7/17/70, Ralph Graves, "How They Unearthed the Tiger Cages."
125. Baltimore Sun, 7/18/70, Gene Oskie, "Doctor describes Torture at Viet Interrogation Center."
126. The Washington Daily News, 7/18)70, Ray Cromley, "Con Son's Brutality."
127. St. Louis Daily Record, 7/18/70, Andrew Tully, "Vietnam-U.S. Money Down A Rat Hole."
128. New York Times, 7/19/70, Gloria Emerson, "'Tailor Relieves Con Son Ordeal."
129. Major Mirola Fact Sheet To F. Walton, 7/19/70, "Viet Cong Attacks on correctional centers."
130. Time, 7/20/70, "Vietnam -The Cages of Con Son Island."
131. Washington Post, 7/21/70, "Con Son and Salvaging The Truth," George Wilson.
132. Geneva, AP, International Red Cross "Inspections of Con Son Correctional Camps."
133. LTC. Ramon Sloan Memo to F. Walton, 7/21/70, "Interview Of American Society of Friends (Quakers)/ Quang Ngai."
134. Prime Minister South Vietnam Press Release, 7/21/70, "Con Son and Other correctional centers."
135. Congressional Record -volume 116-Part 19, July 21, 1970 -July 29, 1970 -Pages 2551355-26488, "Congressman Crane Reports on Con Son."
136. New York Times, 7/22/70, James Sterba, "Vietnam to Alter Tiger Cage Cells."
137. New York Times, 7/25/70, Red Cross on "POW Treatment in Con Son Prison," Robert M. Smith.

138. Chicago Tribune, 7/24/70, Press Service, "Congressman Raps Viet Prison Critics."
139. Louisville Courier Journal, editorial, 7/24/70, "Let Walton Tell Us About Con Son."
140. Sam Pesacreta Memo to Byron Engle, 7/24/70, "Coverage of Rep. Phillip Crane's press Conference about Con Son."
141. Berkeley to Walton, 7/25/70, "GVN Ineptitude in Handling of the Con Son Crisis."
142. Walton Fact Sheet, 7/27/70, Revised: "Sector Discussion Paper of Public Safety."
143. Bordenkircher listing, by name, of each POW on Con Son Island as of 27 July 70.
144. Congressional Record -House -7/22/70, "Question of Personal Privilege" Hawkins vs. Crane regarding Con Son Island."
145. National Review , 7/28/70, "Prisoners and Prisoners."
146. Chicago Tribune, 7/28/70, Capitol Views, "Chalk up another Hard Lesson ," Willard Edwards.
147. Congressional Record, Vol. 116, No. 129, 7/29/70, "Congressman Crane Reports on Con Son."
148. Manopoli Memo to F. Walton, "Con Son Prison and South Vietnam's Corrections System," 7/29/70.
149. R.H. Nooter, USAID/V, letter To J. Munroe, OPS/W, "Seven Responses To Inquiry of the Moss Committee," 7/29/70.
150. Geneva, 7/30/70, "Red Cross Limited In Visit Con Son."
151. Hard Times Aug. 10/17/70, # 85, Joe Stork, "AID'S Office of Public Safety," 14 pgs.
152. Berkeley Memo to W. Colby, August 1, 1970, "Provides a Synopsis of the CONDEL Con Son visits and their aftermath."
153. Press Release, Rep. William L. Dickenson, Alabama, 8/5/70, "Con Son Island."
154. Memorandum of conversation, 8/7/70 between Minister of Justice, Le Van Thu & Wm. Colby, 15 pgs, "Concerning Con Son An Tri Sentencing."
155. Miscellaneous personal letters to Frank Walton, 8/10/70, from COMUS/ MCV (Commanding Officer Military United States/Military Command-Vietnam)
156. OPS Fact Sheet, "The US Corrections and Detention Advisory Programs in Vietnam," 8/7/70.
157. Congressional Record, E7522, 8/11/70, "Facts on Con Son Prison," Fatr Daniel Lyons
158. Colby to Ambbassador Bunker "Background Information on Con Son." 8/12/70, 15 pages
159. Berkeley Memo to McPhie, 8/13/70, "Preparation for Walton appearance in Washington before Moss Committee."
160. Berkeley to Walton, 8/13/70, "Status of UN/US Investigation of Tiger Cage Matters."
161. American Embassy Memo to F. Walton, 8/14/70, "More Tiger Cage Allegations" from Gong Luan Newspaper.
162. Leland McPhie to Walton, 8/14/70, "Correction/Detention Division Monthly Report."
163. Human Events, August 15, 1970, "What I Saw at Con Son," by Phillip M. Crane.
164. San Francisco Examiner, 8/18/70, AP wire service, "New Tiger Cages At Con Son."
165. Los Angeles Herald-Examiner 7/28/70, "Tiger Cage Report not true, says Congressman."
166. Embassy Cable 1915, State 135976, "Students say Government Leaders Reneging on Promise to Destroy Tiger Cages."
167. Secor to Berkeley Memo, 6/20/70. "Tiger Cages."
168. GAO Request info on "500 prisoners moved from Con Son to Saigon," 8/21/70.
169. Berkeley to Sanh, 8/21/70, "Request Frank Bormann visit Con Son Island."
170. Sworn statement of Frank Walton to Elwood Martin, General Accounting

Office, "Correction/Detention Program," 8/21/70.
171. Berkeley to Colby to Gen. Khiem, 10/21/70, "Adverse Publicity on Con Son."
172. Mirolla to Berkeley, 8/24/70, "Trip Report To Thu Duc."
173. Berkeley Memo to Walton, 8/24/70, "Trip to Con Son."
174. Colonel Brigand, Memo to Chief of Staff, 8/24/70, "GAO Investigation into Con Son Island Transfer of Prisoners."
175. Embassy To Secretary of State, 8/24/70, No. 13675 "Status of 'Tiger Cages'"
176. Berkeley to Walton, 8/24/70, "Report of Disturbance at Thu Duc Correction Center."
177. Chester Taylor to Walton, 8/25/70, "Keep up good work"
178. Tinsang News, 8/26/70, "Representatives Kiev Mong Thu denounces Col. Ve."
179. LTC. Sloan to Walton, 8/26/70, "Confinement Facilities for U.S. Forces Prisoners."
180. Prime Minister to III Corps Commander, No.633/ BDPT3/KH/45, 8/28/70, "Special Support for Con Son Island Administration."
181. Washington Post, 8/31/70, Jack Anderson, "Prisoners Tortured in SV Jails."
182. Berkeley Presentation to 44 province Public Safety Advisors, 8/31/70, 4 pgs.
183. UPI Cable, 8/31/70, Astronaut Frank Bormann visit to Con Son Island.
184. Embassy Cable to Secretary of State, 13201, 8/31/70, "Public Safety Funding Assistance to South Vietnam."
185. UPI Saigon, 9/1/70, "40 POW's Escape Pho Quoc Island,"
186. U.S. Embassy cable to State Department, 9/2/70, "Vietnamese Prisons/ New Students Report."
187. Smith to Walton, 9/4/70, "Moss Subcommittee Members."
188. Berkeley to McCann/Manopoli, 9/12/70, "Priorities in Work Assignments."
189. Berkeley Fact Sheet, 9/13/70, "Historical View of Struggle to Obtain OPS/C&D Personnel."
190. McCann to Berkeley, 9/21/70, "PSD Meeting-RE:Con Son."
191. House Of Representatives, 9/22/70, "Speech of Frank Bormann to Joint Meeting of the Two Houses Of Congress."
192. Berkeley Memo to Walton:, 9/24/70, "Don Luce."
193. C&D Fact Sheet, 9/24/70, "Correction Facilities Visited by C&D Advisors"
194. Saigon News Dispatch, 9/25/70, Michael Morrow, "Two Officials of Viet Corrections Speak Out."
195. Bordenkircher Memo to Director of Correction, 10/12/70, "Establishment of National Correction Reformatory Units."
196. Saigon News Service, a Letter from Don Luce, 10/20/70.
197. Berkeley to Walton, 10/19/70, "The Critical Situation In the Corrections System as Regards Brutality and The Treatment of Prisoners."
198. OPS Fact Sheet, 10/21/70, "Vietnam PSO Seniority Listing."
199. Bordenkircher to Walton, 10/27/70, "Quaker Report-Quang Nqai."
200. The Progressive, 10/27/70, Tom Harkin, "The Congressional Jury that Convicted Itself,"
201. Bordenkircher to Colby, 11/1/70, "GVN Inter/Ministry Support of DOC - Con Son."
202. C&D Fact Sheet, Bordenkircher, 11/2/70, "Correction Centers Project - -Inmate Welfare."
203. Firnstahl to Walton, 11/1/70, typed poem "Advisors Lament."
204. Bordenkircher to Berkeley, 11/2/70, "Prisoners In Turmoil -Personal Viewpoint."
205. Secor Memo to Berkeley, 11/9/70, "Allegations of Brutality and Torture in Correction Centers."
206. Time, 11/1/70, "Print and Be Seized."
207. O. Gordon Young to Berkeley, 11/13/70, "Preliminary Report on Con Son Resources."

208. Newsweek, 11/30/70, "Hanoi's Pawns: The Prisoner of War."
209. Fact Sheet, Bordenkircher, 12/2/70, "Internal Security Problem Areas in C&D Relative to Phoenix."
210. New York Times, 12/3/70, "Riot in Women's Prison In South Vietnam Reported."
211. Bordenkircher, Fact Sheet, 12/11/70, "Correction and Detention Facilities."
212. The Overseas Weekly, 12/12/70, Jack Anderson, "The Struggle For Status."
213. Secor to Berkeley, 12/17/70, "Incident Involving U.S. Citizens held in Chi Hoa Correction Center." (Bordenkircher defusing situation -precipitating 2nd medal & letter "job well done."
214. U.S. News & World Report, 12/21/70, "Growing Menace to Vietnam: Red Spies in the South."
215. John Meyers to Berkeley, 12/28/70, "Con Son Correction Center Update."
216. T. F. Oberlein Memo to Walton, 12/28/70, "Inspection/Evaluation of Construction Projects at Con Son."
217. Project Status & Accomplishments Report, 1970, Correction Centers 730-11-710-753   218. Correction & Detention Division End of Year Report-1968-70.
219. U.S. EMBASSY Memo, 1/1/71, "Chronology of Events Leading to GVN Refusal to Review Press Card of Don Luce."
220. Berkeley Cable to Secretary of State, 1/1/71, "Status of Con Son." 40 pgs.
221. Walton Memo to W. Colby, 1/6/71, "Capacities & Populations of the GVN Corrections and Detention Systems," 20 pgs. 222. Walton Memo to Colby, 1/14/71, "Reporting System To Minister Review Parole Release System." 15 pgs.
223. Berkeley Memo to Walton, 2/1/71, "History of the U.S. Correction & Detention Advisory Programs in Vietnam," 11 pgs.
224. Engle to OPS/Vietnam, 2/12/71, "Conversation with Congressman Montgomery.
225. Walton letter to Colonel Sanh, 2/20/71, "Physical Examination Of Prisoners."
226. Press clippings, 2/19/71-2/21/71 "Work Started on New Cells at Con Son."
227. C&D Fact Sheet, 3/1/71, "The Tiger Cages of Con Son "
228. C&D Fact Sheet, 3/1/71, "List of Self-Help Projects of the Detention Program."
229. C&D Fact Sheet, 3/1/71, "Major Accomplishments Of C&D Advisory Programs..."
230. C&D Fact Sheet, 3/1/71, "Con Son Prison's & South Vietnam Corrections System."
231. DEPCORDS Talking Paper, by Berkeley, 3/1/71, "Modification of the Tiger Cages and Related GVN Prison Matters."
232. Black Times, Albany California, editorial, 3/4/71, "$400,000 for What?!"
233. Berkeley Memo to Colby, 3/16/71, "Con Son Trip of 14 March 71," 20 pages.
234. Washington Post, 3/19/71, Page Ad, International Committee to Free South Vietnamese Political Prisoners from Detention, Torture and Death."
235. OPS C&D Fact Sheet, 4/1/71, "Con Son & The Correctional System."
236. Col. Ve to Walton, 4/1/71, "Displeasure of all U.S. war media reports on Con Son."
237. U.S. News & World Report, 9/27/71, "Why U.S. Prisons are Exploding."
238. Walton memo, 6/20/72, "David Marsh of Newsweek said to me he knew of Harkin's plan to set up Con Son..."
239. Distributed by King Features Syndicate, 7/24/74, "These Days -Postscript to The Tiger Cage," by John Chamberlain.
240. OPS Fact Sheet, 3/6/73, USAID Assistance to Civic Security Forces.
241. OPS Fact Sheet, 4/18/73, 6 pgs, "U.S. Assistance to Directorate Corrections, GVN."
242. OPS Fact Sheet, 4/20/73, "US Assistance to National Police, Jail Administration Activity, GVN."

243. Hannah letter To Lee Hamilton, 5/29/73, "The Corrections Project-GVN."
244. Washington Post, 4/28/73, Jacquis Leslie, "VC Saigon Exchange Civilian POWS."
245. Goin to Harvey to Regula, 6/21/73, "Allegations of Mistreatment of political prisoners."
246. OPS Fact Sheet, 6/30/73, "The Correction Program 1970-1973"
247. OPS Fact Sheet, 8/23/73, "Civilian Prisoners-SV," 6 pgs
248. OPS Fact Sheet, 9/27/73, "Status of Activities Previously a Part of the Public Safety Program in Vietnam."
249. OPS Fact Sheet, 7/1/74, "Public Safety-South Vietnam."
250. Goin to Harvey to Patman , 10/2/74, "Training of Foreign Police Officers in U.S."
251. Washington Post 1/15/75, Jack Anderson, "New Data on CIA -Police School Ties."
252. Washington Post, 5/6/75, "Tiger Cages Emptied."
253. Washington Post, 8/6/79, "Doubt Cast on Paralysis of Tiger Cage Inmates."
254. Washington Post, 10/7/82, Truong Nhu Tang "The Liberation of Vietnam."
255. Washington Post, 8/2/83, "General Shocked at Vietnam Assassinations."
256. Los Angeles Times, 11/15/83, George McArthur, "Vietnam's Political Prisoners."
257. Washington Post, 2/13/88, "Vietnam Releases Political Prisoners," Murray Hiebert.
258. Insight, 12/23/91, "Attack From the Left, 'Tom Harkin Runs for President."
259. "Transcription of Taped Interview of Don Luce," Shirley Bordenkircher, 12/11/92 (Accompanied by Jerry Snider)
260. "Working notes, records, tape recordings, interviews, correspondence, ET AL, S. Bordenkircher research," 61 pgs
261. Con Son press clippings, C&D staff, 200 pgs, 1970.
262. "Prison in South Vietnam," translation of the writings of 30 students, The Committee for Struggle Against Oppression of Student's, 1969.
263. "Con Son Fact Sheets, 7/7/70, C&D Staff. 80 pages.
264. "Translation of Prisoner's Memoirs of Con Son," author unknown, unpublished
265. "OPS Fact Sheets (2 Vol.) For DEPCORDS Briefing to State, 1970, 50 Pages.
266. "Legal System, Republic of Vietnam, May 1967, by GVN Ministry of Justice & Public Administration, USAID/Saigon, published by USAID/ CORDS.
267. "The Rehabilitation Systems of Vietnam," Frank E. Walton & Bill Benson, 10/63, published by OPS/Saigon.
268. "Background Information Relating to Southeast Asia and Vietnam," Committee on Foreign Relations, U.S. Government Printing Office, July 1967
269. "C & D Fact Sheets, " Bordenkircher, 1968.
270. "Briefing File-OPS/Saigon -OPS Staff, 1968.
271. "The Code of Criminal Procedure -(Draft) The Republic of Vietnam, USAID, Public Administration.
272. "Prisons In South Vietnam." unpublished, 30 students & Don Luce.
273. "Con Son Archipelago," unpublished, Nguyen Van Ve & Bordenkircher
274. "Frank E. Walton Responds to Moss Sub-Committee." August 1970, Two Books, 800 pages. Contains all C&D data. (Unpublished)

BOOKS

275. "The Great Tiger Cage Frame-up," draft Frank Walton, 1975.   276. "America In Vietnam," Guenter Lewy, Oxford University Press.
277. "The Phoenix Program," Douglas Valentine, Morrow, 1990
278. "Decent Interval," Frank Snepp, Random House.
279. "The Ten Thousand Day War," Michael Maclear, St. Martins Press
280. "The Unheard Voices," Luce & Summer, Cornell University Press.
281. "Honorable Men-My Life in the CIA," William Colby, Simon & Schuster.
282. "Lost Victory," William Colby, Contemporary Books.
283. "Investigation Into Vietnam AID Program," Hearings before Committee on

Government Operations, House of Representatives, U.S. Printing Office, 7/17/70

284. "U.S. Involvement In Southeast Asia," Findings Of the House Subcommittee investigation into Southeast Asia, July 6, 1970, U.S. Government Printing Office.

285. "Hostages of War," Homer Brown & Don Luce, Indochina Mobile Education Project, January 1973.

286. "Background Information Relating to Southeast Asia and Vietnam," Committee on Foreign Relations, U.S. Senate. U.S. Government Printing Office, July 1967.

287. U.S. House of Representatives, RPT 91-1276, 91st Congress, 2nd Session, "CONDEL Select Committee Report on Recent Developments in South East Asia," July 6, 1970.

288. 7/1779, "Hearings Before Committee on Government Operations," Harkin ET. AL.

289. "Bureaucracy at War --US Performance in the Vietnam Conflict," Robert Komer, Westview Publishing.

290. "Facing The Phoenix," Zalin Grant, 1991, W. W. Norton & Company.

291. "JFK Wants To Know," Edward B. Chaflin, 1991, William Morrow and Company

292. "A Spy For All Seasons" Duane R. Clarridge w/ Digby Diehl, Scribner, 1997, 159-161

MISCELLANEOUS

293. "Come With Me to Macedonia," Lucius Amelius Paulus, 168 B.C.

294. "The Advisor's Lament," author unknown.

295. "RAMPARTS" magazine, Vol 6 #3, October 1967, "Pacification in Vietnam"

GLOSSARY & ACRONYMS

AID: *Agency for International Development - Division of the U.S. Department of State.*

APC: *The Accelerated Pacification Campaign. Began 11/68 by William Colby*

ARVN: *Army of the Republic of Vietnam (South)*

Attrition: *The wearing away of enemy forces to the point where they are either unable, or unwilling to continue fighting*

CAS: *Saigon office for CIA*

CD: *Civilian Detainee. Civilians detained military forces.*

C&D: *Corrections and Detention Branch of the Public Safety Directorate, CORDS,administratively under ICEX-SIDE (PHOENIX)*

CFS: *Country Field Submission. A narrative statement as part of annual budget presentation.*

Chieu Hoi: *Open Arms program - amnesty offered to VC defectors*

CI: *counterinsurgency*

CIA: *Central Intelligence Agency*

COMUS: *Vietnam, Commander of U.S. military forces, Vietnam*

CONDEL: *Congressional Delegation*

COSMUS/MACV: *Commander, U. S. Military Assistance Command, Vietnam*

Counterinsurgency: *Military, paramilitary, political, economical, psychological, and civic actions taken by a government to defeat subversive insurgency*

CORDS: *Civil Operations and Revolutionary Development. Changed to Civil Operations and Rural Development by Ambassador Colby. Coordinated U.S. Military, civilian operations and advisory programs under one command.*

CPDC: *Central Pacification and Development Council. Formed in 1968 by Ambassador Colby. Subordinate to Ambassador Bunker and Generals Westmoreland and Abrams.*

DEPCORDS: *Deputy to the MACV Commander & Ambassador Ellsworth Bunker for Civil Operations and Rural Development (CORDS)*

DGNP: *Director General of South Vietnamese National Police whose American counterpart (advisor) was the Director of the Public Safety Directorate (D/PSD-S) Saigon.*

DIOCC: *District Intelligence and Operations Coordination Center in each of 250 districts of South Vietnam. Advised by the CIA. This entity is NOT a jail or a prison, nor is the term synonymous with either jail or prison. A facility utilized only in time of war at the District level.*

DISTRICT: *District refers to an area of governmental structure or control akin to a county in the U.S.*

DRV: *Democratic Republic of Vietnam (North)*

GVN: *Government of South Vietnam*

ICEX: *Intelligence Coordination and Exploitation. The original name for Phoenix.*

IPA: *International Police Academy. Located at 3600 M Street, Washington, D.C. The training component of the Office of Public Safety, Washington, D.C., (OPS/W).*

JAIL: *NOT a term synonymous with prison. A facility where suspected lawbreakers are incarcerated until court decides their fate, & where sentenced criminals serve terms less than one year and one day.*

MAAG: *Military Assistance Advisory Group*

MACV: *Military Assistance Command, Vietnam. Established 2/62 - the unified command under the Commander-in-Chief, Pacific.*

MAP: *Military Assistance Program*

MOI: *Minister of Interior - South Vietnam*

MSTS: *Military Sea Transport Service*

MSUG: *Michigan State University Group. Original U.S. advisory and technical assistance group under contract with the U.S. State Department (1954).*

NLF: *National Liberation Front. Anti government dissidents & insurgents.*

NVA: *North Vietnamese Army - army regulars.*

NVN: *North Vietnam*

RVN: *Republic of Vietnam (South)*

PAR: *Project Appraisal Report. Required annual evaluation of an advisory project.*

PBS: *Project Budget Submission.*

Phoung Hoang: *Mythological bird of conjugal love appearing in times of peace.*

PIC: *Provincial Interrogation Center advised only by covert advi-*

term synonymous with a jail, or prison. PIC's were a province confinement facility utilized only in time of war.

PIP: *Project Implementation Plan. A time-phased expression of work to be done, resources required, and results expected during the feasible life of the project. It sets the standard for meaningful project evaluation.*

PolAd: *Political Advisor*

POW: *prisoner of war*

PRISON: *A term NOT synonymous with jail. A facility where a lawbreaker is incarcerated for any sentence exceeding one year. During wartime, criminals were held in prisons to await sentence/ trials, under An Tri law, until more jails were built.*

PROVINCE, PROVINCIAL: *In SV refers to an area of government structure/control akin to a state in the U.S.*

PSD: *A directorate within CORDS to advise the National Police*

PSCD: *Pacification Security Coordination Division of CORDS (CIA).*

PSYOPS: *Psychological Operations*

PsyWar: *Psychological Warfare*

RF/PF: *Regional and Popular Forces of South Vietnam. A National Guard under control of province and district chiefs.*

SIDE: *Screening, Interrogation, and Detention of the Viet Cong Infrastructure*

SVN: *South Vietnam*

TS: *Top secret connector with Phoenix (formerly ICEX)*

USAID: *U. S. Agency for International Development*

VC or VCI: *Viet Cong Clandestine, Vietnamese Communist or Viet Cong Infrastructure. Communist party members, National Liberation Front Officers, Viet Cong, and North Vietnam Saboteurs and terrorists not carrying arms when arrested.*

VCS: *Vietnamese civilians suspected of being a member of the VCI.*

index

240

ORDER FORM

Send additional copies of **TIGER CAGES**: *An Untold Story* to:

Name_____

Company_____

Address_____

City, St. Zip_____

Daytime phone_____

Please send ___ copies of **TIGER CAGE** at $14.95 @   _____

Shipping $3.00 for first book, $1.00 @ additional book   _____

WV residents add $ .92 tax per book   _____

                                                    Total   _____

Payment:__Check ___Mastercard/Visa/Discover

Card #_____Exp Date ____

Signature _____

E-mail us at **onus2sab@ovis.net** *to ask about our quantity discounts on orders of 5 copies or more.*
P. O. Box 114, Cameron, WV

TIGER CAGE:

Con Son Island, a penal colony in the South China Sea, is where a young congressional aide, now Senator Tom Harkin of Iowa, purported to discover the tiger cages. The resultant expose on South Vietnam's civilian prisons caught the attention of the international press, elevating the aide to expert status and the cages to infamy.

There is, however, an authentic expert on South Vietnam's prisons & the tiger cages, who has, since that incident, stood silent. He is the man who was there—for five years as the Senior U. S. Advisor to the South Vietnamese Director of Corrections. His story is historically relevant. Whether or not it is ideologically relevant is a judgment readers must make for themselves.

The Bordenkirchers have simplified the bureaucratic hierarchies of Vietnam, mapped out CIA & Phoenix involvement, defined Corrections & Detention, ICEX, & the Office of Public Safety, the mission of each; and infused the whole with humor and style.

Bordenkircher is currently Chair and Associate Professor of Criminal Justice at West Liberty State College in West Virginia. He has served as Warden at three maximum security prisons, as a County Sheriff and as a police chief, and is a court certified expert. He and his wife, Shirley, this book's lead author, collaborate on select private investigations. She continues to work independently on other literary projects.

ISBN 0-9661771-4-2

51495

9 780966 177145

$14.95

abby publishing